SOMETHING
FOR YOU
TO DO

Biblical Perspectives on 'Calling', 'Craftsmanship' and 'Finding your Element' (it's not all about ministry and mission)

By Iain R. Dunbar

Oxford, UK

Published by New Generation Publishing in 2021

Copyright © Iain R. Dunbar 2020

First Edition

Paperback ISBN: 978-1-80031-406-1
Ebook ISBN: 978-1-80031-405-4

www.newgeneration-publishing.com

New Generation Publishing

CHAPTER 7 MODELLING GOD'S CHARACTER – CULTURE AND GENDER

CHAPTER 8 MODELLING GOD'S CHARACTER – WATCHMEN AND 'STANDING WITH' 127

Acknowledgements

Love and thanks to my wife, **Dawn**, who has stood with me for nearly 40 years. She says I am progressively getting easier to live with, and for that I am thankful. Over all this time, she has consistently sought the Lord, committed herself to prayer and dispensed love and wisdom to those around her. She has contributed more to this book than she realises – bringing valuable insights from her studies and daily readings and, during our frequent discussions has shed new light, at just the right moment, on the very things I have been wrestling with.

I also owe a great debt of gratitude to my daughter, **Joy**, not just for inheriting substantially the same taste in music as me but for the development editing process – she has painstakingly reviewed each chapter, patiently explained what I cannot say or what needs to be said differently, frequently suggested a better ordering of the content and often offered new thoughts and insights to enrich it or to supply what was not there.

Introduction

God is a craftsman who is never idle and not usually silent. He creates with passion and with care and attention to detail and He made us in His image. His express intention is that we might own Him as Father, understand His ways and be involved in the fulfilling of His purposes. Although we are not worthy of such involvement, He takes the initiative to 'call' people to both short and long-term tasks. Sometimes He uses those who don't know Him but most often the 'calls' come to those of the 'called-out people', with whom He is already forging relationship and to whom He wants to pass on His craftsmanship. Short-term 'commissions' may be stepping stones to a longer term 'vocation'.

The craftsman in Him has created a longing in us to be craftsmen – to produce quality work and to achieve lasting results. Is God *only* interested in us applying ourselves in that way in ministry or mission situations? No. He is interested in the builder and the carpenter and the project manager and the administrator and the nurse and the teacher and the carer and the parent doing a job with skill and with passion and creating high-quality products and lasting results.

The career that we train for, the aptitudes that we develop, the skills we acquire and the practical abilities that we hone are not incidental to God's purposes. God does not just *tolerate* us plastering walls or designing bridges or nursing the sick or teaching a class, as long as we also stand on a soapbox or wear a sandwich board or use some of our disposable income to go on short-term mission. No, God takes an acute interest in our skillset *for its own sake*. He is interested in plastering excellence, in the rich education that comes to children from inspired teaching, in the healing qualities of nursing carers and both the complex calculations and the flowing lines that make up a bridge design and He calls people to do that stuff.

So, what is the purpose of such calls and who will they benefit? He wants the world to benefit from a huge variety of skills, exercised wherever He places one of His children. He also wants the worker to benefit from doing the work and from the opportunity to grow and develop in the doing. As to which aptitudes and skills are to be applied and by whom, wherever possible He intends the benefit to all parties to be enhanced by giving the task to someone whose aptitudes and personal passions are going to collide in the doing of it.

The starting point is to love God with all our heart, all our soul and all our strength and to sacrifice our lives on the altar of His plans and purposes and the specific callings He directs at us. His primary calling is to a 'life in Christ' and for us to exhibit a whole series of persistent attributes that are in keeping with that life. His secondary callings are to specific works and activities that capture our individuality and uniqueness and give us the opportunity to create high-quality products and lasting results.

Although the emphasis in much of the writing about 'calling' is misleading, often suggesting that ministry and mission are the only things you can legitimately be called to, I have no desire to downgrade such activity. If we follow God's leading for our lives, the attributes acquired through our primary calling are most likely to propel us into that, in some form. However, as far as secondary callings to both short and long-term activities are concerned, there is huge variety to what God gives people to do and the breadth and depth of the skillsets with which He gifts them is staggering. We can appreciate a little of this richness by looking at two parts of the Old Testament:

In Exodus we have the account of God's call of Moses, followed by Israel's miraculous rescue from slavery in Egypt, the destruction of their Egyptian captors and the emergence of a new nation, living under a completely new set of laws. When I say 'nation', Exodus 12:37-38 tells us there were 600,000 men, plus women and children plus a mixed multitude (of non-Jews, including a lot of Egyptians who had come to believe in the God of Israel) – so, at least 1 million people. They travel into the desert and, at Sinai, they receive a comprehensive rule book, first hand from God, plus a detailed set of instructions for constructing the tabernacle and all its associated furniture and finery.

Whenever I read these chapters, I am overwhelmed by the precision and detail and awed by God's reasoning – He never does anything without a clear purpose and never insists on something without good reason. The laws cover the nation's religious, economic and business life, as well as matters relating to governance and administration, community, social justice, leisure and festivals. To say that this new way of living was different to what they had known in Egypt is a massive understatement. Just how different is described a little further on, in Exodus 33:16, when Moses says to God:

'How shall it be known that I have found favour in your sight, I and your people? Is it not in your going with us, so that *we are distinct, I and your people, from every other people on the face of the earth*?'

As to the people that God calls to perform specific tasks; between chapters 16 and 31 of Exodus we see the emergence of national leaders, spiritual leaders, military leaders, a hierarchy of judges and administrators, some outstanding craftsmen and a group of skilled tradespeople.

We already know about Moses, God's right-hand man and the national leader, and about his brother Aaron, who was a Levite and chief priest and the mouthpiece when Moses was tongue-tied. But another couple of highlights from these chapters tell us about a number of other people called to perform

4

important roles. In Exodus 18:8-27 Moses' father-in-law, Jethro, gives him wise advice about the daily judging of disputes and other civil matters – Moses was becoming exhausted and needed to appoint 'able men from all the people, men who fear God, who are trustworthy and hate a bribe, and place such men over the people as chiefs of thousands, of hundreds, of fifties, and of tens' (verse 21). These are the qualities that God needs to see evidence of before He can give someone something really useful to do.

Then, immediately after God has finished explaining how the people are to approach Him on a daily basis, through the ministry of the priests, He says to Moses:

'See, I have called by name Bezalel, son of Uri... and I have filled him with the Spirit of God, with ability and intelligence, with knowledge and all craftsmanship, to devise artistic designs, to work in gold, silver and bronze, in cutting stones for setting, and in carving wood, to work in every craft. And behold I have appointed with him Oholiab, son of Ahisamach... and I have given to all able men ability, that they may make all that I have commanded you.' (Exodus 31:1-6)

These practical trades, and those who perform them, are as valuable to God as is the leadership and the priestly service because God does all things well and everything He has ordained needs to be done properly, with skill and passion and to a standard where He can say, 'It is good'.

Later, in 1 Chronicles 12, we find David, a 'type' of Jesus, who has been anointed to be king but is still unable to move about freely because Saul is stalking the countryside intent on killing him. At this time, a great many men came and joined themselves to David because they knew that God was with him. They are called 'the mighty men' (verse 1) and, together, they are referred to as 'a great army, like an army of God.' (verse 22) This chapter give us vital clues as to the level and variety of expertise that was gathered. There were:

- Benjaminites who 'were bowmen and could shoot arrows and sling stones with either the right or the left hand';
- Gadites, 'experienced warriors, expert with shield and spear, whose faces were like the faces of lions and who were swift as gazelles upon the mountains... the least was a match for a hundred men and the greatest for a thousand';
- Men of Issachar whom God had gifted, we are told, with 'understanding of the times, to know what Israel ought to do'.

Why did they come? Verse 38a says, 'All these, men of war, arrayed in battle order, possessing special skills, came to Hebron with a whole heart to make David king over all Israel.' They came because God stirred their hearts to be part of the team, and to contribute their individual expertise in order to achieve His will and purpose.

What was the outcome? Verses 38b-40 say, 'all... were of a single mind to make David king. And they were there with David... eating and drinking, for their brothers had made preparation for them... for there was joy in Israel.'

Calling is all about God instructing men and women about what He wants them to do. It is about Him stirring their hearts to be useful and to dedicate their particular skill set to His cause.

It is also about those people, despite the enormity of the challenge and whatever difficulties might ensue, deriving great joy from what they are doing.

Biographies

The stories of how six different people have responded to the call of God are distributed throughout the book. These are integral to the message and, rather than interrupting the flow of argument, when taken together they illustrate most of the core principles. What has happened in their lives cannot be neatly broken down into elements that cleanly illustrate one point of principle or another but their real-life, human experience upholds the biblical argument.

Each story is very different from the next – as different as one individual is from the next – and every effort has been made to present a true account of the sometimes tortuous and frequently non-linear journey that people take towards successful fulfilment of a call. Each has been told with the full cooperation of the individual or their living representatives. In some cases, biographical details have deliberately been left out in order to protect either the individual or those that they know.

These people were not hard to find – indeed, there are many, many more whose stories I could have used. They are all very ordinary people, four of whom are well known to me and, having spoken to living relatives and friends or another one, I feel like I also know her.

If, having read the first few chapters, you engage the folk around you in conversation about 'calling', as I have done with those around me, you will find that many have had moments of epiphany and, even if they haven't associated it with the particular terminology I have used, also wondered what in the wide world they might have been 'made for'.

Some author limitations

I am not a Hebrew or Greek scholar and so, in keeping with other mere mortals, I rely on commentaries and the written claims of those who do possess that scholarship. It is interesting, however, that even those with scholarship can make assumptions or follow convention and end up adopting a misleading position or fail to realize that other parts of scripture contradict the interpretation they have adopted. Please therefore check my references, question my interpretation and look for contradictions or other supporting examples.

It is possible that, for some, the text may contain what is regarded as 'sexist comment'. There is no exclusivity intended – God 'calls' both men and women and if I say 'man', it is likely that I am talking about 'mankind'. I use words like 'craftsman/men' and 'watchman/men' because those are the words that occur in the Bible and they are not meant in an exclusively male sense. I also use the term 'adoption as sons' or 'sonship' because it is the way that, e.g. in Ephesians, Paul expresses our predestined position in Christ. I am comfortable with using 'He' or 'Him' to describe God because, again, it's the pronoun used throughout all the main translations of the Bible. No restrictions are implied, in principle, due to gender and the examples that I use throughout feature both men and women.

The writing comes from my own study. However, where I have knowingly reproduced someone else's thoughts, taken directly from another source, it is acknowledged. It is almost inevitable that, without being conscious of the process, I've adapted someone else's thoughts for my own purposes and not acknowledged it. Apologies if anyone reading this recognizes that process.

References

Biblical quotes/references are taken from the English Standard Version (ESV) or the New King James Version (NKJV), unless indicated otherwise:

- Scripture quotations from the ESV® Bible (The Holy Bible, English Standard Version®), copyright © 2001 by Crossway, a publishing ministry of Good News Publishers. Used by Permission. All rights reserved.
- Scripture quotations from the New King James Version. Copyright © 1982 by Thomas Nelson, Inc. Used by permission. All rights reserved.

In several places I have used a translation of the New Testament by a Jewish professor of philosophy called Heinz Cassirer (Cassirer, 1989). He was a classics scholar, who taught at Glasgow University and Oxford (Corpus Christi) and accepted Jesus as Messiah relatively late in life, having determined to read both Old and New Testaments. He then set out to translate the NT and to apply a Jewish lens to the way it is expressed, with the result that his translation is both scholarly and refreshing.

I have also used translations by Alec Motyer of both Isaiah (Motyer, 2011) and the Psalms (Motyer, 2016). Alec was the former Principal of Trinity College, Bristol and a widely respected scholar, who spent his life studying the Bible, writing, preaching and lecturing.

Chapter 1

What We Do Matters

If God made us 'special', why are quite a lot of us miserable?

A great many people, those with faith and those without, when questioned, will admit to having an in-built sense of purpose, even 'specialness', that has not found an outlet and still needs to be drawn out and clarified. This should not come as a shock because all men and women have been made in the image of God and therefore imbued with purpose, whether they actively acknowledge Him or not.

However, writers, coaches and consultants, in both the secular and Christian worlds, all agree that the majority of people from thirties up to retiring age, when questioned about their life and career choices, admit that they have not really enjoyed or felt fulfilled in what they have done. This is not merely people expressing something in a negative way that suggests, if they put their mind to it, they would be able to 'sort it out', it is a much more deep-seated dissatisfaction with the outcomes of life so far.

Each of us, throughout life, has to make a series of decisions about what we spend most of our waking hours engaged in. We either feel fulfilled in that activity or not and the evidence seems to be that a significant majority of people do not.

If the lack of enjoyment were purely due to inherited personality traits, our upbringing or the positive and negative things that have happened in life thus far, most of us would probably entertain the hope, even the expectation, that God could do something about it – perhaps by us confiding in someone who genuinely cares and will pray for us, or seeking some counselling, or investing in more 'constructive' relationships, or pulling back from 'destructive' habits, or some combination of all of those.

However, where dissatisfaction over career choices or 'what we spend our lives *doing*' is concerned, there does not appear to be the same level of hope or expectation that, if we submit it to Him, God can do something about it. Instead there is a sort of resignation that says, 'this is the way it is and it's unlikely to change'. You may not consider yourself a part of that group but I have heard that resigned tone countless times and most of those speaking did not even seem aware of a theoretical mechanism for addressing the situation.

In terms of outward demeanour, people tell me that the fictional character I most resemble is Eeyore, the gloomy donkey in Winnie the Pooh. Much as I love A.A. Milne's stories, I've been trying my whole life to shake off this particular association. I think it must have something to do with the way I say 'Hello' because I phoned my daughter just yesterday and, after I had uttered that one word, she dissolved into laughter and then asked me if there was anything wrong. Nothing was wrong – I was actually feeling quite positive!

As to what is more deep-seated, there have been periods of time in my life when I have indeed been miserable – not enjoying what I have done for a living and unable to switch off from it in order to throw myself into other, more pleasurable activity outside the workplace. For many years, I wistfully longed for a better understanding of what God thinks about it all but didn't actively pursue an answer. When I did ask Him and got urgent about it, He began to give some understanding of His purpose for people in general and I began to realize what was on His heart for me in particular. Then, having followed His leading and made a couple of fairly significant shifts into more 'profitable' activity (that is, profitable in the non-financial sense!), I committed myself to studying what the Bible says on the subject of 'calling' and, so as to be better able to assist others, trained as an executive coach.

The type of coaching I practise does not to tell people what they should do but rather helps them tell a coherent story, be it personal or corporate, in order to make sense of what has happened in their lives so far. It then assists them to transition into a new phase of life and effectiveness. In order to achieve any level of success, I have to know what questions to ask, be able to create a relaxed and secure environment for people to talk about themselves, be interested in them and 'present' with them, be relentlessly positive and, lastly, be astute enough to frame and reframe what I'm hearing in such a way that the narrator comes to understand his/her options and has the confidence to explore them.

I focus on asking people particular kinds of questions and I have no difficulty being interested in the answers because, as soon as they start talking about their real selves and about the things across their lives they have not only enjoyed doing but were achievements to be proud of, they 'come alive' and inhabit the story. It is not possible not to be captivated. The only problem is that, for the most part, the achievements that 'light people up' and propel them into impassioned storytelling are too rarely related to their work life or what they spend most of their waking hours doing.

Learning to discern

The concept of 'calling', when raised in conversation, is usually met with a surprising amount of recognition and understanding but, despite living with a lack of fulfilment, most people are strangely reluctant to explore the subject seriously. The key reasons for this seem to be a) they intuitively *know* that 'calling' is a broad concept and encompasses craftsmanship of all kinds but, at the same time, a much narrower definition is being used in the available Christian literature, and b) they *know* their own calling is not to a form of Christian ministry and so the available Christian literature probably won't help.

Now, you may be thinking at this point, 'He has missed another, blindingly obvious, key reason – namely, that people have enough hassle without wanting to get sucked into some intensely pressurised quest for "the thing I am meant to be doing with my life".' And anyway, you might argue, I don't want to become that person who walks around all the time saying, 'thus says the Lord' when it's as clear as the nose on your face that He hasn't said it! Well, trust me, I do not want you to become that person. Neither do I have any intention of applying undue pressure on you to find 'your thing'.

As it happens, I don't believe it's primarily about us finding 'our thing', it's actually about developing a relationship with God, in which there's regular communication, a growing sensitivity to His promptings and an ability to make good and wise decisions 'in peace'. As a result, we will begin to appreciate how interested He is in lifting us out of misery and giving us a succession of things to do that are useful and that we will enjoy.

For those who are practised at communicating with God and, being aware of their own weaknesses, also able to 'weigh' what they hear, finding out what He wants them to do can be as simple as Him speaking, followed by them hearing and then getting on with it! But God knows we are not all at that place – many of us are poor at hearing what He is saying and we need training. So, He may take the initiative and present us with new opportunities that trigger our interest, nudge us back towards engagement with Him and tempt us into action.

If we take the bait, the quality of the ongoing validation we receive from those actions or the unmistakeable sense of the rightness of what we are doing or, conversely, a sense of being outside our comfort zone will be clues to discovering His guidance. Of course, there are dangers lurking here – just because something 'feels right' doesn't necessarily make it right and just because we feel some discomfort doesn't necessarily make it wrong – but God is interested in the decision-making process. He wants us to 'learn to discern', which means going beyond the feelings and beyond the seemingly obvious and, when faced with alternatives, be able to recognize the difference between a sense of 'shalom' (peace, wellbeing, tranquillity) and a sense of 'dis-ease'.

God has things for us to do whether we are younger or older – age is no barrier to usefulness, in either direction. Those of us who are older, if we have not felt fulfilled in what we have done or are doing, may feel stuck in that state and have given up on there being more chances – not so, our God has no shortage of innovative ideas. Some may recall a time when they thought they sensed a calling but, either through their own fault or someone else's, it didn't come to anything and has been lost – not so, our God does not let His word fall to the ground.

Those who are younger may already be disillusioned by economic uncertainty and lack of substantial career opportunities but our God has made a habit of calling young people to vital roles during, and often in preparation for, times of great political and economic upheaval: Samuel is thought to have been about eleven years old; Joseph and Jeremiah were around seventeen years old; Esther was in her late teens or early twenties; Mary in her mid-teens; and the Disciples in their early twenties. The needs now are at least as great as were the needs then and God's enterprise and creativity are not diminished.

Interestingly, the current generation of graduates and young professionals, when talking about career decision-making, have adopted a conceptual framework using vocabulary such as 'vocational discernment', 'understanding your call', 'passion, gifts & talent', 'doing what brings you joy'. These are largely secular people using terminology we might previously have thought of as 'spiritual' and it needs to be reclaimed.

I would submit that three things are therefore necessary:

- to present what the Bible *really* says about calling and craftsmanship;
- to understand what *God* is passionate about and how He wants to employ us – after all, the only works of lasting value are those that He initiates;
- to talk both to older people (before it's too late) and to younger people (before they get cynical) about how to hear God and 'find their element'.

What do I mean by 'find their element'? Sir Ken Robinson created the best definition: it is that place where 'your natural aptitude meets your personal passion' (Robinson, 2010). And God is the only one who knows where that place is and how to get there, for each person made in His image.

Are there not enough books about calling already?

I am not in the least pessimistic about God managing to work out His purpose for you and I. If we respond to Him, it will happen exactly as He intends because, as Jesus said in Matthew 24:35, 'Heaven and earth will pass away, but my words will not pass away'. Having said that, (and this is not Eeyore reverting to type) I am not optimistic that you will get the right message about 'calling' by reading most of the existing books on the subject.

My dis-ease stems from what is missing, and therefore misleading, in much of the material already written. As alluded to in the section above, this disease is shared by a great many other people, although not many have openly articulated it.

Most books and articles, despite saying some useful things, seem to fall into one or both of the following traps:

i) Either they completely omit from the argument some of the important, biblical aspects of calling and imply that the only valid calls are to Christian ministry or mission;

ii) Or they suggest that a person, by employing a certain patented methodology, can discover the call on his/her life for themselves and can then 'be it' or 'do it' or 'go there'.

The first is actually a huge distortion of both God's purposes and man's uniqueness and the second is the exact opposite of the truth.

As to trap i), Os Guinness got it right in his book *The Call* (Guinness, 1998) – there are four main ways in which the concept of 'a call' or 'a calling' is used in the Bible:

1) calling out to capture someone's attention;
2) calling someone or something by a name;
3) the 'called-out people' – a calling out of the world and into the body of Christ;
4) the call to live by kingdom principles and to undertake specific tasks (the former taking precedence over the latter and the latter built on the former).

Most books on 'calling', written from a biblical standpoint, ignore all but point three and a bit of point four. They highlight our calling to be disciples of Christ (which is right, because it's the essential starting point) but then focus only on how we should use our gifts, skills, education, experience and time in ministry (to the body of Christ) and in mission (to the world).

They don't acknowledge the full implication of God having created each person for specific purposes and that He is intimately concerned with our whole lives. Hence, most writing fails to provide any guidance as to how we understand what our gifts and skills are; how and why we as individuals are different from all those around us; how we can find things to do that utilise our passions and match our individuality; and what career or vocation we should pursue.

In short, point four gets distorted, imposing limits on the list of 'specific tasks' to which we can legitimately be called, making it all about ministry and mission and failing to acknowledge the value of a trade or the performance of a practical skill. Whereas, in God's economy, these latter two can be infused with as much kingdom purpose as the former two. We will look more closely at this four-fold framework in Chapter 3.

As to trap ii), Rick Warren said, in *The Purpose Driven Life* (Warren, 2002), 'I have read many books that suggest ways to discover the purpose of my life. All of them could be classified as "self-help" books'. The self-help message is more prevalent now than when Rick wrote that at the start of this century. John the Baptist, when questioned about his own call, took no personal credit – he said, 'There is nothing a man can receive except what has been granted to him by heaven.' (John 3:27)

We can muddle along by ourselves, use various tools to try and analyse our personal characteristics and then look for tasks that employ some or all of those characteristics. However, although using tools (e.g. to define personality type and/or motivated abilities) can be helpful, and analysing how we got to where we are is a useful exercise, that kind of data can only provide clues.

God is the one who issues calls and He dictates their content because He already knows *everything* about us – the strengths, the limitations, the experience, the triumphs and the failures, the aspirations and the doubts. His calls and commissions are crafted to take us forward to 'sonship' and He uses them to move us along the road towards that goal. In other words, they are one of the most important mechanisms that He uses for our sanctification.

The tricky element to this is that understanding God's calls and commissions doesn't happen by our effort – they can only be received by revelation. We therefore need to hear what He is saying to us and that means believing that He wants to speak and then developing listening skills and a process of testing and confirmation. As we take courage and learn to listen we will find, in the words of the late Francis Schaeffer, 'He is there and He is not silent.'

Inherited craftsmanship & a new identity

Like any attentive father who loves His sons and daughters, God's desire is to show people how to do stuff and to pass on both His craftsmanship and His ways. He wants to apprentice us to Him and to stand with us as we acquire the skills. However, too few people attest to God speaking to them, on a regular basis, to direct them to what they should do, the projects they should take on, the tasks they should perform. Very few can testify to having pursued a vocational 'calling'. Not enough can testify to God having given them one or more strategically important tasks, as they've sought Him to make them useful.

When He speaks, God usually calls things into being that are not yet fully formed. We obviously see it in creation but it is also evident, time and again, throughout scripture as He calls people to things they have never done before and which, at least at the outset, they think they are not capable of. We must therefore be ready to develop into what we are not yet and be prepared to acquire new skills.

This may seem scary but there is no need to panic because special doses of grace will *always* follow a call – God knows that for us to fulfil any call, change and growth will inevitably be required but that our resolve for such a process is usually weak. He is committed both to the sanctification and to the 'continuous personal and professional development' of His sons and daughters and so, as with the calls themselves, the doses of grace that He administers will be specifically tailored to the needs of each individual.

Left to our own devices, we are most likely to do what seven of the eleven remaining disciples did, after Jesus' resurrection. As reported in John 21, feeling unsure and not knowing what to do, they did what they always did – the only thing that they knew how to do – they went fishing. Likewise, if we are not sure of the plan or we don't feel comfortable, we will tend to continue doing the things that seem obvious and which require only our existing skills. As was the case on this occasion, when Jesus met the disciples after they had had another night of fruitless toil, it needs Jesus to intervene in our lives, to create a new agenda and to give us confidence to step out in a new direction.

There is a whole chapter later on in the book about 'Identity', given that it is a perennially hot topic. What a person believes to be their identity is built from such things as where they came from, who they are and what they do but God has made each one of us with a unique set of attributes and He is not limited by location, history, societal influence or acquired experience. He knows what He intends us to become and He is the only one who knows how to match the calls specifically to the person called.

Our true identity is found, paradoxically, by being willing to lose the one we've built for ourselves and then by letting Him rebuild it. We will not know what it is to be truly useful, let alone find that place where natural aptitude coincides with personal passion, unless we are doing stuff that matches who we are and what we were made for.

It is therefore no surprise that, at various times in our lives, we have moments of epiphany that seem to provide a clue to our purpose. Those moments are usually accompanied by a great longing to fulfil that purpose. The sense of epiphany, be it strong or mild, along with the sense of purposefulness that follows, point to God being involved – He is sharing His own purposes with us. But here is the corollary; if God's purposes depend in part on our being willing to heed His calls, and we don't do so, then tasks that He intended to be performed in a unique fashion will not be performed in that way and possibly not at all.

Of course, each individual is limited in what he/she can achieve and it is not God's intention to lay too great a burden on any one person but He wants you and I to be part of His work and there are elements of what we each contribute that cannot be provided by anyone else.

He has amazingly creative ways of getting the job done, that often involve people's respective callings having to dovetail together, in order to achieve a complementary, collaborative and collective outcome. This means we each must operate according to the permissions given and within the sphere of influence to which we've been assigned. Herein lies one of the secrets of what the New Testament calls 'the body' – each member is free to hear God for him/herself but is encouraged to test and to fulfil their 'callings' in an appropriate (Church) context. Where there is a desire not to stifle the individual, but to see the body of Christ operate as God intends, He will enable those respective callings to be worked out in a corporate context and the whole will turn out to be more than the sum of the parts.

So, to summarise: in contrast to the lack of enjoyment and fulfilment reported by so many, if all the following statements hold true...

- God is persistent in His communication with men and women;
- Each person is uniquely fashioned and He tailors His handling and guidance of each one accordingly;
- There are links between a person's calling and his/her identity;
- God's application of grace to each individual is both relentless and prudent;

...then God is committed to matching what He gives us to do to our unique personhood and thus, following God's calls will be the surest route both to finding our true identity and to learning the art of true collaboration. We might even find ourselves 'in our element'.

Don't expect a 'Theology of Work'

My definition of 'a sense of calling' is, 'a God-given awareness, that is compelling and that I cannot ignore, of a particular role I need to play or a set of functions I need to perform. A sense of purpose that seems to have its own momentum and propels me forward, despite my not yet having all the skills and experience necessary for its fulfilment.'

What this definition doesn't say is almost as important as what it does say. It does not say whether the calling is, or should be, my career and it does not say whether or not I will be remunerated for my efforts. This is because a consideration of 'calling' is 'higher' than concerns over what I do for a living and how much I get paid for what I do.

For that reason, it is not my intention, and it is probably not appropriate, to provide a 'theology of work'. Firstly, there are many other people, better qualified and more eloquent than me, who have written or are currently writing on that subject and secondly, I hope to convince you that, contrary to what you might read in many books about 'calling' or 'vocation', if God is interested in issuing 'calls' to *everyone* (as opposed to a select few), then focusing on Him and what He has to say should take precedence over seeking specific answers to particular work-related questions. In fact, to focus on particular work-related questions might be a distraction from the main event.

Having said that, there may be many different, work-related scenarios that make someone decide to pick up a book about 'calling'. For example:

- You may be coming to it as a recent graduate, eager to develop your skills and abilities for a noble cause, and wanting to find the right career;
- You may have begun a career but it didn't work out, or you have fallen foul of an economic downturn, and now want to be sure of the next decision;
- You might be in a job that is extremely unfulfilling and you don't know how long you can stick it out;
- You might be quite successful but you know that, earlier in life, you received a call that you did not follow up and it is nagging at you;
- You may feel called to something that, under normal circumstances, would be most unlikely to pay the bills and you are therefore conflicted.

Conventional career counselling might lead to *a solution* but it is more desirable to look for *the right solution*. And, as useful as a theology of work undoubtedly is, it should not be a primary focus when considering what your calling might be.

If God approves of a wide variety of both practical and intellectual skills and abilities and it is legitimate to be called into a wide variety of roles and professions, and if He is the only one who truly knows what each is best suited to and, knowing all our strengths, limitations, successes and failures, He still has our highest welfare and best interests at heart, then we can definitely trust Him to give us the *right* careers advice.

Ideally, seeking a 'calling' should transcend the human desire to choose our own path and will demand the laying down of our own agenda in favour of His opinion. Accordingly, we should not impose (even by accident) any kind of restriction on what God might choose for an individual, but rather encourage each person to seek God for themselves.

When we look at the many biblical examples of people whom God called, we find the career outcomes to be wide ranging. Here are just three to be going on with:

Paul was a tentmaker by trade but called to be an apostle – Acts 18:2-4. He took many years both to come to terms with that calling and to be prepared by God for living it out. He chose to maintain his trade so as not to be a financial burden on the churches that he planted. So, his paid work subsidised the practice of his calling.

Matthew was a tax collector when Jesus called him to become a disciple. Although tax-collecting was extremely lucrative, it says in Matthew 9:9 that he left it and followed Jesus and we hear nothing further about how he supported himself. In other words, his calling had a significantly detrimental effect on his ability to earn.

Huram-abi was a master craftsman, sent by Hiram, king of Tyre, to Solomon. A remarkable man, in whom God had put 'a spirit of skill' (see Exodus 28:3 for the first reference to this concept), who was tasked with taking charge of the building of both the temple and of Solomon's house. We are told that he was 'trained to work in gold, silver, bronze, iron, stone, and wood, and in purple, blue and crimson fabrics and fine linen, and to do all sorts of engraving and execute any design that may be assigned him'. We know he was paid for his leadership and his expertise and that this calling was exactly in line with his existing skill set. Nevertheless, it required him to extend those skills and to learn new techniques because he had to engineer structures and fabricate vessels that had never been made before.

Recognition and reward

I have been trying to say that the nature of the work that someone does should ideally follow from their receipt of a calling. However, you may consider that, hitherto, you have not experienced any clear leading and have had little or no choice about what you 'do'. You may have followed what seemed like the obvious path, or even the *only* path, and have made pragmatic decisions about what will provide a secure livelihood.

We all have legitimate concerns about earning a livelihood, about what we do and how we do it, about whether we enjoy what we do, and about the level of remuneration we receive for the doing. The Bible also makes it clear that God is similarly concerned, on our behalf, about all of that.

Right back in the beginning, in Gen 2, He gave the man and his wife the mandate to work and He has not rescinded it, despite the entry of sin and the difficulties that poses. As my friend Chris Gillies (who is publishing a book called *Love your Work*) says, 'God intends us to continue in creative work, being fruitful and having dominion over things that would otherwise run wild, serving and protecting creation' (Work Redeemed is Service to God, 2015).

In the New Testament, Jesus uses 'work language' – for example, in John 5, after performing a healing on the Sabbath, and being taken to task by the religious Jews, He says, *'My Father is working until now, and I am working.'* Then, further on in the New Testament, we who have chosen relationship with Jesus are invited to work in creative partnership: Paul says, in 1 Corinthians 3:6-9, 'I planted, Apollos watered, but God gave the growth. So, neither he who plants nor he who waters is anything, but only God who gives the growth.

He who plants and he who waters are one, *and each will receive his wages according to his labour. For we are God's fellow workers.* You are God's field, God's building.'

In the conference paper mentioned above, Chris Gillies comments on the work language that Jesus and Paul both use and suggests that, *'God's chosen method is to partner with us, as if we were the heirs to the family business, working alongside Him to build His kingdom.'* My thesis is that God's calls will encompass a very wide range of human skills and work contexts and whatever He calls us to will have kingdom-building value. That value, along with the creativity He releases in us and the outcomes He engineers, appear to take precedence over considerations about levels of remuneration and the recognition we might otherwise have looked for.

Work redeemed

Many of us will be familiar with the passage in Matthew 6 about 'not being anxious about our lives' and 'looking at the birds of the air... how our Heavenly Father feeds them' and we know that it concludes by exhorting us to 'seek first the kingdom of God and his righteousness'. Making the *right* career decisions requires us to get God's mind on it and, whereas He often challenges us to go on an adventure by issuing a new 'call', He will sometimes tell us to stay where we are and urge us to call on Him to transform the situation in some way.

Chris Gillies' argument is helpful in clarifying the point:

So, if God works and He created us to work, and if work in the garden [of Eden] was originally good, but became hard toil as a result of the fall, then it follows that Christ's blood, the cross and His resurrection have the power to redeem our work.

When we examine how this redemption operates in the ministry of Jesus, in the work of the early church, and indeed also in its application today, we see that this is not about returning to a very basic simple life as lived by Adam and Eve, but rather it's about a renewal and restoration of work as it is experienced in the present. Jesus, in healing the sick, in causing Zacchaeus the tax collector to change his life, in confronting the Pharisees, in his handling of the adulteress, in all of his teaching about money and possessions, is addressing the world and society as he found it... and from where he found it, he challenges society to reform, not regress.

...whilst planting churches and preaching the gospel, Paul continued to work. In Acts 18:3 we learn that his trade was making tents. Far from abandoning this trade, he practiced it on his travels, making a crucial connection with Aquila and Priscilla as a consequence, and ensuring that he was not a financial drain on the churches he planted and visited.

In Col 3:23-24 he says, 'Whatever you do, work at it with all your heart, as working for the Lord, not for men, since you know that you will receive an inheritance from the Lord as a reward. It is the Lord Christ you are serving.' This advice, given by Paul to bondservants, demonstrates the transforming potential of the Gospel. Once we are born again, as a new creation in Christ, then our work - and the reason for it - is transformed.

So, the most basic of jobs, and indeed all kinds of work, are to be considered as service to God. The Greek word for 'whatever' is a wide-ranging word, implying that every task is encompassed, suggesting that this goes beyond the household chores performed by Greek slaves and applies to all kinds of work. This restores dignity and value to manual work. It also causes us to think again about how and why we do our work.

The question regarding our work should no longer be 'What job can I do that will give me the most money, status or satisfaction?' Instead, the question should now be 'How can I, with my existing abilities and opportunities, be of greatest service to God's Kingdom'. (Work Redeemed is Service to God, 2015)

God is relaxed about the outcome

Each long-term call or short-term commission that God directs at an individual or a group arrives with His absolute assurance that He is behind it and has the power and skill to make it happen. If He tells you to go out and do something, the outcome is all but guaranteed AS LONG AS we put our faith in Him and trust Him to work it out His way.

We have an unfortunate tendency to panic, to be overwhelmed, to imagine all the ways that something might go wrong and to prepare for the worst but God is relaxed because, whatever it is, He knows that He can do it. Let's briefly consider a person to whom God came and spoke whilst he was scared stiff, doing his best to keep his head below the parapet and definitely not in the market for a difficult project. He didn't actually want a project of any kind.

Judges 6 tells us that Gideon was met by an angel whilst frantically trying to beat out wheat in a winepress, for fear of the Midianites. The angel didn't get into the winepress with him, he came to sit under the oak (terebinth) at Ophrah, which was Gideon's family home. A terebinth is a large, spreading tree and, if a family had such a tree on their land, it would be common to sit under it for shelter and for rest, particularly at the end of the day. Such a tree came to symbolise family and strength and security and durability, indeed all the things that Israel in general, and Gideon in particular, had lost sight of due to Midian's terror tactics.

Look at the difference in body language – the angel's action and whole demeanour suggests resting in safety after the work has been done and it is in marked contrast to Gideon's frenzied and inefficient activity. The angel had come to present a fait accompli, as far as the problem of the Midianites was concerned. He was effectively saying, 'it has been done' or 'the outcome is assured'. Hence, the Lord's words to Gideon in v12, 'The Lord is with you, O mighty man of valour.' And again, in v16, 'I will be with you and you shall strike the Midianites as one man.'

The Lord coming and presenting himself in this way is actually a throwback to Genesis 18:1, where God comes to Abraham, under the oaks at Mamre, to tell him what has been decided and will happen imminently to Sodom and Gomorrah. In Genesis the destruction of Sodom and Gomorrah had been decreed and here in Judges the decision as to how the Midianites would be overthrown had been made and their removal was as good as accomplished already.

Nobody is suggesting that God only gives us easy things to do but, when we receive a call, God has already determined the what and the how and we need not worry about how *we* are going to 'pull it off' – because *we* are *not* going to pull it off. Gideon did not see the significance of the angel's behaviour, did not correctly interpret his body language, and did not take God's word at face value. He needed a lot more convincing that the call was genuine and then, once he had finally agreed, had to be shown that the victory was not about might or weight of numbers.

God always takes responsibility for the things He asks us to do – He is the senior partner and He will make it happen. The wonderful part about all this is that, although He could do it Himself, He chooses to give us a part to play. He has our sanctification and our 'partnership in the family business' in view. He wants us to experience 'fulfilment' in the doing and to know the difference between purposeless or fruitless activity and lasting achievement.

Three hoped-for results of reading this book

Here are three things that I would be delighted for you to take away from my treatment of the subject of 'calling':

1. A realization that God issues calls much more frequently than many people might have imagined and that, if you ask Him, He will tell you *what* He wants you to do and *how* He wants you to do it.
2. An understanding that accepting Jesus' Lordship means you cannot expect Him to cooperate with your personal plans for either career or spiritual development – He has kingdom plans and they should take precedence. Submitting the planning to Him and obeying the resulting calls is the best way to go and is an assured route to accomplishing something lasting and to gaining a payoff that is fulfilling.
3. A preparedness to take courage, once He has spoken, and to call on Him to make it happen, whether or not you already have the necessary skills & experience, because He knows better and He can supply what's not there yet.

Bio #1 - Tim

Tim Morfin is the CEO of a national Christian charity, focussed on equipping the local church to support struggling children, by tackling issues around school exclusion, emotional wellbeing and holiday hunger. Many quotations used here are taken from Tim's book, *Out of the Ordinary*, which tells the story of the charity (Morfin, 2015).

It began officially in 1998, soon after Tim and a small team of people, associated with his local church, had seen a significant breakthrough with one young person. That young person had been engaged in an epic struggle with the 'system' for several years and the breakthrough proved that, with faith, prayer, perseverance and not a little skill, it was possible to turn someone's life around and arrest the destructive cycle of emotional disturbance, behavioural crisis, relationship breakdown and exclusion from school.

Tim had discovered that 'struggling individuals who, for whatever reason, were not accessing school would engage with [his] team.' Describing the success, he says, 'the idea of not only providing fun stuff to do after school but also a programme of education actually made a difference to behaviour and the ability to relate... So much of what we were doing was about helping [him] to learn how to learn – building the disciplines that would not only help a successful return to school, but also give him the best chance of making it in the world of work.'

At the time the charity started operations, Tim was working full-time for a major pharmaceutical company, 'doing all sorts of business stuff: sales, project management, marketing, business planning, [followed by] a role in the management of learning and development'. As such, it was God's way of providing '[me with] one of the best leadership development programmes available'.

His leadership skills had first been exercised at the age of fifteen when he became grumpy and frustrated with the youth group at his local church. It was, for Tim, the first of a series of occasions on which he has been confronted by a need and has said to himself, 'we must be able to do better than this'.

The church had been planted by his father, on a housing estate in Hull, and the youth group was being run by his parents at the time. As we all know, it's unwise to voice dissatisfaction with a situation unless you are also prepared to do something about it. To his surprise, Tim's father gave him permission to 'lead a group of other teenagers to plan and organize events for kids in the local area.'

This introduction to leadership, though born out of frustration, taught him an enormous amount and credit must go to a father whose patient guiding and mentoring skills extended to handing over the responsibility for one of his projects to his fifteen-year-old son.

Tim went to university some way from home but, having been immersed in the local church and in youth work and evangelism on a large, challenging housing estate since he was very young, his extra-curricular activity in this new place focussed on youth work with local young people, in an area at least as challenging as that at home.

At the end of his course of study, he elected not to go back home to live, using the word 'call' to describe his decision – 'youth work with local young people was a significant part of God's call to me to stay... It wasn't a flash of lightning type of call, just a strong sense that I was being given an insight into the needs of a city that I couldn't ignore.' (Morfin, 2015)

We should examine Tim's decision-making process a little more closely because we need to understand what he means, both by 'call' and by 'needs... that I couldn't ignore'.

As to the latter, he describes it this way, '[I am'] someone who has been made by God to enjoy action. I began to see more and more that giving my... time [to] these kids was worship to God.... I think about the teenagers who can't read the Bible or the words on the screen, or whose hyperactivity means they can't sit for ten minutes, let alone for the length of a church meeting.... What hope [is] there for this generation? And how do God's people respond if they find themselves in the middle of this kind of desolation? From such apparent hopelessness came the passion for disengaged children which has become the heartbeat of [the charity].'

As to his use of the word 'call', Tim talks about keeping a prayer diary – making notes of the things he has prayed for and writing down what he believes God has said to him. He is not only comfortable with the notion of God speaking to him, he expects it to happen, and not long before formalising the charity God spoke to him from 1 Thessalonians 5:24: 'The one who calls you is faithful and he will do it'. The diary entry reads, 'Calls not called. Present tense – not just a historical calling but a constant guiding and instruction.'

His expectation of a relationship with God is for it to involve continual communication and ongoing guidance. He describes a growing conviction regarding the work that God was 'calling' him to undertake but qualifies the use of that terminology: 'I believe the "calling" word can be overplayed. We are all called to live like Jesus and be good news. It is just living it and doing it. I don't think that there is anything super-special about the calling of those of us involved in this work. It seems to me that whatever we are asked to do by God, it is often born amidst frustration and desperation to see things change. God has put in me an ability to imagine things being different, and a concern for the church to do things differently. I saw that there are eternal things at stake, and that lives can be physically changed, hope brought and peace restored in this lifetime.'

The language that Tim uses here is entirely in keeping with the message of the upcoming chapters of this book – we will set out the various ways in which the word 'calling' is used in the Bible and establish that we are, first and foremost, called to a relationship with God that progressively makes us more like Jesus. We are to exhibit certain persistent attributes that He works into us by His Spirit and then we are to undertake tasks that He either points us towards or instructs us to initiate or places directly in our path for us to fall over.

Tim's choice of words is helpful in several respects; firstly, wishing to relax the 'calling imperative' takes the pressure off us having to hear some unequivocal word from God before undertaking any form of activity and puts the emphasis back on relationship. What we end up feeling called to do *must* flow from that relationship and, as long as we are engaging with God, the onus is on Him to show us the rightness (or otherwise) of our actions. For Tim, confirmation of that rightness has often come during the course of the activity. Secondly, his words point to one of the principal ways that God has used over the years to get his attention – namely, to show him a need that is not being met or a situation that is unresolved and to allow him to feel frustrated, or even desperate, about it. Is he affected the same way by every need and every situation? No. There are certain kinds of need that God seems to have made Tim particularly sensitive to and which trigger his determination to act. It will not be exactly the same for you and for me but God is clever and He knows what opportunities or circumstances or need profiles or challenges are most likely to grab each person's attention and to trigger our desire for involvement.

Plenty of people, over the years, have tried to convince Tim that he must have a 'calling' to Church leadership or to be ordained or to some other form of full-time ministry, but he knew that was not God's way for him. He says, 'Throughout my mid-twenties I'd successfully resisted invitations to become a church leader or minister. Despite the confidence of those making the approach to me, I couldn't bring myself to inflict my visionary, strategic, systematic leadership style on a poor unsuspecting congregation! Yet, as the [charity] vision grew in my heart, I began to know that [this] was what God had planned for me.'

This is very common – leaders in the Church often tend to assume that those who exhibit leadership skills must be called to ministry or mission within the context of the Church. Thankfully, although Tim rightly says (above) that he has 'a concern for the church to do things differently', he has practised listening to God and he knows that God has a slightly different outlet for his talents.

Tim is still heavily involved in a local church but he knows that a major portion of his 'ministry' is to be exercised via an organization external to and independent of the Church. And, although it started modestly, the charity has grown into an enterprise that is able both to harness the missional energy of many churches and to appeal to both government and other corporate bodies for support.

The young person whose transformation provided faith and impetus all those years ago is now much older but still going on with God and growing in wisdom and championing the cause. He has been joined by many, many others whose stories of rescue are inspiring and provide proof that this vision came from God and is still enjoying His inspiration.

For Tim personally, there were various defining moments following the start of operations in 1998 – he made a bold choice to reduce his employed days from five to four per week, which made him (at the time) the only male manager working part time in a global company. Then, two years later, an even bolder choice saw him negotiate his way out, as he began to understand that the charity would be his main activity – he knew commitment was very important and that he had to let people know that 'this is the thing'.

There are occasions in life when, as the founder and CEO of The Message Trust says, 'if God doesn't show up, we're stuffed!' Tim's testimony was and is that God speaks and leads and confirms and supports – 'after all, first and foremost, this is His work and not ours; so, our starting point has always been that God will provide. The story continues to include so many of those "if God doesn't show up..." moments and, in doing so, continues to demonstrate God's presence with His people. Each time God provides what we need, we see something more of His heart to reach children and families facing crisis in education.'

If you talk to Tim today, some seventeen years later, his enthusiasm is undimmed and his resolve to rescue children and their families from exclusion, crisis and breakdown is as strong as ever. Among other things, he will tell you about the challenges of continuing to hear God; of the societal and cultural pressures on his organization and on those he is seeking to help; and of the need for teamwork and corporate decision-making in realizing the calling. These are all subjects we will be tackling in the following pages.

Chapter 2

Building a 'Theology of Calling'

In this chapter we will lay out a series of foundational principles. Although each is weight-bearing, as a set they are able to support the whole edifice of reasoned argument in the chapters to come.

Each of the claims made in these pages is now so familiar to me it has become part of the fabric of my understanding but I am not assuming that to be the case for you and I may not have expressed them in the most helpful way. You are therefore invited to consider all seven and to see if they 'ring true'. They need to be tested, not just against human experience and what 'seems right' but whether they measure up against the truth of scripture in its entirety.

One of the things that God said to me in the lead up to this material being written was that it is necessary to be 'rigorous' with what we think He may be revealing to us; with what we yearn for; with the outworking of our dreams and visions; and with our handling of His word. If God says something we can be absolutely confident of it coming to pass and it therefore behoves us to ponder, to question and to investigate until we 'understand aright'.

In establishing a theology of calling, it is important to stay 'grounded' – I have no intention of going off into flights of fancy, but I do believe that God has *enduring* work for every person to do. I will be defending the rightness and the reality of our having been created in God's image, each person unique from every other being in the universe. I am claiming that God has put a sense of destiny in the heart of each one of us and, further than that, He has 'stuff' for each of us to accomplish. What kind of stuff? Stuff that is to be done in a way that only you can do it.

One more thing about remaining grounded... although I believe God wants us to get to grips with the special tasks that He has earmarked for each of us, I know that 'calling' is not just about vocation. There are other, foundational aspects to 'our life in Christ' and the vocational piece is intended to be subordinate to those, as should become clear.

Claim 1: Senses of 'rightness' that are the first inklings of God 'calling us'

Have there been times in your life, however short or however fleeting, when you have been engaged on a project or carrying out a set of actions or involved in an activity and you have said to yourself, 'I think this is me – it feels as though this is what I was made to do'? Or you might have uttered the phrase, 'I'm in my element'. Maybe it wasn't quite as clear as that but have there been times when you definitely felt the 'rightness', the 'fit' and the 'timeliness' of what you were doing?

When someone gets one of those senses, God is almost certainly involved but it is likely that, within a very short time, several other thoughts will try to counter the initial sense – 'that can't be right, I'm not trained to do that' or 'I'm not good enough' or 'I could never make a living doing that' or 'that role/position is too up-front or important or senior for someone like me'.

Whether or not you can answer Yes to the question posed above, have you ever found yourself thinking, 'I'm sure there's something "special" that I am supposed to do with my life – something "different" – something that's not the same as the other people around me?'

Such thoughts and senses are quite common, both in those whom we would call 'believers' or 'people with faith' and in those who characterize themselves as an 'unbeliever'. It is not common, however, for people in either category to follow those thoughts through to a satisfactory conclusion. If you have had at least one 'this is me' or 'I'm different' experience, it is unlikely that you then ran off and declared it to those closest to you, in the way that the teenage Joseph shared his dreams with his father and brothers in Genesis 37. It is more likely that you kept the thoughts to yourself and waited, sometimes for years, to see if corroboration or confirmation would come from somewhere. Indeed, many go into middle or older age carrying a sense of at least partial failure or lack of fulfilment, harbouring 'what if' questions.

In spite of having had the kind of thoughts and senses I'm describing, we all tend to rationalise when it comes to following 'dreams', especially if we have people to look after and responsibilities to fulfil and even more so if the following of dreams will have significant economic consequences.

We are going to talk about why 'this is me' and 'I'm different' thoughts are both biblical and should be pursued. God is in them and they lead, sometimes directly but more often by a slightly circuitous route, to us finding out how our unique shape fits into His purposes. But there is another reason, more important than any individual finding his/her fulfilment, why we need to take the pursuit seriously – God has plans and purposes and He has determined to use men and women in their outworking.

Claim 2: We must be 'about our Father's business'

We will do well to appreciate just how clever God is in plugging the people best suited into prepared roles. We also need to appreciate that this is a matter of life and death – we were not put on this earth to follow our instincts or to determine our own path, we were bought with a price and there is a kingdom to be established, first of all in the individual and then in the wider world.

God's agenda surely has to take priority but it can be difficult to apprehend – a disappointing number of us are operating on instinct and 'hoping for the best'. But what if our 'best' is only second or third best? The best is found by revelation and then realized by obedience but God is infinitely gracious and He gives us clues – each person's design is known to Him and to that individual and there are times when the individual is doing something that matches, or nearly matches, a key element of his/her design. It's a clue and they know it!

Let's just pick up the idea of 'instinct' again for a moment – I will keep returning to the fact that God's intention all along, right from the moment He created man and woman in His own image, was for those things that are instinctive to His nature to become instinctive to ours. In other words, we too should operate according to the principles inherent within the godhead and, in any role we take on or task we perform, we should exhibit the characteristics of His nature.

Although we are created in His image, our ability to model God's character when we do things is not instinctive – it is something we need to get progressively better at. Isaiah 55:8-9 says, 'For my thoughts are not your thoughts, nor are your ways my ways, says the Lord. For as the heavens are higher than the earth, so are my ways higher than your ways, and my thoughts than your thoughts.' That is true but He intends that His ways should become ours in increasing measure as we submit to His Holy Spirit. As we do so, we will undergo character change and things that were formerly alien to our nature will start to become natural to us. Furthermore, He seems to have ordained a significant proportion of the change to take place as we get on with the things He has called us to do.

When considering the way in which someone works out their callings in this world, Jesus was obviously an unusual case! Unlike us, He had the natural attributes of His Father in full measure. We will talk in more detail about these, and how we must learn to model them, in Chapters 6–8 but the Bible indicates that, although still learning and developing, Jesus knew and was pursuing his calling from before the age of twelve. Recall what he said to his parents when they finally found him, sitting among the teachers in the temple, after searching for him for three days: 'Why were you looking for me? Did you not know that I must be about my Father's business?' Luke 2:49. Even at this early stage, the committed relationship with His Heavenly Father eclipsed the one with His earthly parents.

Then, when Jesus began His ministry at the age of thirty, He instinctively did so both in plurality (in teamwork with the Father and the Holy Spirit) and by presenting His Father to the disciples as their Father too. He put 'committed, mutually beneficial relationship' and 'parenthood', both of which are fundamental to God's nature, at the heart of all that He said and did. Both originated back at the beginning – Genesis 2:18-24 has God saying, 'It is not good that the man should be alone; I will make a helper fit for him' and Genesis 1:28 has Him saying, 'Be fruitful and multiply and fill the earth and subdue it' – and both were heralded even before there was a community or a job of work or an aspiration to achieve.

The teamwork involved in Jesus' ministry was obvious to the disciples – in Acts 10:38 Peter testifies that 'God anointed Jesus with the Holy Spirit' and 'God was with Him'. Both the teamwork and the parenthood aspects were clear even to those who hated Him – John 5:18 says, 'This was why the Jews were seeking all the more to kill Him, because not only was He breaking the Sabbath, but he was even calling God his own Father, making Himself equal with God.'

A study of Jesus' interactions with people shows, both by the language He used and the actions He took, that He, like His Heavenly Father, displays the characteristics of both father and mother. This can be seen, for example, in His lament over Jerusalem in Luke 13:34 – 'O Jerusalem, Jerusalem, the city that kills the prophets and stones those who are sent to it! *How often would I have gathered your children together as a hen gathers her brood under her wings*, and you were not willing!'

Throughout his life on earth, Jesus only did what His Father gave him to do and, crucially, He did it in the way His Father would have done it. Again, in John 5 he says, 'I can do nothing on my own. As I hear, I judge, and my judgment is just, because I seek not my own will but the will of him who sent me.' And again, 'Truly, truly, I say to you, the Son can do nothing of his own accord, but only what he sees the Father doing. For whatever the Father does, that the Son does likewise.' Jesus had the Father's nature and He knew not just *what* the Father was doing but *how* He was doing it and was able instinctively to employ those same characteristics.

It is most important that we learn to heed God's promptings because we too must be about our Father's business. There are two main ways to fail:

- We can spend our time and use our talents in pursuit of personal treasure (and each person knows what his/her true motivation is), which will be a waste of our talents because we'll be building a rival kingdom;
- We can bury our talents, out of fear or an unwillingness to take responsibility for who we are.

Either way, it is a refusal to do the specific tasks that God is allocating to us... the things tailored to match who He has deliberately made us to be.

However, if we submit our time and talents to the God who made us, with the desire to build His kingdom, we will find a fitting role in the building process. In Luke 11, where Jesus has just cast out a demon from a dumb man and is instructing the crowds about rival kingdoms, there is a telling verse: Jesus says, 'He who is not on my side opposes me, and he who gathers in his store without having me by his side scatters his goods.' (Cassirer, 1989)

Claim 3: He wants to give us work that is actually enjoyable

In Ephesians 2:10 it says, 'For we are God's handiwork, created as men who have their being in Christ Jesus, in order that we should give ourselves up to the performance of good works which God has prepared beforehand, *so that we might enjoy our lives in the doing of them*.' (Cassirer, 1989)

This is a crucial verse which most translations render as, '...good works, which God prepared beforehand that we should *walk in them*' so, how did Heinz Cassirer arrive at 'enjoy our lives in the doing of them'? The Greek word translated 'walk' is 'περιπατήσωμεν / peripatesomen' and it does mean to walk but is literally 'to tread all around' and so the sense is of maintaining a certain 'walk of life' or 'way of life'. Paul is therefore talking about how I am to spend my whole life engaged in doing what God has already prepared for me and, by definition, that means what God has determined for/matched to/tailored to *me as an individual*.

That is interesting but it still doesn't quite get us to the word 'enjoy'. A clue is in 'good works' – the Greek word for 'good' is 'ἀγαθός / agathos' and it indicates what has originated from God and is being empowered by God. For those who are 'in Christ Jesus', these good works are *His* works, that He accomplishes through us, by means of our faith.

In the same way that Jesus had joy in fulfilling the Father's will and spoke of it to His disciples, when He said, 'If you keep my commandments, you will abide in my love, just as I have kept my Father's commandments [done all that He has told me] and abide in His love. These things I have spoken to you, that my joy may be in you, and that your joy may be full' (John 15:10-11), we too are intended to find joy in the outworking of our lives, by faith.

Heinz Cassirer, with his Jewish lens, detected an unmistakeable sense of Shalom in what Paul is saying about the good works in Ephesians 2 – a 'shalom' that is supposed to indwell the 'walk of life' of the one 'in Christ', who, by His Holy Spirit, reveals and then empowers a whole series of good works that have been pre-prepared. As anyone who is Jewish will tell you, shalom is a great deal more than 'peace' – it is rest, prosperity, wholeness, welfare, completion, fullness and even well-being. There are echoes here of what is declared in Proverbs 8:22-31 about the role of 'wisdom' in creation (surely, in this context, a synonym for Jesus) - 'I was beside him, like a master workman, and I was daily filled with delight, rejoicing before him always' (verse 30). We who are 'in Christ' are called to be like Him in enjoying what we do.

Lastly, this same sense of enjoyment in doing God's will is encapsulated in what David says in Psalm 40:6-8. David, the earthly king and 'type' of Jesus, is first pondering his own response to Yahweh's deliverance – 'In sacrifice and offering you have not delighted, but you have given me an open ear. Burnt offering and sin offering you have not required.' And then he utters the responsive dedication that the true Messianic King would make – 'Then I said, "Behold, I have come; in the scroll of the book it is written of me: *I delight to do your will*, O my God; your law is within my heart".' Alec Motyer's translation of this last verse is, '...in the roll of the book it is written about me; *to do your good pleasure, my God, I delight*' (Motyer, 2016).

There are three things to say about 'enjoying the things that God gives us to do'.

Firstly, it's okay! There are some who think that, in order to be doing God's will, we need to suffer – that the only worthwhile things are hard things. There is no doubt that suffering is often part of the package but what we're talking about here is not 'leisure' or 'only doing what we happen to like doing', it's pointing to a connection between what God gives us to do and the kind of person that we are. The connectedness leads to a sense of purpose and a deep satisfaction, which can be there even if life is difficult.

Secondly, just because you sense God giving you something to do and even though you enjoy doing that project or activity or job, it does not necessarily mean you have found your vocation – but, it's almost certainly a clue to what it might be. There is the 'What' we do but there is also the 'How' we do it and 'Why' we do it to take into consideration. When God made you, He gave you a unique combination of personality traits and gifts/ aptitudes/ skills/ capabilities and motivated abilities – in other words, it might not just have been *what* you did that gave you enjoyment or satisfaction, it might have been *the way* you were allowed to do it or the set of capabilities you were able to employ in the doing of it or *the outcome* of the exercise.

Thirdly, it is possible that you will need a number of such 'clues' before you know for certain what God might be calling you to. A number of different experiences that all *resonate* in some way with *who you are* might build a more accurate picture of what God is trying to tell you. [*Resonance*, in this context, is meant to indicate a heightening of the spiritual senses and/or a stirring of the heart, along with a profound feeling of 'rightness' either at the time or in retrospect.]

Claim 4: God makes 'far-sighted judgment calls' to guide us towards His goal

We are going to talk about us being admitted to God's family, as legitimate heirs, and then how He progressively brings healing and wholeness to us, so that we can fully appreciate our new status and properly participate in what was referred to in Chapter 1 as 'the family business'.

When you become a Christian, there is a personal transaction between you and Jesus – your response to His call – and it results in you being admitted to His family. As Ephesians 1:4-5 says, 'He (the Father) chose us in him (Jesus) before the foundation of the world, that we should be holy and blameless before him. In love He predestined us for adoption as sons through Christ Jesus, according to the purpose of His will'. This notion of being 'adopted into sonship' actually has both an immediate part to it and a future part and, so that you don't just take my word for it, we need to look at the New Testament verses which prove it...

The immediate part: Galatians 4:6-7 says, 'Because *you are sons*, God has sent the Spirit of his Son into our hearts, crying, "Abba! Father!" So, *you are no longer a slave, but a son*, and if a son, then an heir through God.' And Romans 8:16-17 says, 'The Spirit himself bears witness with our spirit that *we are children of God*, and if children, then heirs—heirs of God and fellow heirs with Christ...' So, when Christ died for us, the price was paid, and when we trust him, we are legally and permanently in the family. We can relax in the sure knowledge that we now have all the rights of sonship.

The future part: Romans 8:22-23 says, 'The whole creation has been groaning together in the pains of childbirth until now. And not only the creation, but we ourselves, who have the first fruits of the Spirit, groan inwardly as *we wait eagerly for adoption as sons*, the redemption of our bodies'. So, as well as giving us our legally adopted status, God has also set in motion a process by which we are led, as individuals, by degrees, from our unholy state to maturity. Or, we could see ourselves as in some way 'dysfunctional', and then our dysfunction progressively being healed until we are completely 'whole'. We also know this process by another name – 'sanctification'.

As to the actual mechanism by which God has determined to sanctify or transform us, we need to look at some verses that may be a little difficult to follow at first reading – the point I want to make will come from the italicised portion but I have completed the quote to establish context and to indicate that the end of the matter is for God to bring everything to wholeness 'in Christ': Ephesians 1:7-10 [NKJV] says, 'In Him we have redemption through His blood, the forgiveness of sins, *according to the riches of His grace which He made to abound toward us in all wisdom and prudence*, having made known to us the mystery of His will, according to His good pleasure which He purposed in Himself, that in the dispensation of the fullness of the times He might gather together in one all things in Christ, both which are in heaven and which are on earth—in Him.'

One of the many things that Paul is explaining in this passage is that the riches of God's grace are administered to us, wisely and *prudently*. The word 'prudent' comes from the Latin 'prudens' which means 'far-sighted'. So, this is a calculated process on God's part. Choosing not to abandon us in our inadequacy, He makes good/sensible and far-sighted judgment calls, using all His experience and knowledge, and administers doses of His grace which are intended to move us, bit by bit, towards what He can already envisage us becoming.

As we have stated, this is a process, a journey, an adventure and it's intensely personal. Changing the metaphor slightly; you can expect Him to talk to you at each twist and turn in the road, and at each junction, about the choice of route that He has determined.

As soon as I understood Ephesians 1:8, although I hope I have retained a healthy fear of the Lord, I stopped being afraid of judgment because, although God will never compromise over sin and there is an inevitable reckoning for any who reject Jesus' atoning work, God's judgment is more about continuous assessment than about setting a final exam. For all those who take Him seriously and are His sons and daughters, it's about the consistent application of grace that makes judgments about where we are and where we need to be and, like a satnav, plots the route. So, what should it be like for us to take that route?

We all know that life is not all plain sailing. We know that there will be difficulty and opposition and some suffering along the way. But, recalling the thought from Ephesians 2:10, that good works of the kingdom should be enjoyed, it is important to grasp that God's best intention for the work(s) we do, throughout the course of each one's individual odyssey, is that they be personally chosen and fulfilling.

Most people who are seeking to be led by God understand that, even in difficulty, it is possible to know that you are in the right place, doing the right things. However, I am taking it at least one step further and saying that the notion of hearing and responding to God's callings is central to the process of sanctification and the One who is guiding us along the route has made it possible to find 'shalom' (a sense of rightness, peace and wellbeing), at each stage.

Claim 5: We are to offer our lives on an 'Altar acceptable to God'

To make this point, I am going to use someone else's words and so I need to preface them with a little (auto)biographical background. Back in the early 1980s, when I got married, my wife's parents, though British, were living and working in Israel. He was a doctor and she a nurse. They spoke Hebrew and attended what was called the Messianic Assembly, at a time when there were only about 400 believers in the whole country. I had some appreciation of the biblical languages but these two 'inherited parents' kick-started my education about aspects of the Jewish mindset and gave me an appreciation of the place of the Jewish nation in God's purposes.

Today there are many thousands of Jews in Israel who acknowledge Jesus [Yeshua] as Lord. Daniel Yahav is one of those, serving as pastor of the Peniel Fellowship in Tiberias, beside the Sea of Galilee. Daniel has had a very interesting pilgrimage, seeking to follow a sequence of calls from God, which took him from church ministry into founding a successful business and then back again to the church.

It is important for those of us in the Gentile world to pursue an understanding of the Jewish perspective on the subject of calling. God issued His first 'calls' to the Jews and the biblical accounts of their fulfilment, though inspired by a sovereign God, describe a Jewish culture and necessarily have a Jewish flavour.

Daniel recently published a series of teachings entitled 'An altar acceptable to God', expounding a passage in Exodus 20:22-24 which says, 'Thus you shall say to the people of Israel: "You have seen for yourselves that I have talked with you from heaven. You shall not make gods of silver to be with me, nor shall you make for yourselves gods of gold. An altar of earth you shall make for me and sacrifice on it your burnt offerings and your peace offerings, your sheep and your oxen. In every place where I cause my name to be remembered I will come to you and bless you".'

Daniel comments on these verses as follows:

The Law speaks to us in pictures and shadows, but the fulfilment of them is in the New Covenant through Yeshua (Colossians 2:16-7, Hebrews 10:1). These pictures are of great value, teaching us deep spiritual truths if we correctly understand them, and they can make it easier for us to remember these truths.

In Hebrews 13:11-12, the writer is making a comparison between Yeshua and the sacrifice on the Day of Atonement. Yeshua offered Himself as a sacrifice on the cross, and so the cross was His altar. In the same way, we as His followers, are called to offer our lives to God. In the gospel of John, Yeshua expresses that He came to fulfil that which His Father gave Him to do. (John 17:4). In another place He said that He doesn't do anything except that which the Father reveals to Him. All the deeds that He did were what the Father had sent Him to do - leading to the final sacrifice on the cross. Yeshua poured out His life on this altar of service which the Father had given Him to fulfil. Sometimes He didn't sleep at night. We read that when He was in Jerusalem He was hungry in the morning, meaning He had not eaten breakfast. In another place He says 'the foxes have dens and the birds have nests but I don't have anywhere to lay My head.' He sacrificed Himself all the way, not just on the cross, in order to fulfil all that the Father had planned for Him.

Paul also speaks in the same way in his letter to the Philippians (2:17). He described himself as being poured out on the altar as a drink offering. All of Paul's life, his calling to bring the good news of the gospel to the Gentiles and also to the Jews, was his sacrifice for God's purposes (Acts 9:15). This was his calling and this was his ministry, it was for this cause that he poured out his life. It was for this that they lashed him with whips on several occasions and for this they stoned him, and for this he was thrown in jail. He was shipwrecked a number of times, he suffered hunger and nakedness, because this was his God-given calling, and this was the altar on which he was continually sacrificing his life.

With this in mind, let's now apply it to our own lives: 'Therefore I urge you, brethren, by the mercies of God to present your bodies as a living sacrifice, holy and acceptable to God, which is your spiritual service of worship. And do not be conformed to this world, but be transformed by the renewing of your mind, so that you may prove what the will of God is, that which is good, and acceptable and perfect' (Romans 12:1). First of all, we see that our lives are a sacrifice, not just our death. We are focusing here on the sacrifice of our daily lives, and not on the drama of death itself.

Paul tells us not to be like the world, but to be transformed by the renewing of our minds, so that we know what God's will is. It is important to realize that only God knows the altar which He has prepared for us because only He knows the deeds that He has prepared for us to do. 'For we are His workmanship, created in the Messiah Yeshua, for good works, which God prepared beforehand that we should walk in them' (Ephesians 2:10).

If you are launching into the army, into a career, into a certain ministry or anything else, and you want to do the maximum possible, this is good, but test your motives before the Lord. Have you sincerely asked God: 'What do You want me to do?' have you said to Him: 'Put me where You want me to be...' If not, and if you are thinking like the world, you will be following your own ambitions. But if your mind has truly been transformed, you will be asking God: 'What is your plan for my life?' If you think like the world, you might have your life mapped out already, from one step to the next. But if you are walking in the Spirit, you will be asking God: 'Lead me to fulfil your purposes for my life'.

This kind of walk before God, is an altar. In fact, only what God has prepared for us, is the altar on which we can sacrifice our lives. Anything else is a distraction and a waste of time. It is possible to go through life, doing many things, being involved in different projects and even 'ministries', making all the decisions, and finally reach the end, only to discover that we have completely missed God's plan for us. Let us be sure that this does not happen, by giving our whole lives over to God, to seek and to do His will, with the understanding that He will take us wherever He chooses, and He will use us according to His *good will, so that we will be sacrificing our lives on the altar He has prepared for us.*

Let's remember what Yeshua said: 'If anyone wishes to come after Me, he must deny himself, and take up his cross daily and follow Me' (Luke 9:23). That cross is the altar on which we sacrifice our lives daily, as we walk in the good deeds that God has prepared for us. It is not an easy place, it would require denying our flesh and sacrificing our comfort.

When we look at the life of Yeshua or Paul, we see that they were men of humility and simplicity (Matthew 11:28-29). God calls us as well, to sacrifice our lives on an altar that is simple and humble, which He has chosen for us. No matter what is our occupation, honourable or simple in the eyes of this world, if we are in a management position or spend our time at home caring for the family God has given us – this is our altar, and we can do our service with a humble heart unto the Lord, with thanksgiving. This will please our Heavenly Father, as Paul says '...whatever you do, do all to the glory of God.' (1 Corinthians 10:31)

If we are faithful in a little, the time may come to move on, and God will give us more. But it will still be an altar, simple and humble. It may be that the Lord will ask us to give up something that is valuable or honourable in the world's eyes in order to do something that is more valuable in His eyes. As long as we are in the place of His choice, doing what He has called us to do, that is worth treasure in heaven. This humble earthen altar on which we sacrifice our lives, will produce gold, silver and precious stones that will stand the test of fire. When Yeshua's eyes of fire will look at our lives, they will test everything we have done. Whatever was not from Him or according to His will, will be burned up and lost, but whatever was from Him and done for His glory by faith, love and sacrifice, will remain for eternity. (Yahav, 2019)

Although Daniel is approaching the subject of calling from a slightly different angle, what he is saying is the same – we are to serve at the Lord's pleasure, humbly, doing what He has determined for us, whatever the cost. We are to be 'about our Father's business.'

Claim 6: God can use whoever He wishes – even unbelievers

Speaking of 'kingdom purpose', we must also reckon with the fact that God, who is the Lord of all creation, can and will use those who do not know him to accomplish his work. A classic example of this is Cyrus, king of Persia, who conquered the Babylonians around 540BC. A couple of years later, he issued a decree allowing the exiled Jews to return to their homeland. Initially, as reported in Ezra and Nehemiah, about 50,000 people made the journey.

However, the book of Isaiah makes clear that Cyrus did not make this decision entirely of his own volition: 'Thus, says the Lord, your Redeemer… who says of Cyrus, "He is my shepherd and he shall fulfil all my purpose";

saying of Jerusalem, "She shall be built," and the temple, "Your foundation shall be laid". Thus, says the Lord to his anointed, to Cyrus, whose right hand I have grasped, to subdue nations before him and to loose the belts of kings, to open doors before him that gates may not be closed: "I will go before you and level the exalted places ... I will give you the treasures of darkness and the hoards in secret places, that you may know that it is I, the Lord, the God of Israel, who call you by your name. For the sake of my servant Jacob, and Israel my chosen, I call you by your name, I name you, though you do not know me. I am the Lord, and there is no other, besides me there is no God; I equip you, though you do not know me..."' (Isaiah 44:28 to Isaiah 45:5)

This would suggest that, not only did God direct Cyrus's decision, for the sake of His own people, but the rise of Cyrus as a conqueror of nations and all his other successes were God's sovereign work.

In the following chapters, we will see examples of God 'calling' both believers and non-believers to accomplish His purposes. The language quoted above, in Isaiah 44 & 45, is instructive; Cyrus' name, which probably came either from the Greek Kyros, which means 'far-sighted' [the Greek form of the Persian Kūrush] or from Kyrios, which means 'lord', was given to him by God and then God called out to him, by name, getting his attention and directing him at the right time to act in the interests of Israel.

As we will see in Chapter 4, when we talk about the names that people are called, it was normal for a person to be given a name that 'sounds like' either the circumstances surrounding their birth or an aspect of their intended purpose. Cyrus/Kyros sounds like 'Kairos', one of the Greek words for 'time' – not chronological or sequential time, which was 'Chronos', but rather 'the opportune or appropriate time'. Kairos is all about discerning the moment when something needs to be done; the opportune time to act. Now, obviously, God always acts at the right time but He had already decreed the length of time the nation of Israel would be in Babylon and He had already determined both the means and the agent of release. Having chosen that agent by name, it's not without the realms of possibility that He gave that name multiple, appropriate meanings.

Claim 7: The 'clues' that God gives need to be interpreted with care

We talked earlier about the 'this is me' moments in life, when God seems to be giving us clues as to what He has made us to do. The correct interpretation of these clues depends on maintaining relationship with God and listening carefully about how to make life decisions. The easiest way to illustrate this is to give a real-life example. The following is the experience of my daughter, Joy, who had what she describes as epiphanies earlier in her life, that seemed, at first, to be pointing in a particular direction. But, after several God-inspired career moves, in a different direction, and further questioning of His intentions, their purpose became clear. These are her own words:

'From early childhood, I felt like I was meant to be a teacher. My favourite thing at school was to finish my work early and then go around helping other people who'd got stuck. I even complained once to a teacher about how badly he was explaining simultaneous equations and happily took to the whiteboard when he replied with (a rather cross) "Well you have a go then!"

'I definitely felt that teaching was what God had made me for. I'd even had prophetic words about it. It felt "obvious". But, when it was time to make actual decisions, during and after university, I felt God directing me to unexpected options.

'A significant reason for choosing my university was its practice of students spending their third year on a placement in industry, before returning to complete the course. I had intended, from the outset, to take a teaching placement, but later found that the university had withdrawn that option and I had to look for an alternative.

'God most definitely then guided me towards joining a particular company, in the Oxford area, and having loved the project management job I ended up with, they offered me a permanent role in Oxford after graduating. This was also unexpected because I knew I would be moving to Leeds, as I was engaged and my fiancé was settled there, and the company in Oxford had no connection to Leeds.

'I obviously concluded that I would not be accepting the job but, at exactly the right moment, the company won a major contract, opened a Leeds office and were suddenly able to offer a graduate project manager role based in that location. To my surprise, I felt God lead me to accept it. But, I assumed this was a temporary measure – an easier way to start married life than taking on a PGCE immediately.

'Nine months later I was offered another, quite different, job. This time the focus was on business development and it felt like, if I accepted it, the ship would sail on teaching. On the one hand, I had what I felt God had said generally (but consistently) over many years about who I was – about being a teacher. Then, on the other hand, there was what He said to me specifically about this job offer, which was two things: firstly, that He wanted me to be about my Father's business (my dad had connections with the company) and secondly, from Ezekiel 47 where the river flowing from the temple becomes progressively deeper, I felt He was saying that He was going to bless the company and it would become increasingly successful.

'I decided that I had to go with what God was saying *now*. I assumed that I had either got it wrong previously about the whole teaching thing or that, if I hadn't, then probably it was going to look different to how I'd imagined. I decided I'd just have to wait and see what God did.

'More than ten years on, I am really confident I heard God correctly about those decisions. Amongst other things, the sales revenue of the company I went to work for increased by around 50–100% each year for several years, in exactly the way I felt God had told me it would from the passage in Ezekiel.

'In the end, the project management and business development roles turned out to be God's very specific training course and preparation for my current job. I became aware that a Christian charity, working with children, needed someone with my qualifications and, when I read the job description, felt for the first time like "this is a job that is completely designed for me". God confirmed the rightness of it in several ways: through a passage from the story of Gideon; through a picture where I had been slogging up a mountain, but was now climbing down into a valley filled with fruit trees, where He was indicating a new season of "ease" and fruitfulness; and through a profound sense of resonance as I prepared for the interview.

'I was amazed that God could find me a job that was so tailored to *what* I like doing, to *how* I like doing it, to *the outcomes* I am motivated by, and that would also enable me to earn enough to help support my family. And I have been equally amazed, in the years since, by how specifically the experience of those earlier roles seems to have been designed to show me how to do things that I would need later on.

'However, about a year ago, I felt God reminding me about what he'd said about being a teacher. I felt He was challenging me that I shouldn't have let go of it so completely. It wasn't that the decisions were wrong – they were right. And it wasn't that I shouldn't have put the timing and outworking into His hands – that was right too. Rather, it was that when God speaks, we are to treasure those things in our hearts, just as Mary did with testimonies of the shepherds and the magi that were shared with her on their visits in the early days of Jesus' life.

'A little while later, two separate people, neither of whom were well known to me, and apropos of nothing, said to me on the same day, "You're a teacher, aren't you?" The literal answer was "no" but something in my spirit kept saying "Yes!" and I realized that I really, really wanted to be teaching people about Jesus.

'I lead the children's ministry at our church and so I get to teach kids about Jesus a lot and I started to realize just how important a part of my calling that is, but also that I am called to be teaching adults too. I asked for an opportunity to speak at our church and it has felt very natural and "right" each time I've had a go – almost a relief to have that outlet and be able to "be myself" in that way.

'I know if I'd taken what I understood about myself and what I felt God had said, without listening to Him about specific decisions, I'd have become a classroom teacher. I'm certain that, even though that might have been okay, it wouldn't have been the best. I'm also sure that there is more to come in the outworking of the part of my calling to "be a teacher". This time I'm praying more actively about it and asking God to show me when and where I should be serving Him in that way.'

Summary and some working definitions

Hopefully, the above sequence of claims forms an understandable basis for what will follow. The arguments presented either make sense or they do not! If they do, there ought to be a growing incentive to move forward and to explore what God is really saying about 'calling'. To assist with that, let me suggest working definitions of 'calling', 'purpose', one's 'element' and 'God's normative calling process':

- A sense of calling – A God-given awareness, that is compelling and that I cannot ignore, of a particular role I need to play or a set of functions I need to perform. A sense of purpose that seems to have its own momentum and propels me forward, despite my not yet having all the skills and experience necessary for its fulfilment.
- Being in one's element – The experience of doing something where I'm expressing my unique attributes such that my natural aptitude coincides with my personal passion.
- God's normative calling process – When God issues calls to men and women, He is initiating strategic, day-to-day communication with individuals so that, by the prudent application of His grace, they can experience continuous personal and professional development and thereby be enabled to do useful, 'lasting' things that they enjoy and which achieve His kingdom purposes.
- Purpose – the underlying reasons (whether or not fully known) that provide impetus for pursuing a commission or a call.

Chapter 3

A Biblical Framework for Understanding Calling

Defining 'calling'

The dictionary definitions of 'calling' tend to focus on its vocational nature: 'a strong wish to do a job, usually one that's socially valuable'; 'an activity that is a person's most important job, especially one that the person has a strong interest in and ability for'; 'a strong urge towards a particular way of life or career – a vocation.'

The biblical definition of 'calling', however, is much broader – there are actually several parts to the definition, describing different aspects of 'calling', which must *all* be understood if we are to have a balanced view. The common factor in all aspects is that they are anchored in God speaking to us and in us hearing Him correctly and then deciding to obey what He tells us to do.

Understanding the will of God happens by revelation – as Romans 10:17 says, 'faith comes from hearing'. But, 'hearing God' seems to be a skill that is sadly lacking in the Church, both in an individual and a corporate sense and it is not often taught. In order for each of us to do God's will, we need to be practised at testing and looking for confirmation of what we believe He is saying to us. It is also advisable to have wise and prayerful people at our disposal, from time to time, to assist.

Personal decision-making is hard enough but it is even more difficult to make right decisions in a corporate context (be it within a marriage or a family or a business or in a church group) and equally important to have testing mechanisms in place, along with a willingness to consider and debate alternatives, to expect confirmations and to seek consensus.

There is enormous value to be derived from actively seeking God for revelation and then learning to distinguish His voice from all the other, competing voices.

The Os Guinness Framework (with a couple of tweaks & illustrations)

The following basic framework for defining the word 'Calling', as it is used in the Bible, has been borrowed from Os Guinness, with his permission (Guinness, 1998). I have used this because it is the most balanced of all that I've yet come across. Os suggests four different ways in which the word 'calling' is used. Other than the four main headings, wherever his words are used they are indicated by quotation marks:

1. The Hebrew for 'call' has the same everyday meaning as our English word

When we call out to someone we are attracting their attention – it is a relational thing and has had that meaning since Old Testament times. Thus, right from the beginning, God has been in communication with us and that communication works in both directions:

Men (believers and unbelievers) and other creatures call out to God

- '[God] provides food for the cattle and for the young ravens when they call', Psalm 147:9;
- 'Consecrate a fast; call a solemn assembly. Gather the elders and all the inhabitants of the land to the house of the Lord your God, and cry/call out to the Lord', Joel 1:14;
- '...but let man and beast be covered with sackcloth, and let them call out mightily to God. Let everyone turn from his evil way and from the violence that is in his hands', Jonah 3:8;
- 'But Naaman was angry and went away, saying, "Behold, I thought that he would surely come out to me and stand and call upon the name of the Lord his God, and wave his hand over the place and cure the leper".' 2Kings 5:11.

God calls out to men

- In Eden – 'But the Lord God called to the man and said to him, "Where are you?"' Genesis 3:9;
- The burning bush – 'When the Lord saw that he turned aside to see, God called to him out of the bush, "Moses, Moses!" And he said, "Here I am."' Exodus 3:4;

- Jesus and the children – 'But Jesus called them to him, saying, "Let the children come to me, and do not hinder them, for to such belongs the kingdom of God."' Luke 18:16.

2. We 'call' both people and things by a name

A name is a label or description which identifies something or someone and makes it or them distinct from other things or people. The name identifies its owner but is not just intended as a tag, it also carries a sense of 'calling something into being'.

In the Bible, created objects are given names, individual people are given names and corporate entities (groups or nations) are given names. For example:

- **Things** – 'God called the light "day" and the darkness he called "night".' Genesis 1:5;
- **Individuals** – 'He called His disciples… Simon, whom he named (called) Peter, and Andrew his brother…" Luke 6:13-14. "And I tell you, you are Peter, and on this rock, I will build my church, and the gates of hell shall not prevail against it."' Matthew 16:18;
- **Corporate Entities** – God gave the nation the name 'Israel' and thereby constituted it and them as his people. He did this by changing Jacob's name to Israel back in Genesis and then telling him that from him would come a great nation. A very interesting name/identity thing then happens in a verse at the end of Genesis, when Jacob is dying and calls his twelve sons to him to bless them. He says, 'Assemble and listen, O sons of *Jacob*, listen to *Israel* your father.' Genesis 49:2. They had been born to Jacob but they were being blessed by Israel.

Throughout the Bible there are also 'City States', which stand as symbols of man's corporate endeavours and which, when called by a name, gain an identity and character of their own. For example: Nineveh is 'the bloody city' (Nahum 3:1); Babylon is 'the mother of harlots' (Revelation 17:5); Tyre is 'the jubilant city' (Isaiah 23:7); Jerusalem is Ariel, 'the lion of God' (Isaiah 29:1).

Keep in mind that in two of the examples I have used (Simon/Peter and Jacob/Israel) there is a change of name. The new name, in each case, describes something of the calling or destiny of the individual/group. God does this far more often than you might have thought – it seems to be a habit of His to declare His purpose for someone by naming them or re-naming them. Accordingly, it is extremely important to grasp the point that the act of naming someone also carries a sense of 'calling something into being'.

When God calls us, He is not labelling a finished work, He is kicking off a sequence of events. The call is to someone who is not yet what He wants them to be and therefore someone upon whom He intends to lavish grace. By definition, they don't have all the requisite skills and experience at the outset and, of course, they lack confidence and need to be moulded and made whole and equipped – that's the nature of calling.

3. God 'calls people to Himself as followers of Christ'

This aspect of calling 'is almost synonymous with salvation'. The followers of Jesus, as a whole, are a community of the 'called-out ones' (a possible meaning of the word 'ecclesia', the Greek word for church). For example:

- 'To all who are in Rome, beloved of God, called to be saints: Grace to you...' Romans 1:7;
- 'And it shall come to pass in the place where it was said to them, "You are not My people", there they shall be called sons of the living God.' Romans 9:26;
- 'To the church of God which is at Corinth, to those who are sanctified in Christ Jesus, called to be saints, with all who in every place call on the name of Jesus Christ our Lord, both theirs and ours.' 1 Corinthians 1:2;
- [Speaking of Unity in the Church] 'I, therefore, the prisoner of the Lord, beseech you to walk worthy of the calling with which you were called...' Ephesians 4:1.

4. Jesus calls His followers A) to live according to kingdom principles and B) to undertake specific tasks:

It is only at this stage in the framework that we begin to consider the things God might want us to do and, even then, the callings that God issues are usually directed at followers of Christ, whose lives are at least beginning to be transformed. It's not that a particular standard has to be reached before we can do anything – we are all miles away from being 'righteous' – but lasting value is dependent on Him having His way, rather than us insisting on our own way.

As we will see, the God who made us in His image always intended that we exhibit the instinctive qualities of His own nature in what we do. But, because of our fallen nature, those qualities can't become evident unless we are 'in Christ', practising the right behaviours and attitudes and letting the Holy Spirit work them into our being.

Called to a quality of life in Christ, characterized by certain persistent attributes

Here are a few of those qualities, the descriptions of which are fairly self-explanatory. They are offered in the order in which they are found in the New Testament:

- **Freedom** – Galatians 5:13 'For you were *called* to freedom, brothers. Only do not use your freedom as an opportunity for the flesh, but through love serve one another';
- **Hope** – Ephesians 1:18 'Having the eyes of your hearts enlightened, that you may know what is the hope to which He has *called* you, what are the riches of his glorious inheritance in the saints'; Ephesians 4:4 'There is one body and one spirit – just as you were called to the one hope that belongs to your call – one Lord, one faith, one baptism, one God and Father of all';
- **Peace & Thankfulness** – Colossians 3:15 'And let the peace of Christ rule in your hearts, to which indeed you were *called* in one body. And be thankful';
- **Eternal Life** – 1Timothy 6:12 'Fight the good fight of the faith. Take hold of the eternal life to which you were *called* and about which you made the good confession in the presence of many witnesses';
- **Holiness** – 2Timothy 1:9 'God, who saved us and *called* us to a holy calling, not because of our works but because of his own purpose and grace, which he gave us in Christ Jesus before the ages began'; 1Thessalonians 4:7 'For God has not *called* us for impurity, but in holiness';
- **Suffering** – 1Peter 2:21 'For to this you have been *called*, because Christ also suffered for you, leaving you an example, so that you might follow in his footsteps';
- **Blessing (not reviling)** – 1Peter 3:9 'Do not repay evil for evil or reviling for reviling, but on the contrary, bless, for to this you were *called* that you may obtain a blessing';
- **Eternal Glory & Excellence** – 1Peter 5:10 'And after you have suffered a little while, the God of all grace, who has *called* you to his eternal glory in Christ, will himself restore, confirm, strengthen and establish you'; 2Peter 1:3 'His divine power has granted to us all things that pertain to life and godliness, through the knowledge of him who *called* us to his own glory and excellence...'

If someone is bent on exhibiting evidence of this combination of attributes or characteristics, they will become increasingly sensitive to God's promptings, more likely to hear Him clearly and prone to following His instructions accurately. In short, they will become people to whom God can entrust useful and important tasks.

God is a role model who instinctively operates according to His own nature and wants that nature to be ours as well. The attributes listed above are only possible because God's essential nature – who He is – supports them. They betray the kind of person He is and He cannot be other than that. When He made man[kind], we had His essential nature built into us and it was immediately assumed that we would operate accordingly.

Called to work(s), be it commission or vocation

In the Bible, we don't find the words 'calling' or 'called' regularly used when someone undertakes a specific task or a role. What we do find repeatedly, however, is God speaking to people and giving them instructions about *what* He wants them to do and *how* He wants them to do it. In other words, all the right language is used and, furthermore, what God reveals to someone and the instructions He gives are always specific to the individual, who most often will have to work with one or more others to accomplish the task.

We will be looking at a wide variety of examples of this in the coming chapters, exploring the nature of the call in each case, pointing out the ways in which God gets an individual's attention (the first meaning of calling from the framework) and indicating how God names or renames an individual in line with their calling (the second meaning of calling from the framework).

As Paul wrote to the followers of Christ at Colossae: 'Whatever you do, work at it with all your heart, as working for the Lord, not for men' (Colossians 3:23). This verse doesn't differentiate between work that someone is obliged to do and work that someone feels called to do – instead, it is pointing to another 'persistent attribute' that needs to be built into us; something that, once again, is instinctive to God's own nature and which He wants to become instinctive to ours. Namely, a commitment to excellence because God is a craftsman and He cannot be anything else – it is not in His nature to do an 'adequate' job and He doesn't ever say, 'that will do'.

When God made the world and everything in it, His assessment, at each stage, was that 'it was good' – see Genesis 1:3, 10, 12, 18, 21, 25. In Genesis 1:31, He says, 'it was very good.' We are to adopt that same focus when undertaking *any* task of work. Such an attitude, if persistent, will build quality and excellence into whatever we do.

Look again at Ephesians 2:10 – 'For we are His workmanship, created in Christ Jesus for good works, which God prepared beforehand, that we should walk in them.' This affirms what we have said above; about us being created, in His image, for good works that are only possible when we are 'in Christ' and having His essential attributes built into our nature.

Called primarily to some*one* rather than to some*thing*

We began to establish this principle at Point 2 in the framework above – being called *by name*. There is individuality and purpose built into who we are. 'Who we are' matters to us and it matters to God and so the relationship we have with Him is intensely personal.

Being 'called to' a set of tasks sounds a bit clinical but the process is actually meant to be organic, happening as an extension to relationship; a natural outworking of our wanting to be 'about our Father's business'. It should make all the difference in the world to me that I am called '*by Him*'. Equally, when I am 'called to' a task, I can see purpose in it but the question is, whose purpose? I am arguing throughout this book that it is our Father's work and it should make all the difference in the world that I do it '*for Him*'.

Calling is increasingly being talked about in secular circles and, in that context, the term is limited to some vocation to which a person aspires, because it employs their perceived skill set and encapsulates both their interests and the particular way they wish to be useful.

Although there is such a thing as 'common grace' and it would be true to say that some human aspirations have aspects of God's character clearly in evidence, to regard 'calling' as a secular concept would be to strip it of its true meaning. If you deny the God who inspires it and gives it purpose, you also impose catastrophic human limitations on the value of the result.

For the person of faith or the 'believer', a 'calling' is a great deal more than whatever the secular world might aspire to:

Firstly, being anchored in a relationship with Jesus Christ and the Father (Point 3 of the framework) it is born out of that relationship. If there is no relationship of son or daughter to a Father, there is no awareness of revelation, no sanctifying process and no kingdom purpose to the calling.

Secondly, where a relationship with God does exist, calling is primarily to establish the foundational attributes of life in God's family (Point 4A) – the exhibiting of characteristics that are inextricably part of and should be a natural consequence of that life.

Thirdly, unless those foundational attributes are present, or at least are being acquired, the calling to specific tasks, be they short or long-term, is fraught with difficulty and potentially doomed to disaster, because the callings (by definition) are issued by God, are His work and are dependent on Him for their successful outworking. Someone who has no interest in their life exhibiting the evidence of relationship with God is hardly likely to produce lasting results.

Os Guinness rightly points out that the two strands of the meaning of calling, set out in Point 4, 'are the basis for a vital distinction between a Primary and a Secondary calling. Our Primary calling as followers of Christ is by him, to him, and for him. First and foremost, we are called to Some*one* (God), <u>not</u> to some*thing* (such as motherhood, politics, or teaching) and <u>not</u> to some*where* (such as the inner city or Outer Mongolia).'

This is clearly illustrated in Philippians 3, where Paul sets out his impeccable credentials – 'If anyone else thinks he has reason for confidence in the flesh, I have more: circumcised on the eighth day, of the people of Israel, of the tribe of Benjamin, a Hebrew of Hebrews; as to the law, a Pharisee etc.' But, he then says, '...whatever gain I had, I counted as loss for the sake of Christ. Indeed, I count everything as loss because of the surpassing worth of knowing Christ Jesus my Lord.' Paul is straining towards faith in Christ, a participation in His sufferings and knowing the power of His resurrection and, in doing so, is prepared to lose everything else.

Os Guinness goes on to say, 'Our Secondary callings, be they homemaking or the law or the practice of art history [or a particular task or ministry], are always the secondary consideration [because God is sovereign and He alone can make us into what we are intended to be]. As indicated, Secondary things are "callings" rather than the "calling." They are our personal answer to God's address, our response to God's summons.

'This vital distinction between primary and secondary calling carries with it two challenges: firstly, to hold the two together and secondly, to ensure that they are kept in the right order. We can say that secondary calling matters, but only because the primary calling matters most.' [*The bracketed words are mine.*]

At this juncture, although I fully concur with the four-fold usage of the word 'calling' in the Bible and, at Point 4, wholeheartedly agree with the need to promote the primary calling above the secondary, I have to take a slightly different position to the one Os adopts (and which he expounds in his book *The Call*), that only a very few people have express, or what he calls supernatural, callings from the Lord.

He is by no means denying that clear and supernatural callings happen but he appears to be saying that God only speaks to a small percentage of people to give them specific tasks to perform and, although we should be open to that word coming, we should not necessarily expect it to happen. Accordingly, we should just get on with doing whatever we do, and do all to the glory of God, using all the giftedness and resources at our disposal.

Now, there is truth and wisdom in these statements as they relate to the discovery of our giftedness, the summoning of all our resources and the doing all to the glory of God within the spheres of influence that have been afforded to us. But, my reading of the Bible suggests that it is not just the few who can and will have God speak to them specifically about what He wants them to do. My reading of scripture suggests that we should not be passive in our listening but actively seeking for God's word to illuminate our path on a day-to-day basis because He has things for *everyone* to do.

If we hold to the opinion that God only speaks in order to hand out long-term vocations, and that He only does that for a very few, we may be tempted to down tools and become static, as we wait for some commanding voice from heaven. However, whilst God does hand out long-term vocations (and not just to a few), the truth is that He is much more likely to give us a whole series of short-term projects (what I am calling 'commissions') that could lead to that vocation.

Furthermore, the relationship we have with Him and our experience of Him speaking to us is meant to have a natural and relaxed air about it. So, the accent ought not to be on the dynamic and the dramatic, instead we can be getting on with the work in front of us, waiting patiently for Him to show us the specific short and long-term tasks of His choosing, confident that they will resonate with our individuality.

Rightly relating to that Some*one*

There is a potential conflict in what has been said so far in this chapter about 'calling', if we don't properly understand the nature of our relationship with God. That's because there are actually two different types of relationship we are required to have, simultaneously, with the God who calls us.

Whether God calls us to a short-term task or to our life's work, we have already stated that it is *His* work that He is giving us to do, which makes Him the boss or the manager and it makes our first kind of relationship a means to the desired outcome that God has for the task(s).

However, we also said above that someone who, in carrying out the task(s), has no interest in their life exhibiting the evidence of committed relationship with God is hardly likely to produce lasting results. The word for 'relationship' in that sentence is pointing to what is formed when we respond to Jesus and start to 'follow Him'. This is the second, and much more intimate, kind of relationship where we begin to acquire some of the attributes of His character and it is therefore altogether different to the first.

Somehow, we need to pursue both these relationship types *at the same time* and, in order to make this a little clearer, I need to enlist the help of my friend Tom Marshall. Tom, a New Zealander, was one of the clearest thinkers and best communicators I ever met. He died a number of years ago but I still think about him often. I also regularly refer to the books that he wrote – among them was one called 'Right Relationships' and the terminology that he uses for the two kinds of relationship is 'instrumental' and 'consummatory'. He says:

'In the creation mandate [in Genesis 1:26-28], the command and authority are given to man, male and female and multiplied man, that is to humankind as a whole. To steward creation is to be a co-operative undertaking in which men and women combine their efforts and resources to do together what they would never be able to accomplish on their own. Note that co-operation, not

competition is at the beginning. This type of relationship can also be called **instrumental**, _that is a means to an end_. Individuals may enter into co-operative relationships to reach a goal, attain an objective, complete a common task, achieve a purpose. The relationship is an instrument to that end and without the existence of the goal or purpose there would be nothing to cause the people to relate.

'In Genesis 2:18 we have something quite different. God looked at Adam and said, "It is not good for man to be alone, I will make a helper suitable for him." Here we have a relationship that is not co-operative but social, it is not instrumental but **consummatory**, that is the relationship is not a means to an end, it is _an end in itself_. This is the beginning of relationships that are "good" in themselves, that is, they need no external goal or purpose to justify their existence.

'Man was made first of all for relationship with God and there are therefore some aspects of that relationship that have no counterpart with his [our] relationship with other human beings. Worship is one; its exclusive object is God alone and to give worship to anyone or anything other than God is idolatry. In many [other] ways, however, the dynamics of our relationship with God are the same as the dynamics of our relationship with other people.

'Firstly, our relationship with God is the most instrumental of all – it is for a purpose, the most exalted of all purposes... God's purpose from all eternity is the establishment of the Kingdom, a goal so great that Jesus said it is like treasure hidden in a field. If a man once sees it, he will sell everything he possesses for it... Make no mistake, God does not need us. He is sovereign and he can do anything he wants anytime he wants. God is omnipotent, he is omniscient and he is eternal. You cannot overpower God, you cannot outsmart God and you cannot outlast God. But that is a sovereignty that does not satisfy the heart of God. The only sovereignty that satisfies his heart is the sovereignty of Fatherhood, that is having his purposes accomplished by sons and daughters who do it just because it is the Father's will. That will keep us motivated all our life, and all the life to come.

'But secondly, our relationship with God is also the most consummatory of all. To know him is the supreme end of all existence. If we know Christ only for the benefits his salvation brings, we do not yet really know him. Jesus Christ is so holy and so attractive that if we saw him we would love him even if he was not our redeemer. As Paul said, "I count everything a loss compared to the surpassing greatness of knowing Christ Jesus my Lord." Yet, amazingly, God ascribes these same consummatory qualities to his relationship with us because he chooses to be our friend – "Abraham my friend", said God in Isaiah 41:8 and "You are my friends", said Jesus in John 15:4.' (Marshall, 1989)

Conflict will inevitably result if we pursue both kinds of relationship, simultaneously, on a human level – for example, if we find ourselves working for someone who is also our friend. We have to be careful not to let the two get entwined or both are ruined – the job does not get done and the friendship is lost.

But, with God, there need not be conflict. Knowing about the two types of relationship should help us to see Him for who He really is: He is not subject to the constraints of fallen humanity and is able to hold both His sovereignty over us and His friendship with us in creative tension, in the same way that He holds many other, seemingly opposite, things in tension – such as Lordship vs Servanthood and Wrath vs Grace.

It is His express intention that we grasp these truths and come to understand His nature and His ways. And it is our response to His callings and our willingness to work together with Him towards their outcomes that is the most efficient vehicle for that to happen.

Sovereignty and friendship – a creative combination

He has set up home with us and pledged to stand with us and to teach us skills. So, we don't sit separate to Him, respond to an injunction from on high to do something, and then operate out of blind obedience to a sovereign God who defines the rules but doesn't really care for the one performing the task. On the contrary, His aim is that we undertake the task together and then together we look at the outcome and say, 'It is good'.

The qualities that His sovereignty has called each of us to exhibit do not make us all turn out alike, but instead they are the surest way to the emergence and the blossoming of our uniqueness. Associating with the one who made us allows His friendship to peel away the layers and to cause us to be seen for the individual someone that we are.

Although He understands the struggle for security and our need to earn a livelihood and although He does not condemn us if, as a result, we don't really enjoy what we do, there is a better way. His care for us extends to *how* we spend our time and energy; *how* we earn our living; *what* we turn our talents to and *what precisely* we produce. His preference is, if faith permits, for us to become captivated by His entrepreneurial nature and to commit to a bit of risk and the possibility of change. To do so, in response to His sovereignty, makes us dependent on His friendship but gives us a shot at 'shalom'.

If, in our decision-making process so far, we have failed to discern Him saying anything definite and, as a result, have concluded that He is not in the habit of speaking to people about their career choices or the outlets for their skills & abilities, what challenges does that present? Knowing it is unsafe to argue from the absence of something, unless there's a clear injunction against that something, and weighing the biblical evidence that God *does* communicate with people and *does* give them very specific things to do, suggests we need to ask ourselves some additional questions:

- If I haven't heard anything, did I actually ask Him?
- If I asked Him and didn't hear anything, what were my expectations?
- Have I been putting limits on the way He is allowed to get my attention or on the kind of thing He is allowed to say?
- Did I actually sense something but then dismiss it because it either 'didn't seem right' or would have been too risky?
- Did I go and seek out anybody else, to assist me in praying for understanding or to provide confirmation?

My conclusions, concerning God's sovereignty over us and His friendship with us, are that we are more important to Him than we know; He has more invested in us than we can imagine; and He has given each of us a unique combination of capabilities for a reason.

Personal reflections: Initial stirrings, long delays and coming to terms with calling

I grew up in a Christian environment, being taken to a Presbyterian church when I was very young and then attending an Independent Evangelical church from the start of secondary school. It was rare, in the latter, for people to talk about 'calling' but, when they did, it was always in the context of being called into the ministry or onto the mission field. I didn't know that there was any other kind.

People didn't tend to talk about enjoying their work – it was a functional thing, a necessity, and something that conferred status and security. You got educated in order to get a job and there was some sort of pecking order for the professions, with the most status being conferred upon lawyers and doctors and scientists and the least status attaching to such as plumbers and bricklayers.

My education felt like a conveyor belt – if you did reasonably well at certain subjects at GCSE, you were encouraged to pursue them at A-level and then, if you got good enough grades at A-level, you went on to a university. By the time you had chosen a subject for university, you were all but destined to pursue a career in something related to it, especially if it was a science subject. All the while, I was also unconsciously looking for my father's approval – he was an electronic engineer and so my choice of physics went down well, even though it has always been a conversation-stopper if I'm asked what I studied!

Looking back on the process, I know I was not really mature enough to know my own mind and be able to question the assumptions that those around me were making. I accept responsibility for the decisions that were made but, although I was more intrigued by the structure and management of organizations than by the work of a technical specialist, I allowed myself to follow a very theoretical path and to emerge as a physicist.

In my first job, I was reasonably competent in the role of physicist but not really good enough and, despite it being fairly obvious to me that there were better ways of running not just the department but the division and the whole company, there was an established but immovable practice of only ever promoting people into management roles on the basis of scientific excellence! It was disastrous for how the company was managed and it was disastrous for me.

I can safely say that there was no real enjoyment in that first career but, before I moved on, I did experience the first clues as to what might be 'my thing'. It happened outside the workplace, in the context of the Church, where I was learning some profound lessons. It is important to relate that I was now attending a Baptist church and it grew, over the time I was there, from about 100 to 450 members. It was a much more dynamic environment than my workplace – lots of thinking, discussing and debating and lots of teaching and organizational management opportunities. I had opportunity to preach and teach, to lead groups and to take part in the governance of the organization as a whole. The Church planted two congregations in that period and I became the pastor of the second, doing that job alongside my regular employment for a period of three years.

During that time, there were many occasions when I was aware of a coming together between, on the one hand, what I had the *aptitude* to do and, on the other, a particular aspect of what I had a *passion* to be doing. It happened in preaching, whenever I had a good command of the subject matter, felt free to explain concepts and practical applications and then saw people 'light up' with a new understanding. It happened in managing a team whenever I was able to plug someone into a role that suited their capabilities and aspirations and then see them thrive. And it happened in the process of corporate decision-making, whenever we were able to debate an issue and then come to a consensus about the way forward.

I can't overemphasise the importance of learning to make right decisions, both individually and corporately. Life is one long series of decisions and the person of faith has to find a way of getting God's opinion on all the important ones. We cannot afford not to ask Him because His ways are not our ways and, if we assume we know what His answer will be, we will often make errors. Even in two sets of exactly similar circumstances, He is likely to come up with a different solution the second time – see 2Samuel 5:17-25 for an example of just that. I think God sometimes does it just to keep us dependent on Him but, in John 10:3-5, Jesus emphasises the importance of us learning to recognize His voice – 'The sheep hear His voice, and He calls His own sheep by name and leads them out... a stranger they will not follow, but they will flee from him, for they do not know the voice of strangers.'

Different Churches have adopted different forms of governance and decision-making, with policy being decided by, for example, a small group of leaders or by a hierarchy of leaders or perhaps by all the members together. Theoretically, the more people involved in the process of trying to discern 'what God is saying' the more difficult it is to arrive at the 'right' decision. The period over which I learned more about decision-making than at any other time in my life was as a member of a Baptist church in the N. of England.

A Baptist church, with one or more pastors and possibly both elders and deacons, is intended to be governed by the 'church meeting' – a regular gathering of all those who are local members – at which all major decisions are made. I say, 'intended to be governed' because it is a sad fact that many use the church meeting only to ratify decisions which have already been taken by a small leadership group. There are also churches, which are part of the Baptist denomination, where many important decisions are never even submitted to the members' meeting.

In contrast, the church that my wife and I were members of, and out of which was planted the congregation that I pastored, was very unusual. The senior pastor, Nigel Wright, later went on to be Principal of Spurgeon's College, but during his time with us we actually looked forward to church meetings because we felt we could trust both the leaders and the members to seek God for the right answers

I recall many occasions where a difficult decision had to be made and, going into the meeting, different people were known to hold strong but differing opinions. On almost every occasion a consensus was reached, sometimes after much disagreement, but there was always testimony about minds being changed and a realization of what God wanted.

I happen to believe that debate is vital – it is healthy for opposing positions to be taken, opinions aired and consideration given to alternative courses of action before a decision is come to. However, that only works where there's respect for one another and, crucially, a corporate commitment to hearing what God might be saying in it all. I owe an enormous debt of gratitude to Nigel for helping me, over a few short years, to learn so much on this subject. It also became the foundation for my wife and I, for a lifetime of decision-making in our marriage.

[For Nigel's own treatment of the decision-making principles alluded to here, please see: *Challenge to Change* by Nigel Wright – ch4, 'The Centre of Gravity' – pp91–132. Kingsway Publications Ltd. 1991]

In the years that followed, I gradually edged towards a work life that contained more of what I wanted to do and less of what I simply had the capability to do, but most career decisions were still pragmatic, rather than aspirational. It was a painstaking and often frustrating process, with small gains from time to time, and only very slowly did I come to understand the importance of following a calling.

So, it is not that I have been harbouring a desire to write on this subject for my whole life and just waiting for the right moment. The material did not actually start to come together until much more recently – a full twenty-five years after an experience that triggered a profound epiphany. The experience happened at a point when I had been working for a living for nearly fifteen years and not really enjoying it and was triggered by a short-term project that came about unexpectedly.

The company I was working for decided to send some of us to a consultancy, whose business it was to analyse personality types – not through short, sharp tests but by gathering lots of real, personal data. I not only enjoyed going through the process, I was riveted by the methodology and the way that the reporting on each participant treated them as unique individuals. It was so opposite to the stereotyping that is typical of many testing regimes.

The report the consultant, Nick Isbister, produced for me was and still is a treasured item. The Q&A and interview experience awakened something and convinced me that I too wanted to be involved in helping people to uncover their uniqueness and to understand 'who they are'. My enthusiasm got me to the point of being offered training to become a consultant and, although I knew the significance of what had happened to me and that it should be followed through, I also knew that it would require a change of career direction, ongoing education and a lot of uncertainty. Having been offered a priceless opportunity to make that change, I bottled it.

I am not the first to do that and I won't be the last but, in my case, God gave me another chance. Twenty-five years after the epiphany I found myself, quite 'by chance', talking to Nick, the consultant through whom the original project had come about and, lo and behold, his set of methodologies was now altogether more comprehensive and compelling than before. I again submitted to the coaching process, in order to understand the changes of method and to test the veracity of the previous results. When, miraculously, the opportunity to train as a coach was offered once again, the right decision was relatively easy to make. Then the problems began.

Daniel Yahav, in Chapter 2, was talking about an altar, of God's making, on which we are to sacrifice our lives. That's serious language and when we reckon with it seriously it gives God permission to eliminate the bits He doesn't like. God may love me just as I am but, as someone once said, 'He has no intention of leaving you just as you am.' I belatedly made the decision to follow this new course and almost immediately God got serious about a pile of things in my life that needed to be sorted out. Did He do that because He is cruel and heartless? No, He did it because He knows that, given half a chance, I'll mess up the long-awaited new start by trying to do it my way.

Quite often we are unaware of how damaged we are and oblivious to what God will require for a call to be successful. Hence, we may be oblivious to what is not there in us, but needs to be there. That was definitely true in my case, especially regarding the relational side of life – I was often aloof but not deliberately so and, compared to most, struggled to initiate conversation.

Following the second experience of being 'coached', I went through about three years of God progressively putting His finger on my attitudes and ways of operating and the ways in which I was not relating to people well and, all the while, He was also pointing out things in His word that I had not properly appreciated before. That three-year Bible study is substantially where the material for this book has come from.

Bio #2 – Josh

By any standard measure, Josh has been very successful. He is skilled at sports, especially football and golf; possesses a full set of GCSEs and three good A-levels, including Geography and Economics; has a First Class degree from Bath in 'Coaching, Education and Sports Development'; is qualified as a teacher; was married at twenty-two; and was appointed head of the PE department in a large comprehensive school at the age of twenty-five, all the while seeking God for his will and committed to following it to the best of his ability.

Josh has been a Christian from an early age and, although always in the thick of things and not unacquainted with mischief, he was no stranger to having to stand out from the crowd if it meant doing what God wanted rather than doing what was popular. Among other things it had him going to parties with his school friends but being very careful how much he drank and then looking out for the vulnerable and, if necessary, making sure they got home safely.

Such actions are characteristic of the way he has always naturally cared for people – a trait that has made sure he is never short of loyal friends. He is now thirty-two, has two young children and is grappling with a sense of calling that first made itself known when he was sixteen, way back before any of the serious studying was done or career decisions made.

Given the timing of that first 'call', when he was only half his current age, how has it taken so long to be coming to fruition? This is a common misconception about 'calling'. We automatically think that, once we get one, it will be full steam ahead to its realization. But that is rarely the case – it is much more common for time to elapse and several more epiphanic moments to occur, each giving further clues to the nature, the context and the means of outworking of the call, before there is the necessary clarity to move forward.

Another reason for the 'delay' is that God calls people who are not fully formed, to positions and activities for which they are not qualified at the time. Such people will almost always have some character traits and experience that are in keeping with God's intentions but they will also have character traits and habits that are incompatible and they are likely to need some additional skills and experience before they can be successful in the intended role.

We have used the word 'successful' a couple of times. When considering the subject of calling, what actually represents 'success' for an individual is worthy of debate. Josh would acknowledge and is grateful for his apparent success to date. But, although he has enjoyed many aspects of his professional and church life so far, he would also say that he has a lingering sense of unfulfillment and, for him, the criteria for success include the ability to realize the calling that he first received at sixteen and which has been reaffirmed several times since.

Josh's first epiphanic moment happened at a meeting for young people at his church, when the subject was 'Leadership and Prophecy'. Up to this point he had been moving steadily into accepting increasing levels of responsibility in the Church context but, whilst listening to someone wax lyrical about leadership, he clearly 'heard' God say, 'I call my leaders and I anoint my leaders.' It was not an audible voice but it was a clear impression and he can recall it in those precise words.

However, what he heard did not have the effect on him that you might expect – rather than confirm his current trajectory, he found himself recoiling from the idea of taking on further responsibility. The negative reaction was triggered by what he had experienced for himself – people in a church context appearing to lead without God or without a servant heart – and then exacerbated by what subsequently happened to a friend, who was forced out of his leadership position by someone imposing their will on the organization. He thought to himself, 'I don't want to lead people in the wrong direction, it's all too difficult' and he backed away.

For part of his time at university, Josh attended a small church where the negative feelings were compounded because he thought the leadership was neither acting wisely nor shepherding the people adequately and he himself didn't feel 'safe'. He had to leave that place and find safe ground.

During this time, he didn't talk through the feelings he was having with anybody, preferring to avoid responsibility. In truth, there was nobody he felt he could trust to stand with him and process it and it was easier to withdraw. But, towards the end of his university course he found a church where he was able to enjoy a measure of relaxation, where the leaders had a different spirit to those he'd known before, and in the period prior to and after graduating the fear of responsibility gradually began to wane. He even took speaking opportunities and found himself getting excited about communicating.

Josh's second epiphany didn't happen until the age of twenty-nine, on a Sunday morning when he had taken the family to church and had been helping with one of the children's groups. He re-joined the service towards the end, at the point when a young couple, who had been serving the church for three years, whilst studying theology, were giving testimony of how God had called them both out of the secular work place in London, to train in preparation for planting a church.

He says, 'I started to weep as they explained their story. Then they invited some members of the church to come up in preparation for a time of prayer ministry. As a small group of people (around 10–12) walked to the front and turned to face the congregation, I felt God say, "I'm going to give you a flock like these – look after them." After this I continued to weep and went forward for prayer. However, when asked by a member of the church leadership to speak out what God had said to me, I was unable to do so, because I was too afraid. I'm not sure why but I knew that verbalising a call to lead God's people was a marker in the sand and I didn't feel ready.'

Once again, despite knowing it was God, the effect of what God said felt overwhelming – it seemed too big and his confidence to declare it melted away.

In the months that followed, he again found himself being asked to do various things in the church. The problem was that, although the church worked extremely hard to provide opportunities for both Josh and his wife and although he had a growing desire to speak to and to care for people, he had to turn some things down because he still did not feel it was the right time to take on more responsibility and he felt uncomfortable about some of the initiatives that were being taken. This confused him and caused some consternation among the leadership of the church and, as a result, he knew he was no longer 'in favour' and the opportunities dried up.

Then, somebody who had come to the town not long previously, to run a small fellowship, and whom Josh had met once or twice, invited him for coffee. In the days leading up to the meeting, Josh knew that it was going to be an important meeting and that he was going to be asked to speak at this person's fellowship.

So, at the age of thirty, what Josh would describe as the third epiphany came as he had coffee with his friend and, as he had sensed, he was asked to go and speak. He took his wife along on the Sunday morning in question and afterwards, reflecting on how they felt, they agreed that, although they were 'square pegs in round holes' in their current church, it was not the right moment to move. They therefore resolved to remain where they were until the situation became clearer.

Soon afterwards, the couple who ran the little fellowship came to Josh's house for dinner and, in the course of the conversation, said that they saw Josh and his wife as shepherds and asked if they would consider joining them.

The process of leaving one church to join another was not straightforward – there were difficulties but, to his credit, Josh was not prepared to allow any misunderstanding to occur and he worked hard to preserve good relationships and to ensure that no one felt slighted.

He also engineered a meeting between the leaders of the 'old' church and the person running the 'new' fellowship and there is now mutual respect between the parties and close ties between the churches.

His fourth and final epiphany (to date) came under slightly strange conditions – Josh was sitting at the bedside of his ninety-four-year-old grandmother, watching over her, just a couple of days before she died. She

61

was an amazing woman who had lived wholeheartedly for Jesus but she was not really conscious at this stage. Josh was reading and praying and God began to speak to him – he relates as follows, 'Firstly, I saw a picture of a mountain that was too steep to climb and again I was moved to tears. It was partly the realization of the enormity of the task, which would be impossible to complete without the supernatural guidance and strengthening of God.

'Then the scene in *The Lord of the Rings* came to mind, where Gandalf is on the bridge, faced by the Balrog. But, unlike the film scene (which I later watched again on YouTube), I saw myself as a frail old person (like Granny) viewing the Balrog barring my way on the narrow path and knowing that I had to find a way past it. I felt as though the Balrog represented idolatry (including the tendency to make ministry an idol), the wretchedness of man and the never-ending needs of people. I knew I would not be able to face those and persevere through them without the power of God.'

During that same period of sitting and watching, Josh's grandmother asked him to get her a drink of water – it was one of the last things she said, and peculiarly apt, although it was not that question that triggered his sense of God speaking.

Although his evolving sense of calling has accelerated over the last couple of years, this is an unfinished story. At the time of writing, Josh is helping to lead the small fellowship, week by week, and taking opportunities both to preach and to get alongside young people and students. He continues in full-time teaching but is waiting to see what God says next. Gradually, he is being equipped and is developing skills. He is trusting that God knows the process and will take the necessary initiatives.

Chapter 4

What is in a Name?

When God gives a name to something or to someone, He has come to a decision about what it/they will become – so it is not just a matter of 'being what they are' and 'doing what they do', but also of *becoming what they are not yet, but are called to be'*. This was the case with all the biblical characters we have listed so far and a great many more that we could list.

By calling someone into a relationship and then giving them useful things to do, God injects purpose into the relationship. The biblical narrative also shows that, for each person, a story begins to unfold. God is the great author and He knows that every plot has twists and turns – often we depart from the path all by ourselves but sometimes He intervenes to take the story in a different direction. Either way, God is not phased. If someone ignores the script and stops responding to His prompts, He is likely to give second and third chances, even if considerable time has been lost.

Names are important to the story, not just because each is a unique individual but because He gives them their identity, knows their name and sometimes reveals new aspects to that identity by changing their name.

Names of things – meaning through association with function

Names of objects are, or become, associated with function or purpose. Some names of objects are little more than labels, such as the word 'knife'. It is of uncertain origin, might have been a person's name before it was associated with a type of object and doesn't really describe what that object is or does.

Sometimes a name does sort of describe what the object is intended for but has taken at least two stages of meaning to emerge as what we know today e.g. 'plate', which was originally from the Greek 'platus' meaning flat or broad and referred to a flat sheet of metal or glass in the 13th C., only becoming the word to describe an eating dish in the 15th C.

On the other hand, for the avoidance of doubt, some devices have been created for a specific purpose, with a name deliberately chosen to describe what that device does, e.g. 'lawnmower'!

Names of people – with meaning not usually, or at least initially, reflective of personality or calling(s)

Names of people, when chosen by God, reflect the purpose He has determined for them or at least a key characteristic of that purpose. In our society, we have largely lost the habit of deliberately naming a child because of what that name means. However, most biblical names are related in some way to the circumstances of a person's birth and God seems to love playing with words.

For example, look at the sons of Jacob, whose names identify the 12 tribes of Israel – the narrative starts in Genesis 29:31 – of which we will cite the first three as examples:

Reuben means 'See a son' because his mother, Leah, knew she was hated and said, 'The Lord has looked on my affliction and now my husband will love me';

Simeon sounds like the Hebrew for 'Heard' because Leah said, 'The Lord has heard that I am hated and has given me this son also.';

Levi sounds like the Hebrew for 'Attached' because Leah said, 'Now this time my husband will be attached to me, because I have borne him three sons', and so on.

Skipping on to the time when Jacob's second wife, Rachel, was finally permitted by God to have children, she bore a son whose life was to take some unexpected twists and turns and whose name would be changed when he succeeded to the role God had had for him all along:

Joseph's name means 'May he add' and also sounds like the Hebrew for 'Taken away' because Rachel said, 'God has taken away my reproach' and also, 'May the Lord add to me another son!' Was she also being prophetic, given that Joseph was subsequently 'taken away' by Midianite traders to Egypt? Then, when God's call was revealed, Joseph's name was changed by Pharaoh to Zaphenath-paneah, which means 'One who discovers hidden things' or 'Revealer of secrets'. As such, it reflected the way God had spoken to Joseph throughout his life and described an essential characteristic of his gifting.

Although Jacob's sons may appear to have been given names solely of their parents' choosing, I hesitate to conclude that there was no forethought on God's part – we are told in Revelation that the New Jerusalem will have twelve gates, each bearing the name of one of the tribes. Perhaps His intended meaning will become clear in due course.

Names of people – with meaning that does reflect God's purpose from the outset

For example, **Elijah** means 'My God is YHWH' or 'God the Lord'. Elijah became Israel's greatest prophet due to his obedience in speaking God's word, repeatedly and uncompromisingly, to those in authority, even at risk of his own life, and in acting on the word in such a way that unless God showed up he was in deep trouble.

Yet, in James 5:17 it says, 'Elijah was a man with a nature like ours, and he prayed fervently that it might not rain, and for three years and six months it did not rain on the earth.' We must not therefore think ourselves too different to those we read about in the Bible – God used ordinary people to do extraordinary things. It was their reaction to receiving God's word that made them extraordinary – their hearts were stirred and they obeyed.

There were occasions when God specifically directed someone to give their child a prophetic name. For example, **Isaiah's children** were named, at God's direction, to emphasise the message He was speaking to the nation: Maher-shalal-hash-baz means 'The spoil speeds, the prey hastens' because God had said to Isaiah, '… before the boy knows how to cry "My father" or "My mother", the wealth of Damascus and the spoil of Samaria will be carried away before the king of Assyria', Isaiah 8:4.

There is another example of this that is even more interesting… **Hosea** was told to take a prostitute as his wife and then, when she had a daughter, God told him, 'Call her name Lo-Ruhamah [which means "Not having obtained mercy" or "Not pitied"], for I will no longer have mercy on the house of Israel, but I will utterly take them away…' Hosea 1:6,8.

Hosea's wife then bore a son and God told him, 'Call his name Lo-Ammi [which means "Not My People"] for you are not my people, and I am not your God.' Hosea 1:9. As we will see, below, God later instructed Hosea to make changes to both names. The alterations appear slight but represent a monumental shift in God's view of and purpose for His people.

God's habit of deliberately changing a person's name

Called and re-called

This may seem like a strange concept but, as we have already seen, the meaning of a name is important to God and what we 'call' someone does matter. There are also twists and turns in a person's story – our lives are dynamic, by definition.

Like the soon to be appointed disciples, Peter and Andrew, James and John, we may be living out the only life we have known, without particular reference to God's leading, just doing what seems obvious, and then God intervenes and gives us a new and different purpose. To accompany that purpose, He may give us a different name, as Jesus did to Peter, James and John, but not to Andrew.

Alternatively, like Jacob's son Joseph, we might appear to have a place in God's purpose or have been set on a course by Him and then find the circumstances of life being irrevocably altered. It might be, as in Joseph's case, because we are a little naïve and make enemies of people who are stronger than we are. Or, we might fall foul of human institutions or experience economic downturn or, through no obvious fault of our own, be badly let down. Or, the changes could come about by our own volition (because we think we know better) or as a result of a series of poor decisions. Whatever the reason, we find ourselves wandering off in a different direction, only to have God intervene at a later date and 're-call' us.

The biblical text clearly identifies at least forty people whose names were changed or who were also known by an alternative name. Some of these people were re-named by a human agency, i.e. it was not God himself who did it. Even so, in a surprising number of cases, whether or not at God's direct agency, the new name did reflect God's purpose for them, illustrating that God was controlling the process and directing someone who didn't know Him to do His bidding.

First of all, the following people's name change clearly reflected something of what they were called to:

Abram/Abraham – in Genesis 17, God changed it from 'Exalted Father' to 'Father of a Multitude';

Joseph/Barnabas – in Acts 4, the apostles changed it from 'He will add' or 'God increases' to 'Son of Encouragement';

Ben-Oni/Benjamin – in Genesis 35, Jacob changed it from what Rachel called him, as she was dying, 'Son of my sorrow', to 'Son of my right hand';

Jacob/Israel – in Genesis 32, God changed it from 'Supplanter' to 'He strives with God';

James & John/Boanerges – in Mark 3, Jesus changed their name to 'Sons of Thunder';

Hoshea/Joshua – in Numbers 13, Moses changed it from *Hawšēʿ* (Oh Save!) to *Yahwšūʿ* (Yahweh is salvation);

Simon/Peter – in Matthew 16, Jesus changed it from 'Listen' or 'He has heard' to 'Rock';

Saul/Paul – in Acts 13, Saul, which means 'Asked for' or 'Prayed for', is called Paul, which means 'Small' or 'Humble', for the first time. The names were interchangeable;

Jedediah/Solomon – in 2 Samuel 12, David called him 'Peace' but Nathan the prophet said the Lord had named him 'Beloved of the Lord'.

Then there are those whose name was altered by someone other than God but the change was still a reflection of what God intended:

Mattaniah/Zedekiah – 'Hope of the Lord' changed to 'God's Justice'. During the war between the Chaldeans and Israel, King Nebuchadnezzar carried many people off to Babylon and then, due to continued Jewish resistance, he came back and besieged Jerusalem.

The exact chronology of attack and defeat and of the three-stage exiling of the Jews is a little difficult to work out but, prior to the final sacking of Jerusalem and its destruction, whilst Jeremiah continued to prophesy and thereby make a nuisance of himself, Jeremiah 37:1-2 tells us: 'Zedekiah the son of Josiah, whom Nebuchadnezzar king of Babylon made king in the land of Judah, reigned instead of Coniah (also known as Jehoiachin)... But neither he nor his servants nor the people of the land listened to the words of the Lord that he spoke through Jeremiah the prophet.'

So, Nebuchadnezzar got rid of Jehoiachin and installed Zedekiah. But, that wasn't quite the whole story – 2Kings 24:17 says, 'The king of Babylon made Mattaniah (meaning "Hope of the Lord"), and who was Jehoiachin's uncle, king in his place, *and changed his name* to Zedekiah (meaning "God's justice")'.

In making this change, Nebuchadnezzar was unwittingly confirming the fulfilment of God's will for Jerusalem. God had spoken through Jeremiah that, despite the wish of the nobles and the prophets, there would be *no hope* [no Mattaniah] for a nation that had despised God's ways and all they could hope for was *God's just reward* [Zedekiah] for their apostasy. Zedekiah then duly presided over the final chapter of Jerusalem's resistance to Babylon.

Joseph/Zaphenath-Paneah – 'Taken away' changed to 'Revealer of Secrets'. We have already spoken about Joseph above and so there is no need to tell the whole story again but look at the wonderful play on words that Joseph's original name represents. Rachel meant 'taken away' in the sense that God had finally given her a child and thereby had 'taken away her reproach'. But God knew that Joseph would be taken away from his home to a foreign land where his true vocation would be revealed and where God's purpose for an entire nation would be worked out.

God's purpose may sometimes seem obscure

Being called by a name that, in some way, reflects God's purpose for us, is a precious thing but God's choices may sometimes seem obscure. Let's take the example of James and John being labelled 'Boanerges' or 'Sons of Thunder'. We would naturally think of that choice as being related primarily to their temperament – a tendency perhaps to be commanding and/or explosive.

However, reading both John's Gospel and his letters we get a very different picture of the man – he has a gentleness and a quiet but deep wisdom. John seems, in the Gospels and in Acts, to be the thoughtful and considered alternative to Peter's more impetuous and direct manner of operation. So, what does 'Boanerges' indicate?

Psalm 29:3 says, 'The voice of the Lord is over the waters; The God of glory thunders; The Lord is over many waters.' And again, in Psalm 18:13, 'The Lord thundered from heaven, and the Most High uttered His voice...' The book of Job is also full of the association between thunder and the voice of God e.g. Job 37:5, 'God thunders marvellously with His voice...' In Job 40:9, God himself says, 'Have you an arm like God? Or can you thunder with a voice like His?' So, in these and other places, notably Ezekiel and Revelation, the voice of the Lord is likened to thunder.

Could it be, therefore, that Jesus' re-naming of James and John had to do with their calling to speak (as it were) with the voice of God, authoritatively and powerfully? It is not necessary to be big and imposing when speaking God's word because, as we know from the account of Elijah, devastating power can come in the form of 'a still small voice'. [I am indebted to my wife for a great many things but she also pointed out this possible interpretation of 'Boanerges'.]

God sometimes reverses His decision

Picking up again the example from Hosea – later in the prophecy God declared his intention to restore his people – to forgive their harlotry and once again to be their God. He then announced a change to or a reversal of the names of Hosea's children - He said, 'And I will have mercy [Ruhamah] on "No Mercy" [Lo-Ruhamah], and I will say to (call) "Not My People" [Lo-Ammi], "You are my people" [Ammi]; and he shall say, "You are my God".' Hosea 2:23

One day God will give us all a new name

To cement this notion of God choosing a name for someone, that reflects what He has determined to make out of them, Revelation 2:17 tells us that He has chosen a special name for every person who will ultimately be with Him; it says, 'To the one who conquers I will give some of the hidden manna, and I will give him a white stone, with a new name written on the stone that no one knows except the one who receives it.'

At the time of the New Heaven and New Earth, we will each come to a new understanding of His intimate knowledge of us, and the uniqueness that He created in us. As Andrew Peterson says, in his song 'The Dark before the Dawn', 'I had a dream that I was waking at the burning edge of dawn; And I could finally believe the King had loved me all along'. It will result in me being given a special name that only He and I know. But, in the here and now, there is also some name-change benefit to be had.

Don't rule out the possibility of it happening to you

Because it is comparatively common, in the Bible, for people to have their names adapted or changed, better to reflect the calling on their lives, we should not overlook the possibility of God doing it to us.

The examples we read about are both 'public' and 'private' in that some people were openly known by their new name but, for others it was something that remained just between them and God.

Either way, if it happens to you, it will be another indicator that God is 'on your case' and it will be further evidence that He is liberating you from what would hold you back and cause you to be ineffective. Some of those hindrances, which contrive to prevent us from ever 'being about His business' and ever truly being useful, are strong and have emerged not just through our own poor decisions but through generations of bad decisions and wrong commitments in our families.

As we become aware of such things, whether in early, middle or later life, it behoves us to call out to God to rid us of them. It is something He loves to do.

Personal reflections on name changing

My given name, Iain, is of Scottish Gaelic origin and corresponds to the English name John. It means 'God is gracious' or 'Gift of God'. So, in terms of meaning it's fine. As to how I came by it, my parents called me after my dad's brother and, in order to distinguish me from him, they also gave me the middle name, Robert. Thereafter, whenever we visited the family in Scotland, my uncle was 'Iain' and I was referred to as 'Iain Robert'. Like many people, I have been happy to tolerate the name I was given but I have not loved it – in my case it is, in part, because people habitually spell it wrong, even when they have known me for a long time.

Surprisingly, God gave me another name several years ago. I certainly wasn't expecting it, I hadn't asked for it and I initially dismissed it. It started with my wife having a strange dream in which, she says, she became aware that I had been reborn, as a child able to walk and talk, with the name Benjamin. For various reasons, not the least being that certain aspects of the dream built on another that she had had many years before, we didn't dismiss it but neither did we talk much more about it or attribute great significance to it.

Then sometime later we were at a meeting for worship and prayer, held monthly at a Christian retreat centre in our locality, and the meeting had just finished. We had been divided into small groups to pray and, as the meeting's moderator was drawing everything to a close, our prayers had not quite finished – in fact one person in our group was still praying for me.

I naturally shy away from expressing my own need and I am often reticent to have people pray for me. I'm not saying that is a right attitude, it's just something that I recognize and have to work against. In the weeks leading up to this meeting, I had been going through a difficult time – unusually anxious and very aware of my failures.

My wife says that, as the prayer for me came to an end and whilst I had my head bowed, one of the staff of the centre walked over and joined in. We hardly know her but, when she spoke, I recognized her voice and knew that she hadn't been part of the group until that moment. She asked whether she could pray the 'Blessing of Benjamin' over me. She then quoted Deuteronomy 33:12, 'The beloved of the Lord dwells in safety. The High God surrounds him all day long, and dwells between his shoulders.' She spoke it slowly, not once but four or five times. It is a slightly obscure but striking verse, one that I was not familiar with but which seemed exactly appropriate for the moment. It was the kind of moment when you think to yourself, 'where did that come from?'

I obviously went home with the verse in my head and looked it up again. Apart from knowing that Benjamin means, 'son of my right hand', I wasn't aware of God's specific intent and resolved to wait and see. Then, a while later, I woke up one morning thinking about an old rhyme which lists the characteristics of children born on different days of the week. I recalled someone reciting it to me when I was very, very young.

Monday's Child

Monday's child is fair of face
Tuesday's child is full of grace,
Wednesday's child is full of woe,
Thursday's child has far to go,
Friday's child is loving and giving,
Saturday's child works hard for a living,
But the child who is born on the Sabbath Day
Is bonny and blithe and good and gay.

I now know it to be a fortune telling song from the 19th C, which is supposed to tell a child's character or future from his or her day of birth, but masquerades as an aid to remembering the days of the week. No need to guess which day I was born on – yes, a Wednesday! Strangely, that diagnosis had remained on the periphery of my subconscious all this time.

Therefore, an aspect of what God was and is saying through this re-naming might be found in the way in which Benjamin got his name – as we stated above: in Genesis 35, Jacob changed it from Ben-Oni to Benjamin because Rachel, when she was weak and dying, called him 'Son of my sorrow'. Jacob was unwilling to leave him with that label and re-named him 'Son of my right hand'.

God is always looking for ways to move us from negative to positive; from uselessness to fruitfulness; from woe to purpose. In His grace, at a time when I was striving towards purpose and trying to lay aside the hindrances of the past, He saw fit to give me hope and it is my hope that I'll be found, even at this late stage of life, at His right hand and making a useful contribution to the kingdom.

Chapter 5

What God Calls Us to and Why

Beware of bias

Over the course of Church history, some bias has been applied both to the possible definition of 'calling' and to the translation of the Hebrew words for 'wisdom' or 'skill'. Depending on which tradition you come from, it is therefore possible to acquire imbalance in one direction or another.

There are four biases to be aware of:

- A 'calling' from God doesn't have to be related to 'the ministry' or other form of 'Christian work';
- The nature of the activity God calls us to frequently involves practical skills – He regards those more highly than we might have thought;
- Callings are not only long-term, life-changing, vocational things, they can be to short term, but nevertheless significant, activities;
- Callings are initiated by God himself and they come to us by revelation – they are not assumed or self-determined. A successful outcome will require our effort but is wholly dependent on God intervening at every stage – 'self-help' is no help at all.

Each of these will be considered in turn, with a view to acquiring a biblical understanding of what 'calling' really is and, conversely, what it definitely isn't!

What is 'Christian work'?

The concept of 'vocation' was apparently only rarely discussed prior to the Reformation but has come back into vogue since that time. However, back then it was not viewed in quite the same way as we might talk about 'vocation' today.

Many in the Church, over the centuries, had warned against the secularizing of 'vocation', believing it to be something indelibly linked to our spiritual life, leading to their conferring vocational legitimacy only on certain types of activity – usually the ecclesial or monastic.

The reformers, in trying to set the record straight and yet not detract from the value of spiritual life, held that all of life could be viewed as vocation – in other words, absolutely every sphere of life and every possible action is religiously and morally meaningful, as a God-given avenue through which we respond obediently to the call of God, in order to serve our neighbour – but, they redressed the previous imbalance, placing honour and dignity on everyday tasks and seeking to elevate the common trades. Indeed, both Luther and Calvin saw the labours of the cobbler and the preacher as equally holy and equally valued by God, if undertaken in faith.

Reformation ethics helpfully established a benchmark of 'Faith active in love through one's callings', which came out of the Reformers' correct insistence that 'the human self stands inescapably before God, and must assess all other role-options from that standpoint.' In other words, they rightly asserted that it is incumbent upon every individual believer to look for and respond to God's 'callings' personally.

Today we think of 'vocation' more in terms of discerning those specific activities that God has determined for us and which mark out His preferred path of service for us personally.

Having said that, much of the discussion in the Christian world today, on 'vocational calling', still appears to be centred on being called to 'Christian work' or 'the ministry' or 'the mission field', focusing on evangelism, preaching, teaching, church-planting and the like and attaching little importance to most other practical trades, occupations and activities, with the possible exception of medical practitioners.

To adopt such a focus leads to a very narrow view of 'Christian work'. It not only downgrades the more enlightened views of the reformers but it also lacks biblical credibility. The reformers' view has much to commend it because they rejected the Church/world dichotomy and gave proper dignity to everyday activities. However, although the generalised, 'whole of life being holy' aspect is a good foundation, we must then go on to embrace the possibility of each individual's uniqueness and God's right to call the individual to specific tasks if we want to get closer to a biblically balanced view.

'Christian work' is not only ministry within the body of Christ and mission to the world but vital service to God happens every day in the home and in the work place and through the practice of various forms of craftsmanship.

For a more complete treatment of these issues, please see Douglas J Schuurman's book *Vocation: Discerning Our Callings in Life* (Schuurman, 2004).

'The spirit of skill' & 'Khokhmah'

Although the narrow definition of 'Christian work' obviously does include important activities, it should not surprise us that even a cursory examination of the Bible shows that God approves of a wide range of skills and abilities and shows them to be integral to His purposes.

We have many projects described in scripture e.g. the building of the ark; the tabernacle; Solomon's Temple and his royal palace; the rebuilding of the Walls of Jerusalem etc. What is more, God specified the designs, in fine detail, and required a very high standard of craftsmanship to be applied. In fact, He repeatedly asked people to build structures and to fabricate objects and vessels, the size and complexity of which exceeded anything that had existed up until that time. The Father was commissioning his children, created in His image, to adopt His own standards of craftsmanship.

I came across a very interesting little book called, *The Case for Working with your Hands*, by Michael Crawford. Michael does not write from a 'with-faith standpoint' but he makes many telling observations about craftsmanship, including this father-son thing. He says, 'My own experience in making craft objects is limited to that of the hobbyist, but is perhaps worth relating... I once built a mahogany coffee table on which I spared no expense of effort. At that time, I had no immediate prospect of becoming a father, yet I imagined a child who would form indelible impressions of this table and know that it was his father's work' (Crawford, 2010).

Is that what happens with us? Do we look around us and, knowing that we are children of our Father, begin to yearn to exhibit craftsmanship like He has? Would that we were able to appreciate God's own burning desire to find craftsmen to whom He can pass aspects of His craftsmanship, and have them become proficient at building the kingdom.

God is extremely creative in the way He gets things done, which is reflected in a broad range of callings: as well as His call to craftsmanship on building projects, there were calls to project manage the building process, or to leadership of groups or even nations, or to make a journey, or to establish a family in a particular location, or to subdue/destroy a particular enemy of His people, or to a consistent prophetic demonstration of how the nation was ignoring God's ways.

We have tended to discount some types of activity from being part of a legitimate calling, partly because certain important words have had vital strands of meaning omitted when the biblical text was translated from Hebrew. One such word is 'khokhmah' [sometimes rendered chokmah], which has been translated as 'wisdom' in many versions of the Bible.

The tabernacle

The guys specifically called by God, in Exodus, to be responsible for building the tabernacle and making all the associated objects and clothing are said to have possessed 'khokhmah'. The word is used eight times between Chapter

28 and 36, one of which is, 'He has filled them with *skill* to do every sort of work done by an engraver or by a designer or by an embroiderer... or by a weaver – by any sort of workman or skilled designer.' (Exodus 35:35)

Whilst it isn't wrong to describe it as 'wisdom' and whilst I am acknowledging that practical skill has limited value without proper understanding, good judgment and right choices, we should still be aware that the cerebral has, for a long time, been celebrated above the practical.

Sometimes, when 'khokhmah' is rendered 'wisdom', it is then supported by other words to indicate more practical skills e.g. in 1Kings 7:14, when talking about the craftsman Huram-abi, it says, 'And he was full of *wisdom [khokhmah]*, understanding and skill for making...'

However, the absence of any reference to practical skill, in the translated wording of many passages, means that an unbalanced message can be conveyed in the way those Bible passages are taught – for example, concerning Joshua succeeding Moses, Deuteronomy 34:9 says, 'Joshua the son of Nun was full of the spirit of *wisdom*, for Moses had laid his hands on him. So, the people of Israel obeyed him...' And again, in the preparation for the building of Solomon's Temple and palaces, 1Kings 5:12 says, 'The Lord gave *wisdom* to Solomon, just as He promised him; and there was peace between Hiram and Solomon, and the two of them made a covenant.' As well as being wise, both Joshua and Solomon possessed a wide range of skills, many of which were practical rather than cerebral, and they were variously lauded for their exploits covering strategy, management, warfare, dispute resolution, design and construction etc.

God says a slightly strange thing for the first time in Exodus 28 – He talks about having filled certain persons with 'the spirit of skill'. Personally, until I read this, I didn't know that such a thing existed, but it makes sense, doesn't it? We frequently see people who appear to have an overabundance of talent – usually focussed in one area of expertise, but sometimes across multiple areas – and, although we might compare them with ourselves and feel poor by comparison, and perhaps wonder why we were absent from that queue when such gifts were being distributed, we nevertheless marvel at the capabilities being demonstrated.

Self-pity is the very last thing we should fall prey to at that moment. Every one of us is made in God's image and has extraordinary potential – wishing we could do what someone else is doing is not the order of the day, but rather we should be calling on our Father to visit us, to fill us with the skills of His choosing and to cause us to come into our inheritance. I take 'filled with the spirit of skill' to mean that the Holy Spirit, who sovereignly gifts people according to God's will and purpose, gives particular skills to particular people for the dual purpose of doing God's chosen works and of equipping others to do them. This is of the essence of calling – men and women who long to be useful, seeking God for His sovereign purpose, and seeing Him respond by issuing calls and equipping us with the necessary skills.

Let's look a little more closely at the tabernacle and at those whom God called to build it:

What really interests me about the two principal craftsmen, Oholiab and Bezalel, is that they were masters of a whole host of crafts (not just one or two) and they also had the ability to teach/to pass on those skills to others...

- Exodus 28:3 – 'You shall speak to all the skilful, whom I have filled with the spirit of skill, to make...'
- Exodus 31:1 onwards – 'I have called by name Bezalel... and I have filled him with ability and intelligence, with knowledge and all craftsmanship...'
- Exodus 35:4 – 'And (the Lord) has inspired him (Bezalel) to teach – both him and Oholiab... He has filled them with skill to do every sort of work...'
- Exodus 36:2 onwards – 'And Moses called Bezalel and Oholiab and every craftsman in whose mind the Lord had put skill, everyone whose heart stirred him up to come to do the work....'

It would appear that acquiring the skills necessary for God's chosen task also has to do with one's heart being stirred up to join the task and, judging by the phrase 'every craftsman in whose *mind* the Lord had put skill', somehow 'knowing' that God will impart that skill. The practical ability can, at least in part, then be learned from those who can do it and can teach it.

Solomon's Temple & the Royal Houses

Khokhmah is the word used by David in 1 Chronicles 28:21, when he is passing on God's charge to his son, Solomon. David had received the design of a new temple from God and had gathered a lot of the necessary materials in preparation for his son to build it. David says, 'and with you in all the work will be every willing man who has *skill* for any kind of service.'

Note that it says, 'every willing man'. This is akin to what we read in Exodus 36, 'everyone whose heart stirred him up to do the work'. The call to be part of the project and the willing response is as necessary as possessing the skill [khokhmah]. Subsequently, in 2 Chronicles 1:7, God comes to Solomon and says, 'Ask what I shall give you'. What Solomon asks for and is granted is khokhmah – wisdom and knowledge.

Then, later still, when he writes the Proverbs, Solomon urges all readers 'to pursue' and 'to get' khokhmah. The only prerequisite, according to Proverbs, is that we should have 'a fear of the Lord' – see for example 9:10 & 15:33.

Although, in most places and in most translations, the word 'khokhmah' is only rendered 'wisdom' or 'knowledge' and there's no hint of the practical aspects of its meaning, we now know that those practical aspects are of vital importance to God and must also be understood when we read these accounts. If you haven't read about the building of Solomon's Temple, you need to do so because it was a mightily impressive programme of work, requiring outstanding displays of planning, organization, project management, logistics and craftsmanship. It is described in 1 Kings 5-7 and in 2 Chronicles 2-4.

It took many years to complete the buildings and required a huge number of men and women – planners, project managers, hundreds of craftsmen, about 3,600 overseers/ foremen and more than 150,000 shift workers were employed. The passages quoted above give some insight both into who was appointed and what they had to accomplish.

Central to this endeavour were two persons: One was Hiram, king of Tyre, who had known King David and offered to assist him and to whom Solomon had later written, asking for that assistance:

- And Solomon sent word to Hiram the king of Tyre: 'As you dealt with David my father and sent him cedar to build himself a house to dwell in, so deal with me. Behold, I am about to build a house for the name of the Lord my God and dedicate it to him...' 2 Chronicles 2:3,4
- Then Hiram the king of Tyre answered in a letter that he sent to Solomon, 'Because the Lord loves his people, he has made you king over them.' Hiram also said, 'Blessed be the Lord God of Israel, who made heaven and earth, who has given King David a wise son, who has discretion and understanding, who will build a temple for the Lord and a royal palace for himself.' 2 Chronicles 2:11,12

The other was the master craftsman, Huram-abi, hired to fabricate a whole series of items, on a scale and at a level of quality and workmanship that had never been achieved before:

- '[Solomon said] So now send me a man skilled to work in gold, silver, bronze, and iron, and in purple, crimson, and blue fabrics, trained also in engraving, to be with the skilled workers who are with me in Judah and Jerusalem, whom David my father provided.' 2 Chronicles 2:7
- [Hiram said] 'Now I have sent a skilled man, who has understanding, Huram-abi, the son of a woman of the daughters of Dan, and his father was a man of Tyre. He is trained to work in gold, silver, bronze, iron, stone, and wood, and in purple, blue, and crimson fabrics and fine linen, and to do all sorts of engraving and execute any design that may be assigned him, with your craftsmen, the craftsmen of my lord, David your father.' 2 Chronicles 2:13,14

Look at the astonishing range of skills that Huram-abi possessed and look at the uniqueness of what he accomplished. I like that, having been asked by Solomon to supply someone with certain, specific skills, Hiram presented the king with someone who did all of that and a whole lot more!

Before I am accused of promoting 'practical skills' without discerning between worthy and unworthy outcomes, it is clear that a craftsman could make something of value or something that is worthless in God's eyes.

Let's be clear that the prime reason for writing this book is to encourage people to hear what God is calling them to do and to be. Hence, if God is doing the calling and the equipping, we don't have to question the potential worth of the intended outcome, for example Exodus 35:10 says, 'Let every skilful craftsman among you come and make all that the Lord has commanded.'

On the other hand, there are stern warnings about fashioning things that the Lord has expressly forbidden, for example in Deuteronomy 27:15, 'Cursed be the man who makes a carved or cast metal image, an abomination to the Lord, a thing made by the hands of a craftsman, and sets it up...'

Craftsmanship hiding in plain sight

Clearly, not everything that is made is a temple or a tabernacle or a king's house. So, does it mean that other stuff does not have value? No, not at all. Indeed, I am sometimes looking in a particular corner of the Bible and read about a structure or some equipment that was needed, where we are not provided with any detail about who made it or how long it took to fashion or anything about its design.

For instance, in Nehemiah 8 we are told about a unique day when a generation who had lost touch with the law of God was reintroduced to it. Ezra the scribe brought the Book of the Law of Moses and read it before the assembly of the people, with various other leaders helping the people to understand what was said. In verse 4 it says, 'And Ezra the scribe stood on a wooden platform that they had made for the purpose. And beside him stood Mattithiah, Shema, Anaiah, Uriah, Hilkiah, and Maaseiah on his right hand, and Pedaiah, Mishael, Malchijah, Hashum, Hashbaddanah, Zechariah and Meshullam on his left hand.'

So, that's at least fourteen people standing on a custom-made wooden platform. I wonder who designed it. I wonder what type of wood was used and with what care and precision the joints were cut and fitted. I wonder what height it was – it says in verse 5 that, '...Ezra opened the book in the sight of all the people, for he was above all the people, and as he opened it all the people stood.' I wonder how they ensured that it remained safe and solid. I wonder at the sense of satisfaction the craftsmen would have had when they were standing before the finished work, listening to the law. I'm sure, as they stood there, those craftsmen felt privileged to have fulfilled that 'commission'.

Short and long-term calls

God speaks to people about long-term, life-altering things (which I'm referring to as 'calls' or 'vocations') but also about short-term things that I am referring to as 'commissions'. Why this distinction? Because 'calls' to obey God and to do something particular don't have to be vocationally life changing. Big transformational changes very often come about by making a series of smaller alterations. We rarely take a giant leap from a standing start.

For a short while, after deciding to distinguish calls in this way and to adopt the word 'commissions', I thought a measure of inspiration had overtaken me. Then I found out that Martin Luther used the same terminology! He says, 'Picture before you the humblest state... no one is without some commission and calling, so no one is without some kind of work... so, serve God and keep his commandments...' (Luther, et al., 1955-1986) [Church Postils, Gospel for the Day of St. John the Evangelist (Luther's Works, vol.22)]

As for the shorter term calls that we see in the Bible (those that don't occupy someone for life or even for a significant proportion of their life), there are many... God has specifically commissioned people to build a large boat, or to petition a despotic king to 'let my people go', or to hang onto the coat tails of God's prophet until they receive a double portion of his spirit, or to hang around the temple until they catch a glimpse of the Messiah, or to anoint the Messiah in advance of his burial, or to provide a new tomb for his burial.

Some of these, as indicated above, led to further commissions or to a fundamental change of life's work. Some were just significant episodes in the relationship of the individual with God. In Chapter 9 we look at seven biblical examples of people who received a commission. Interestingly, each of the seven had to fulfil what God gave them to do whilst fending off criticism and opposition from those around. When God gives someone something to do, it is not uncommon for them to have to 'swim against the tide'.

The self-help disease

In Chapter 1, I quoted Rick Warren, whose book *The Purpose Driven Life* has been hugely popular. He said, 'I have read many books that suggest ways to discover the purpose of my life. All of them could be classified as "self-help" books.'

Unfortunately, the problem that Rick highlighted back in 2001 has not gone away – in fact it's worse. Most individuals profess to dislike DIY, in the classic sense, but then, when their own destiny is at stake, they appear compelled to 'be it' or 'do it' or to 'go there' all by themselves. Too many of us seem to have a strange affinity to people who say, 'the answer is inside you somewhere, if you'll only look more carefully and then try harder'. However eloquently that argument is made, it is not true.

A couple of verses from the Gospels go a long way to making the point: Matthew 16:24,25 says, 'If anyone would come after me [Jesus], let him deny himself and take up his cross and follow me. For whoever would save his life will lose it, but whoever loses his life for my sake will find it.' This same discourse is recorded in Mark 8 and one of the popular paraphrases of the New Testament actually renders that bit about saving and losing your life as 'self-help is no help'! It is also pertinent to look again at Ephesians 2:10, which we referred to in Chapter 2 – 'We are *His workmanship* (God's handiwork), created in Christ Jesus for good works...' We are not our own workmanship.

Self-help seems to have three aspects to it:

- The use of one's own efforts and resources to achieve things without relying on others. In particular doing something oneself, rather than seeking professional help.
- People assisting one another.
- Adopting a system designed to assist people in achieving things for themselves.

Adapted from FRANCESC MIRALLES 1

As believers in a Creator-God, who made us in His own image, we are assailed by offers of assistance to find the right career path/ vocation/ thing to do that we also happen to love/ match to our natural aptitudes, or however you want to put it. They come at us from all angles and some of the secular ones are promoted loudly by the Christian lobby. Take one such example – 'ikigai' – it is described as 'a lifestyle that strives to balance the spiritual with the practical, with a balance found at the intersection where your passions and talents converge with the things that the world needs and is willing to pay for.'

Ikigai is a Japanese word that roughly means 'reason for living' and is a very neat way of presenting the relation-ship between lots of pieces of terminology that are common to the discussion about 'calling'.

At its heart, this call to 'find your ikigai' is a secular, self-help frame-work, couched in terms that lends it to being used for pseudo-spiritual purposes.

When I see a diagram like this, I genuinely want to commend whoever has sought to describe a complex set of relationships in a readily approachable form. But, at the same time, it makes me want to examine whether those relationships are actually true; to test it against biblical truth; and, if it reflects truth, to ask the One who knows me if He will help me to find the centre of the diagram, rather than be left to my own devices.

There are some useful things mixed into this philosophy but I fundamentally disagree with ikigai in at least the following ways:

Firstly, its definitions of the word 'vocation' (seen here at the intersection of 'what the world needs' and 'what you can be paid for') and of the word 'mission' – 'vocation' is originally a Christian concept, having *everything* to do with a strong inclination towards a particular career or occupation being 'right' and *nothing* to do with what remuneration might be available for said occupation. Then 'mission' (when used in this context) is a fundamental, underlying calling or strongly felt ambition, that has been given or imparted – in other words, it has to do with why we exist; it's not about us supplying something that is needed simply because it's what we like doing.

Secondly, and more importantly, the declared philosophy of ikigai eliminates the need to consult God about the outcome of your life.

We need to beware because self-help messages can be quite subtle – it is always a good discipline, even after reading some doctrinal or discipleship material which exhorts you to action in some way, to ask yourself...

- who or what is initiating the action I'm supposed to be taking?
- where is the ongoing inspiration supposed to come from?
- whose effort or what system does a successful outcome depend on?

Be especially wary of trite methodologies that give you X steps to success, where 'X' is a small number.

We need to learn to respond to God's initiative and to depend on His equipping and to grasp that the way He does things is very rarely the same as our way. In fact, the biblical evidence is that He almost never does something the same way twice and it's mainly because He wants us to be wholly dependent on Him.

The outworking of all this is a little bit like walking a tightrope – on one side is God's initiative, intervention, enabling and His great strength. Then on the other side is my personal experience and will and determination and my acquired skill set. It is possible, at any time, to err to one side or the other and to overbalance. Where does my effort stop and God's enabling begin?

There is no doubt that my personal commitment and determination, the use of various skills, perhaps some analysis of personal data, possibly a programme of learning, definitely the courage to face change and to overcome obstacles, will all be needed. But the initiative and the inspiration for it all comes from God, as does the methodology.

The language of the Bible, in describing our active relationship with God, seems to be a combination of both master/servant and intuitive partnership: on the one hand, we only ever do what we see our Father doing; we do as we are bidden, fulfilling the master's wishes. And yet, on the other hand, the Holy Spirit is described as 'He who will stand by your side... and will guide you to the whole of the truth.' John 16:7,13 (Cassirer, 1989)

The way to accomplish lasting outcomes requires ears that are always open and a careful, but nevertheless confident, walk of dependence. It cannot be overemphasised that it's His work and He is the only one who knows us well enough to select the activities to which we are best suited. Hence, it is incumbent on us to hear from Him at each stage *and to know that we have heard* – having a good idea isn't good enough and pressure from other people, who either want us to do something or want to influence what we are doing, *must* be tested very carefully.

The link between calling and our sanctification

In Chapter 2 we established that we must be 'about our Father's business' and that for each of us there is an altar of service on which we need to sacrifice our lives. We also established that God makes a series of far-sighted judgment calls when considering how each person can be transformed from a lost soul into one who can fully appreciate their status as an adopted son or daughter.

The Bible calls this process of transformation 'sanctification' and it is hardly ever straightforward! Why? Because the ways of man are nothing like the ways of God and becoming more like Jesus cannot be accomplished by means of human instinct – it needs His tutelage. Neither is it necessary for us to withdraw from society – we can progressively take on Jesus' characteristics in the course of daily life, as we get on with projects and tasks and jobs of work, as we face problems and challenges and as we interact with the people around us.

In what is called Jesus' 'High Priestly Prayer', in John 17, the word for 'sanctify' occurs three times in three verses. Jesus says to His Father, 'I do not ask that you take them (the disciples and others to whom Jesus had revealed the Father) out of the world, but that you keep them from the evil one. They are not of the world, just as I am not of the world. *Sanctify them in the truth; your word is truth*. As you sent me into the world, so I have sent them into the world. *And for their sake I consecrate (sanctify) myself, that they may also be sanctified in truth*', verses 15-19.

The word used here means 'set apart for holy service to God' – Jesus is saying that He has set Himself apart so that we may also be set apart. Sanctification and holiness are extremely closely linked but *how* we are sanctified is not a mystery – just as Jesus watched the Father and only ever did what he saw Him doing, our sanctification comes about through partnering with Jesus and being discipled by Him in whatever tasks He gives us to accomplish.

In John 21, after Jesus' resurrection and after He has given breakfast to seven of the disciples, on the shore of Galilee, Peter and Jesus go for a walk together. Their conversation, in which Jesus carefully recommissions Peter after his three-fold denial, is partially interrupted by Peter noticing John, who is following at a distance. Jesus then tells Peter to disregard the path that He might or might not choose for John and says, 'what is that to you? You follow me!' Both Peter and John had been called to become 'fishers of men' but this exchange with Jesus strongly implies an individual process of coaching/discipling, where someone else is most likely to be taken on a different path. Subsequent events, as recorded by Luke in the Acts of the Apostles, and in the letters of both men, bear out their different positions, roles and responsibilities in God's service.

I believe that God has deliberate strategies for making us like Jesus – the sanctification process for each individual, in terms of *what* tasks we do, is not in fact haphazard or accidental. His far-sighted judgments mean that He understands exactly how to navigate each unique person towards the fullness of 'sonship' and He allocates tasks to each one that are tailor made. He has prepared a specific programme of 'good works' and so issues specific 'calls' that match a person's aptitude and capabilities. He then guides each call through to a conclusion.

The link between calling and modelling God's character

When Jesus was modelling the relationship with His Father for us, and explaining that He only ever did what the Father was doing, His character was (by definition) in all respects perfectly aligned with that of His Father. Jesus operated at all times in partnership with His Father – the Father was intimately involved, participating in what Jesus was doing and revealing His character in the words and actions.

We, who are now progressively to be made like Jesus, must learn about His character and bit by bit come to exhibit or mirror that character. We do not have Jesus' nature in any complete sense and our ability to grasp what God is like is limited by human frailties. However, he is aware of our limitations (Psalm 103:14 says, 'He knows our frame; He remembers that we are dust.') and so His teaching about himself has to be delivered to us, as was the case for Jesus' disciples, in manageable, bite-size chunks and with much repetition.

Accordingly, we can see from the many examples in the Bible, where God gives someone a task to undertake or a call to fulfil, how, in each case, that call either illustrates one or more aspects of God's character (and requires those aspects to be demonstrated in order to complete the task) or contains a motif – a recurring theme or idea or symbol – which is meant to remind the person(s) called of certain character traits every time it occurs.

His habit is to connect with the one who is called and to participate with them in the fulfilment of the call. We need not worry because His express intention is to be 'in it' with us. He knows that 'we are dust' and that He must not only supply every nuance of gifting, on an ongoing basis, if the job is to be done properly but also give us regular reminders of who He is and how He wants the job to be done. If we are to do something 'right' and produce lasting fruit, it will require our dependence. The only alternatives are compromise or failure.

So, what are some examples of this? Many are obvious but, if you look closely, you'll also find some more subtle expressions. We will start with some that are made explicit:

Adam - God's mandate to him and their ongoing relationship should have been so fruitful and satisfying. Genesis 2:10-17 describes the environment that God created and the mandate (or 'call') that Adam was given 'to work the garden and to keep it' – God showed Adam His own creative skill and His ability to produce and to multiply living organisms, inviting the man to learn how to generate new growth and to produce fruit. There are then the interactive episodes where God, having formed every beast and bird, brought each of them to the man and had him give them names and the habit God had of 'walking in the garden' with the man and his wife and sharing with them in the husbandry and management of His creation.

Abraham - God's call is for him to leave his father's home and to journey to somewhere he did not know, because he is to be the father of nations. God, the father of all, who created both the world and mankind from what was null and void (dead), takes him outside and says, 'Look toward heaven, and number the stars, if you are able to... so shall your offspring be' Genesis 15:5. He then waits until Abraham's body is 'as good as dead' (null and void), Romans 4:19, before fulfilling His word. Abraham has many encounters with God and is in the habit of discussing things with Him. You can infer that they will have communicated about 'fatherhood' on a number of occasions and God the Father, who will one day sacrifice His only son on a particular mountain and then raise Him from the dead, takes Abraham to that very mountain and reveals deep things about His fatherhood to him by requiring him to be willing to sacrifice Isaac and then providing a ram, Genesis 22.

Moses – God's call is to 'bring (lead) the children of Israel out of Egypt', Exodus 3:10, and He issues the call by speaking from a burning bush. Fire is a symbol of several things in the Bible but mainly it is to do with God's presence (with overtones of judgment) and His power (to consume and to purify) and His holiness (leaving behind only those things that have substance and will endure). God is asking Moses to be one of the most significant leaders in history, who will execute judgment on Israel's enemies, require ongoing holiness from Israel's people and be there for those people all the way to the land of promise. God then accompanies Moses, appearing repeatedly, to him and the nation, as fire – in the pillar of fire that went in front of them; in descending on the mountain in fire in order to give instruction for living; and in the daily sacrifices that ensured their ability to come close to God without being consumed.

Joshua – After the death of Moses, God calls Joshua to 'arise, go over this Jordan, you and all this people... into the land that I am giving to them...' and He then says, 'No man will be able to stand before you all the days of your life... I will not leave you or forsake you ... only be strong and very courageous', Joshua 1. Now, Joshua had had experience of God's presence and power since he was a young man – he had accompanied Moses up Mount Sinai, when the law was received, and he was a fixture at the tent of meeting when the pillar of cloud, signifying God's presence, rested there. He had also commanded Israel when they defeated the likes of the Amalekites. So, on entering the Promised Land, he is already an experienced leader and a seasoned military commander. However, he has not been in sole leadership before and he needs God's strategy. As he stands by Jericho, dressed for battle, he comes face to face with the Commander of the Lord's armies [Joshua 5:13-15], who tells him what to do and how to do it.

We could continue with Old Testament examples, such as David and several of the prophets but, not wishing to labour the point, let's turn to the New Testament...

The 12 Disciples – Towards the beginning of Jesus' ministry, He taught the people from Simon Peter's boat, moored just off shore, and then asked the crew to 'put out into the deep and let down your nets for a catch'. The fishermen had tried to catch fish all night, without success, but now they were overwhelmed by fish. It was a deeply shocking experience for Simon but Jesus said, 'Do not be afraid; from now on you will be (fishing for) catching men', Luke 5:1-11. Jesus was issuing a call to them but He had just given them a graphic demonstration of His expertise to make it happen and they left their nets and followed Him. Then, in John 21, after Jesus had risen from the dead, because He knew the trauma they had been through and that they would soon be without Him (in a physical sense), He repeated the 'trick' in order to recommission the disciples to fulfil that calling.

A wider group of disciples – Throughout Jesus' ministry He demonstrated His mastery over sin, sickness and death by forgiving people's sins, healing their diseases and disabilities, delivering them from evil spirits and even raising people from the dead. In Luke 9, He sends out the twelve to proclaim the kingdom of God, to heal and to have power over all demons. They go off and use the authority that they have been given. Then, in Luke 10, Jesus appoints and sends out seventy-two others with a similar commission. Afterwards, when the seventy-two return with stories of demons departing from people at the mention of Jesus' name, He is there to receive their report and to share their joy and to give them further instruction.

Even citing just a few examples, it is abundantly clear that the God who calls us has a track record of demonstrating His prowess, in myriad ways, *before* He issues a call and then of providing ongoing encouragement both *during* its outworking and *after* we have completed a particular phase of the mission.

But look at the punchline Jesus issues, in Luke 10:20, after He has been rejoicing with those who have returned victorious, 'Nevertheless, do not rejoice in this, that the spirits are subject to you, but rejoice that your names are written in heaven.' His object is that, in faith and in response to His call, we learn to model His character but the most important thing is always relationship – it's not 'look at what I've done' but rather 'look who I have the privilege of knowing'.

Personal reflections on craftsmanship

I went to the kind of grammar school that required both the local authority and my parents to contribute towards tuition fees. It was a privileged situation, although I didn't appreciate it at the time. To get there, I had to pass a test called the '11+' and then, instead of just enrolling in the grammar school close to home, several of us were encouraged to take an entrance exam for another school that was two bus rides away. The kids in my class at primary school who didn't pass the 11+ went on to what was known as a 'secondary modern school'.

I will refrain from making comment on the limitations of our educational system but, at secondary modern, as well as Maths and English etc., you got to learn and practice 'trades', such as carpentry, plumbing and bricklaying. I got to do French and Latin and Physics. I have always been slightly envious of the kids who were shown how to do something 'useful', a feeling that has endured partly because my father, despite his obvious expertise, wasn't able to involve me in anything practical that he was doing and partly because the woodwork teacher at my school was a psychopath!

Throughout my whole working life, I have been in awe of craftsmanship. Whenever there were skilled tradesmen in our house, I wanted to watch them and talk to them and to ask them questions. To me they were always the people to emulate and my own attempts at DIY have always paled by comparison.

Several years ago, I had another epiphany in a series that stretches back several decades. This one built on a previous experience of being impacted by certain Old Testament passages concerning those who organized and project-managed the building of Solomon's Temple.

What I sensed God pointing out to me was one particular character's role – that of Hiram, king of Tyre, who had loved David, Solomon's father, and had built him a house. Now that Solomon had succeeded David, Hiram agreed, at Solomon's suggestion, to assemble both craftsmen and materials and to manage the process of getting appropriate quantities of both to site. Exactly what God was wanting me to do, when He pointed this out, was not immediately clear but I knew, from that time on, that He was preparing me for a similar role in a project and that, in due course, He would say more.

Whenever you sense God is 'on your case' but the desired outcome 'awaits its time', you can expect Him to steer you through relevant experiences, each of which prepares you in some way for that outcome. He can order the circumstances in wholly secular contexts if necessary and one such example is that, in my work life over the next few years, I was offered the opportunity to recruit a large team of researchers, each of whom needed to have specific qualification and experience. I didn't just need to find and employ them, I had to appoint them, individually and in groups, to work for client companies on both short and long-term assignments. It was fascinating, given that the team, although not constant in size, was usually approx. eighty persons of which up to fifty were engaged at any one time.

I knew that this work was not 'it' – it wasn't the fulfilment of what God had said – but at the same time I knew He was orchestrating something so that I could learn valuable lessons. I also knew that what I was doing had parallels, albeit in small measure, to what Hiram did. That piece of business was very successful but, having built it up, the responsibilities needed to be passed to someone else in the company and, as we began to work out how to do that, the epiphany occurred – I was reading the prophecy of Zechariah early one morning and not suspecting anything when God clearly said, 'I need craftsmen and I want you to go out and find some for me.'

There was no audible voice or angelic presence or dream-like sequence – I was wide awake, sitting on a high stool at the kitchen worktop, and the closest I can come to an explanation is that the words were written up on a blackboard in my mind. It stopped me in my tracks and I waited for Him to say more. But that was it! Another case of knowing the 'what' but not the 'how' or 'when'. It would actually be another eighteen months before God gave me further clues as to how and when.

A more recent encounter with craftsmanship showed me that God not only knows what aptitudes he has hidden in us and what calls He has issued but He also hears the yearnings of our hearts.

At the end of 2018 my youngest son got married and, because he is very tall, he elected to have a suit made for him. I travelled with him one Saturday, several months prior to the wedding, from Oxford to London, to visit a series of bespoke tailors, to look at materials and styles and obtain quotes.

We had six appointments over the course of the day and, in preparation, had listed our criteria for choosing which tailor to engage. It was a great experience to talk to people who clearly knew their trade and at the end of the tour we felt we had been educated. On the train home we marked each tailor out of five, on each of the predetermined criteria, totalled up the scores, and a clear winner emerged from the six.

All the way home, I had the uncomfortable feeling that I too should succumb to the experience of having something made for the wedding. I had gone on the trip because my son asked me to accompany him – I had not gone with any intention of participating – and I use the phrase 'uncomfortable feeling' because we now knew the likely cost of the exercise and I didn't want to tell my wife what I was thinking.

It is worth pointing out that, in terms of corporate decision-making, the different parties who will be affected by a decision, if they have a desire to know what God thinks about the matter, need to ask Him and to trust that He will speak. In my experience, if we are willing to wait before acting, God is always able to resolve this sort of thing in some unequivocal manner. Of the two of us, my wife is the one who most often will have a sense about something that requires us to come to agreement. She is more frequently the initiator or the 'ideas person' and I am the one who lags behind. Nevertheless, if something is right and if we retain an openness to different eventualities, God comes up trumps. He can give confirmation and He can change minds and, crucially, He can give peace concerning an outcome.

I plucked up courage to talk to my wife about the suit and initially we had to agree to differ. But, at least we prayed that God would find a way of bringing us to agreement. It took three days. She found that, after her somewhat frosty initial reaction, the same realization as had come to me then came to settle on her. So, my son and I both embarked on a sequence of consultations for measurement, decision-making, preliminary fittings, alterations and final fittings.

At the end of Chapter 3, I talked about re-connecting with a consultant friend after twenty-five years, re-submitting to a coaching process and finally deciding to follow a calling that I'd sensed those years before but 'bottled out' on. That coaching process was the trigger for God to start to work with a will on the things in me that He deemed deficient and to put things in place that were non-existent. It was a constructive but painful process, involving lots of facing up to the truth and lots of prayer.

As we approached my son's wedding, I'd been undergoing nearly three years of restorative work, didn't know how much more of it would be required and, like you do, I found myself wondering if God really knew what He was playing at! Then two days before we were due to go back to London, for the final suit fitting, I was feeling very restless and unsettled. Late in the evening, unable to rest, I began to think back to the coaching process, which had initially involved me providing written personal data in response to a whole series of interesting questions.

I decided to look out the document and re-read my answers. It took a little while to locate it but, when I started reading, I found that I'd actually supplied two answers to the first question, 'What image or metaphor comes to mind as you think about where you are right now?' I could remember one of the responses quite clearly but it was the other one, that I'd subsequently forgotten all about, that made me stop and take notice – written there, in black and white, were the words, 'I feel like I am at someone else's wedding wearing a suit that doesn't fit.'

So... that was why it was so important for me to submit to the tailor's craftsmanship and God seemed to be saying that the upcoming wedding would represent an element of closure to the process of restoration.

Bio #3 - Wendy

Wendy's father and mother were part of 'The Windrush Generation', arriving in England from Jamaica and Barbados respectively, in 1958 and 1961. He was the son of a landowner, timber merchant and Baptist Church deacon and she was an orphan who had been brought up by her maternal grandmother, a godly woman and lifelong member of the Church of England.

They were both staunchly Christian in their beliefs, each became settled in Oxford, they met in 1962 and Wendy was born in 1964. Although christened in the C of E, Wendy's first real experience of church was neither C of E nor Baptist. She was enrolled in a Sunday school at a local Church of God of Prophesy, at the age of six, and has been associated with the Pentecostal Church ever since.

Today, Wendy is a gifted teacher who is particularly drawn to the students who have struggled most within the education system. She has an uncanny way with them, often enabling both children and adults to make startling progress over a relatively short period of time. She is very clear about her calling, saying that, from her late teens, she has felt called to 'the world', to be a teacher. She testifies to God having said to her, 'teach the children and they will grow in learning' and, over the years, He seems to have allowed the needy ones to cross her path. But, it has been far from easy and at every stage she has faced opposition, much of it racially motivated.

The first real indication of her calling came about when, having attended all-age Sunday school at the Church of God of Prophecy throughout her childhood and teenage years, she was asked to teach a class. On one occasion, at the age of seventeen, she invited a friend to come to church with her and the girl was allocated to the class that Wendy was due to take. After the session, her friend said, 'You should be a teacher' – it was unexpected and it made Wendy stop and take notice.

The second indication came a little while later, when the Church embarked on a new course of study and Wendy was among those asked to prepare classes. She recalls being handed the study booklet, which was entitled, 'Called to Teach'. Again, the words spoke directly to her.

As is so often the case, her path then became winding and a little overgrown. She went into secretarial work and felt unfulfilled – being plagued by a nagging doubt that 'this is not it'. Then, during the '80s, an organization called the Centre for Black and White Christian Partnership was formed [now part of Queens Foundation for Ecumenical Theological Education] and a two-year 'Certificate in Theology' course began, under the auspices of Birmingham University. Wendy applied for it, was accepted and completed the two years. However, before the end she met someone with whom she set up home and they went on to have several children together.

Life for Wendy, in Birmingham, was sometimes traumatic and she also drifted away from the Church during that time. When her relationship broke down and she found herself having to escape with the children, she sensed God telling her to 'go east', which she did and settled in Oxford. The previously completed Certificate in Theology entitled her to enrol on a degree course and she therefore transferred to Westminster College to study for a Bachelor of Theology, achieving the degree in 1998.

At this point, before explaining how Wendy finally made the transition into teaching, we should reflect on her pilgrimage. It would be easy to ask why, having had two occasions on which the 'rightness' of a teaching career seemed to be indicated, did she take such a round-about route?

Such a question is unfair because it is asked with the precious benefit of hindsight and fails to take three common things into account: firstly, we are often limited in our ability to see the 'big picture', especially in relation to our own lives (we find it easier to be objective about another person's situation); secondly, we are limited in how much change we can handle at any one time; and thirdly, God has a say in it and doesn't often take us in a straight line to the intended outcome.

Having moved to Oxford, it was a relief to reconnect with the study of theology and the BA degree she obtained was to be a very useful stepping stone to teacher training. Without it, she would have taken a lot longer to achieve teacher status. Also, earlier experience of the workplace prepared her well for life in schools and colleges.

Wendy also remembers several times when God had spoken to her, as she was growing up: on one occasion, she had a migraine and was alone in her room reading the Bible. God highlighted one verse to her and, as she puts it, 'His presence in the room increased'. At the same time, the migraine melted away. The verse He had pointed out to her was, 'Be diligent (study) to present yourself approved to God, a worker who doesn't need to be ashamed, rightly dividing the word of truth.' 2 Timothy 2:15. Given the clarity of that experience, it is not a surprise that she opted to study theology.

Soon after obtaining her degree something else happened that Wendy describes as being 'significant as it heralded a change in my fortunes'. She met Paul and they married in 1999. He gave her life added solidity and his support was a major factor in enabling her, in her mid-thirties, finally to come to a decision to pursue a teaching career.

Never one to dip a toe gently into the water, if there is an opportunity to dive straight in, she applied for a very competitive training programme called

SCITT [School-Centred Initial Teacher Training]. It could have been seen as a long-shot but somehow Wendy knew she would be accepted and she was. The course lasted one year and the majority of the time was spent in school, in the classroom, alongside a teacher, with learning coming through immersion and critical observation. However, in order to achieve QTS [Qualified Teacher Status], each student also had to undergo a timed skills test, covering maths, English and IT.

Wendy has always had a love of literature, so the language questions held no menace, and she was IT-literate, but maths was another issue altogether. During the early '70s, the government overhauled the primary curriculum and Wendy's school had failed to update its teaching capability adequately, with the result that she had fallen behind in her understanding of maths and had never caught up. For example, despite it being a mandatory part of the curriculum, she was not taught 'fractions' and had resorted to 'avoidance' as a defence mechanism, learning over the years to detest maths.

Knowing that she would have to take the skills test, Wendy did two things – she engaged a tutor and she prayed. Miraculously, she then found that she was able to understand what had befuddled her brain for many years. She passed the test and knew that God had done something significant. Ironically, some of her greatest successes with underachieving students, in the years that followed, have been in the area of mathematics and she now knows that her own struggle was important in bringing her to a better understanding of the children's struggle.

Since becoming qualified and being given her first class of pupils, Wendy has worked in a number of schools and colleges and there have been regular instances of people opposing her. Some have made overtly racist comments and some have acted more subtly; questioning her methods and her capability and subjecting her classes to an oppressive regime of observation and inspection.

Through it all, up to the present day, two things have characterized these episodes – firstly, the students themselves have consistently risen up and defended her – providing the validation that she has needed either via test results that have shown the progress being made or through individuals physically standing up for her and providing verbal testimony to staff or inspectors – and secondly, a series of independent inspectors have commended her for the innovative way she manages to get through to under-achievers.

It is wrong to assume that, when God points you to your calling and you respond to His leading, success will automatically follow and difficulty will be minimised. Wendy's life as a teacher has been hard but God has gifted her with a steely determination and with compassion for her students. She describes herself as, 'a work-woman for Christ in the most practical and unlikely of callings – to teach in the world.'

Over the years, the sense of rightness of her calling has remained fresh and, at the time of writing, Wendy is embarking on a new venture; to establish a company whose purpose is to bring benefit to the community by offering teaching/tutoring both to children who are behind in the key skills of numeracy and literacy, and to adults who lack them. She intends to use this vehicle to provide bespoke lessons for the children and accreditation (e.g. functional skills qualifications or GCSEs) for the adults, so that each student's confidence is built up and his/her chance of success is improved.

Chapter 6

Modelling God's Character – Teamwork and Uniqueness

God designed us to embrace complementarity & teamwork

When God created people and gave them a mandate for how to live, He was careful to build into them both strengths (or specialties) and limitations. He has given every one of us a set of unique characteristics, along with a sense of awareness that, as an individual, we are unique and, in some way, 'special'.

By 'special', I mean that we have a sense of being earmarked for something that only we can do. The fact that such a sense is present leads us to yearn to fulfil our potential. At the same time, as we contemplate and daydream about what we have a heart to accomplish (and if you've never done that, I want to encourage you to do so – it's one of the key things we've been created to do), we realize, in our saner moments, that we lack some of the things necessary for accomplishing the task or reaching the goal or making it happen or however you prefer to put it.

Why do we inherently know that we have the desire and the drive to do stuff but that the stuff we have in mind is likely to require skills and experience and temperamental qualities we do not possess? Firstly, because God almost never calls people to something for which they are fully equipped at the time and secondly, because the limitations He has deliberately built into us are pointing to a need to go out and look for help.

In God's design for mankind, complementarity and teamwork were always intended to be part of the package. From the beginning, He has been issuing a challenge to us not to rely on ourselves alone but to be prepared to work together. At the same time, He provided, in Himself, a model for us to observe, to understand and to follow and He also demonstrated His commitment to come alongside us and to help us rise to the challenge.

In creating us to work together, God was reflecting an essential attribute of the Godhead, namely that He is plural and He operates in plurality and teamwork. As early as Genesis 1:26 He says, "Let *Us* make man in *Our* image, according to *Our* likeness..." Then, in John 15:26, Jesus is talking to the disciples about going back to His Father and describes the action and interaction of three persons – He says, 'But when the Helper [Parakletos] comes, whom I will send to you from the Father, the Spirit of truth who proceeds from the Father, He will testify of Me.'

There are a great many references we could use but these show that God, in His plurality, assumes distinct roles and works in concert, as a team. It is also worth noting that Heinz Cassirer translates John 15:26 as, 'But when *He who will stand with you* comes...' He tends to use this phrase to describe the Holy Spirit because, once again, he wants to illustrate the essential characteristic that sits behind the language – namely that God doesn't just call us to follow Him, He pledges to *stand with* us. We'll discuss this concept further in Chapter 8 but, for now, let's reflect on what happened right from the beginning, in the Garden of Eden – God appears to have been in the habit of walking and talking with the people He had created (Genesis 3:8,9). The phrasing of these verses suggests that this was a regular occurrence, that Adam and Eve were used to Him coming and accustomed to His voice.

Our God is passionate both about developing relationship with each one of us and giving each one tasks to do. He further intends the outworking of those tasks to be done in partnership, with Him and with others of His choosing.

To begin to illustrate this, we will look at a passage of the Old Testament where God picks a team, allocates complementary tasks and divides up responsibilities in order to win a major victory. This account raises the historically thorny problems of female leadership, male responsibility and a potentially compromised outcome. Certain interpretations of the chapter have consistently failed to ring true to me but let me offer an explanation that both addresses those problems and expresses what I think God is trying to say to us about 'calling'.

Teamwork & collaboration - Deborah, Barak, Jael and Sisera

Following the conquering of large sections of the Promised Land and the death of Joshua, many of the original inhabitants of Canaan had not been driven out and, despite many warnings, it says in Judges 2:10,11, 'there arose another generation... who did not know the Lord or the work that He had done for Israel. And the people of Israel did what was evil in the sight of the Lord.' We are then told in verse 16, 'The Lord raised up judges who saved them out of the hand of those who plundered them.'

This was a cyclic occurrence – the people forgot God and did evil; God surrendered them to an enemy, who oppressed them; they cried out to God to save them; God raised up a judge; the people saw the error of their ways and remembered God again.... and repeat.

In Judges 4 and 5 we have the story of one such cycle. Chapter 4 verse 2 says, 'The Lord sold them into the hand of Jabin king of Canaan, who reigned in Hazor. The commander of his army was Sisera.' And then, in verse 4, there is a clear and revealing statement; 'Now Deborah, a prophetess, the wife of Lappidoth, was judging Israel at that time.'

Let's establish the facts – Deborah (a woman) is named as the judge and we have already been told that it was the Lord who raised up judges. So, Deborah has been called by God to judge Israel – He presumably had free rein to choose whomever He wished but He chose Deborah because she was the one He wanted and the one uniquely qualified to do the job at that time.

Deborah is described as 'a prophetess', which is a vital gifting because it implies that she was experienced at hearing God's voice, receiving inspiration, probably seeing visions, understanding His message, appreciating what He intended to do and communicating with the necessary people.

Deborah is also described as being 'the wife of Lappidoth' but several well-respected commentators highlight the fact that 'Lappidoth' may not actually be the name of a person. As Matthew Henry points out, *'She is said to be the wife of Lappidoth; but, the termination not being commonly found in the name of a man, some make this the name of a place: she was a woman of Lappidoth. Others take it appellatively, Lappidoth signifies lamps. The Rabbin say she had employed herself in making wicks for the lamps of the tabernacle; and, having stooped to that mean office for God, she was afterwards thus preferred. Or she was a woman of illuminations, or of splendours, one that was extraordinarily knowing and wise, and so came to be very eminent and illustrious.'* (Henry, 1960)

Whether or not Lappidoth is a real name, we do seem to be afforded some insight into Deborah's character – she was a torch in a dark place, a firebrand in God's hand to dispense His wisdom to a disobedient generation and to goad them into repentance and action.

So, it is entirely in keeping with her call and her gifting that we read, in verse 6, 'She sent and summoned Barak the son of Abinoam from Kedesh-naphtali and said to him, "Has not the Lord, the God of Israel, commanded you, 'Go, gather your men at Mount Tabor, taking 10,000 from the people of Naphtali and the people of Zebulun. And I will draw out Sisera, the general of Jabin's army, to meet you by the river Kishon with his chariots and his troops, and I will give him into your hand'"?'

How did she know time and place and strategy? Because she was God's prophet and He had told her that now was the moment to overthrow Sisera and that Barak was the man commissioned to lead the army against him. As with Gideon, in later chapters of Judges, God also dictated the number of troops required for the task.

Now, a lot of opinions have been offered concerning Barak's response to Deborah... he says, 'If you will go with me, I will go, but if you will not go with me, I will not go.' Suggestions I have variously heard, from pulpits and lecterns up and down the country, include the following: that Barak bottled it; that he forced God to hand the leadership of the campaign to a woman; that it was

Barak's rightful place to be the leader but he was too weak; and (amazingly) that the only reason Deborah was allowed to take the role of judge at all was because she was being 'covered' by a man.

All of those miss the point and deflect attention from the real focus, namely that it was God's work, He picked the team and determined the roles and appointed those best suited to fulfil each role. God was giving each of the team their instructions and it needed all of them to play their part.

It is not in the least unusual that confirmation of a calling or commissioning to an important task should come to someone like Barak indirectly, via a prophetess, rather than by a dream or an angel or a direct sense from God's Spirit. Confirmation is just as likely to come to us by an indirect route today; perhaps via the exercise of a gift of the Spirit in worship or the exposition of a passage of scripture during a sermon or a sense that comes to a friend who is praying for us. The important thing is that, before we embark on something, we have also known God speaking directly to us about it. It's not so much the mechanism by which the call arrives but what we do with it that matters. It is most likely that something God is saying to us will 'resonate' and we'll find ourselves ruminating on it and looking for it to be confirmed. We are never required to undertake a calling on an idle whim or a vague word – God can be relied upon to speak clearly.

The language of Judges 4 indicates that Deborah's word to Barak didn't come 'out of the blue'. It clearly touched something that had been stirring in him – his immediate response and the obvious willingness of all the fighting men to march out after him suggests he was a respected warrior and that God had already been speaking to him. As is usual on these occasions, there was a great temptation to grab the glory, rather than let it go to God himself. Thankfully, neither Deborah nor Barak fell into the trap.

Deborah was true to her position as prophetess and brought God's word to Barak. He, in turn, knew what he had to do but, because he rightly wanted God to go up with him into battle, he knew he also needed Deborah to be there. His response to Deborah was immediate and, far from displaying weakness, shows that he saw Deborah as the embodiment of God's word at that time, that she had been right thus far and that her going with him was tantamount to God going with him. He accepted that it was his job to lead the troops and to fight the battle but, equally, it was her job to hear God's instruction. If advice was needed along the way, he knew that Deborah would seek God for them and that He would speak to her.

Deborah's answer to Barak's conditional request was also immediate, 'I will surely go with you.' To his credit, Barak had eschewed the glory and he didn't alter his stance, even when Deborah warned him that, to do it this way meant it was not his glory that would result but, rather, Sisera would be sold into the hand of a woman (this would turn out to be Jael).

The fact that Barak was rightly focussed on Israel's defeat of Sisera and willing to opt for teamwork over personal heroics is, I think, the main reason he gets a mention in Hebrews 11:32, 'For time would fail me to tell of Gideon, Barak, Samson, Jephthah, of David and Samuel and the prophets – who through faith conquered kingdoms, enforced justice, obtained promises... became mighty in war, put foreign armies to flight...' The corporate nature of the enterprise is also born out in Judges 5:2, where Deborah and Barak together sing a song of victory, 'That the leaders took the lead in Israel, that the people offered themselves willingly, bless the Lord!' Leaders (plural) taking the lead and people (plural) willingly offering to be led.

If you haven't already done so, you need to read the full account in Judges and to see how Sisera finally fell into the hands of a woman. But, there is one more thing to note in this story because it is going to come up again in a little while – if we look at another part of the song, in Judges 5, we are given a vital insight into what God is like.

As we have already said, several times, God made men and women in His image and gives them useful things to do, both individually and together, utilising their unique characteristics and strategically apportioning gifting for the task. But, He also imparts to men and women the essential elements of His own nature that will affect *how* and in what *capacity* we undertake a particular task. Verses 6 & 7 say, 'In the days of Shamgar, son of Anath, in the days of Jael, the highways were deserted, and the travellers walked along the byways. Village life ceased in Israel, until I, Deborah, arose as a mother in Israel.'

It is possibly better rendered '*a mother to Israel*' and it reveals that parenthood is inherent to God's character and therefore fundamental to the character of those made in His image. He didn't just appoint Deborah as prophetess and judge, He made her a mother to His people because that's what they needed. They had forsaken Him as parent and, given that He has the characteristics of both father and mother, He determined the priority was their need of a mother. God doesn't make mistakes – He needed a woman to speak His word to the nation *as a mother would speak* and He needed a man to respond to that word and to lead the people into battle.

It is worth noting at this point that biblical characters, to whom God has given a job, display a wide variety of negative reactions. Although much has been made over the years of Barak's seeming reluctance to go into battle (which as I've explained, was not the case), any qualification or hesitation on his part was mild compared to that of Moses. When God spoke to Moses out of the burning bush, he objected to the job that God was calling him to and, even after God had promised to go with him and told him of all the things He would do to the Egyptians, he still refused and asked that someone else be sent instead.

God was angry with Moses and reluctantly agreed to send Aaron alongside him. Despite the value and comfort of having someone to 'stand with him' and despite all of Aaron's good qualities, this turned out to be the second-best solution. I'm sure there were times after that when Moses knew he should have agreed to God's original proposition, especially when he came down the mountain and found the Israelites dancing round a golden calf!

God speaks but, whilst some are 'quick to listen', many are 'hard of hearing'

What must it be like for a God whose reason for creating us was to be a wise and loving Father, intent on forming relationship with us, injecting purpose into our lives, communicating with us and giving us fulfilling things to do, only to find that His creation either fails to take notice of Him or refuses to do His bidding?

Most of the time we are slow to listen and some of us don't actually expect Him to speak at all. A few even harbour (what I consider to be) the ridiculous notion that God's intervention in our time and space, to bring a 'now word', ceased with the completion of the canon of scripture, as if God's character and intentions suddenly altered at that point. Many today, even in the Church, have also ceased to accept the authority of that canon of scripture.

Some of us do listen, from time to time, but our understanding and application is poor and, for one reason or another, we don't actually obey His leading. If the word He speaks demands that we alter our lifestyle in some way, we are more likely to prefer and to bow to the pressures of the existing demands. If the word He speaks involves us in using or developing new skills and abilities, we will tend to shy away from the learning process or to disbelieve our capability to learn. It is possible to know or at least to have a shrewd idea that God has spoken to us but then to believe that we know better – concluding that He obviously doesn't realize how change-averse we are and how difficult, costly and disruptive the fulfilment of the word will be.

It's like the parable of the sower all over again but, thankfully, there are a few who do deliberately and consistently incline their ear to hear Him and they listen and they try to take seriously what He says. Doing so they discover the depth of His wisdom and progressively appreciate more of His ways. Pushing through the disruption and accepting the changes that He requires means they begin to participate in His purposes.

'He is there and He is not silent' (Schaeffer, 1972)

The relationship between God and man has involved communication from the very start. The Bible is full, from beginning to end, with God speaking to people (by all sorts of different mechanisms) and with men and women calling on God. There is no biblical evidence that God is reluctant to speak to us, indeed I would contend that there is an imperative to listen and to obey.

Conversely, there does seem to be evidence that we can be deaf to His voice or at least slow to hear what He is actually saying. For example:

- Is 65:2,12 (re-quoted by Paul in Romans 10:21) – 'I have stretched out My hands all day long to a rebellious people, who walk in a way that is not good, according to their own thoughts; A people who provoke Me to anger continually to My face...

  When I called, you did not answer; When I spoke, you did not hear, but did evil before My eyes, and chose that in which I do not delight.'
- Isaiah 43 – '(I)called you by name, you are mine... Bring out the people who are blind, yet have eyes, who are deaf, yet have ears!'
- Jeremiah 7:13 – 'When I spoke to you persistently, you did not listen, and when I called you, you did not answer...'
- Zechariah 7:11 – 'But they refused to pay attention and turned a stubborn shoulder and stopped their ears that they might not hear...'
- Matthew 13:15 – Jesus says of the generation to whom he was speaking, that the prophecy of Isaiah has been fulfilled: 'You will indeed hear but never understand, and you will indeed see but never perceive. For this people's heart has grown dull, and with their ears they can barely hear, and their eyes they have closed, lest they should see with their eyes and hear with their ears and understand with their heart and turn, and I would heal them.'

In John 10:3-5, Jesus described what ought to be the norm: 'He who enters by the door is the shepherd of the sheep. To him the gatekeeper opens. The sheep hear his voice, and he calls his own sheep by name and leads them out... and the sheep follow him, for they know his voice. A stranger they will not follow, but they will flee from him, for they do not know the voice of strangers.' He makes it sound very simple and the inference is that He intends it to be a lot simpler than we typically make it.

He has deliberately made each person unique

Have you ever spoken to two people who turned out to be identical in every respect? Even if you know identical twins, you will find that their temperaments and likes/dislikes have differences and those who know them well will be able to tell them apart. The fact that every person is different from every other person is something that we know intuitively to be the case. It can also be tested empirically – by observing and asking Qs of a substantial group of people.

John Medina, in his book *Brain Rules*, explains how every brain is wired differently and asserts that what you do and learn in life also physically changes what your brain looks like – literally rewiring it. He also explains how men's and women's brains are different from each other (Medina, 2008).

However, we should try and gather biblical evidence which illustrates our uniqueness and suggests how God's purpose for each person is also different:

- Jesus says in Luke 12, 'Are not five sparrows sold for two pennies? And not one of them is forgotten before God. *Why, even the hairs of your head are all numbered*. Fear not; you are of more value than many sparrows.' This was intended to reassure the disciples that God cares for us and knows every last detail about us. The closer you zoom in, to compare seemingly similar things, the more difference you see between them and so this verse is a strong indication that God has crafted each individual to be unique.

- In Psalm 139:13-16, David says: 'For you formed my inward parts; you knitted me together in my mother's womb. I praise you, for I am fearfully and wonderfully made. Wonderful are your works; my soul knows it very well. My frame was not hidden from you, when I was being made in secret, intricately woven in the depths of the earth. Your eyes saw my unformed substance; in your book were written, every one of them, the days that were formed for me, when as yet there was none of them.' This is a powerful indicator that God not only took great care to plan each person's form and substance but that He also has a plan for the outworking of our lives.

- In John 21, when Jesus is deep in conversation with Peter, re-commissioning him after the events of the trial and crucifixion and telling him what will happen to him at the end of his life, Peter looks behind and sees John and says to Jesus, 'But Lord, what about this man?' Jesus then says to him, 'If it is my will that he remains till I come, what is that to you? You follow Me.' Jesus has a different path for each one of us to tread and finding it is dependent on us following Him.

- In Mark 13:34, Jesus is explaining to his disciples that nobody knows, not even the angels in heaven, the date and time when He will return. He says, 'It is like a man going on a journey, when he leaves home and puts his servants in charge, *each with his work*, and commands the doorkeeper to stay awake.' Clearly, He is alluding to His own departure, which took place a few weeks later. 'Each with his work' has the sense of each person receiving his own commission to fulfil. These same words also occur in Nehemiah 4:15, when the walls of the city are being rebuilt and each family has its own section to restore.

- In Revelation 2:17 there is a very interesting verse... 'He who has an ear, let him hear what the Spirit says to the churches. To the one who conquers I will give some of the hidden manna, and I will give him a white stone, with a new name written on the stone that no one knows except the one who receives it.' Jesus is saying that those who resist evil and overcome will receive a new name – which only He and they will know. Given what we have already said above – about a name identifying its owner and making that person distinct – this is the clearest indication yet that God can identify each individual and has imbued them with personal characteristics.

All the above passages allude to there being important differences between one person and the next and therefore important differences between one person's work and the next. The argument is upheld by Paul in his teaching on the body in 1 Corinthians 12. The passage has frequently, wrongly been used to suggest there is a short hierarchy of valid spiritual gifts and we should each determine which one is ours. Nothing could be further from the truth – it is supposed to show us that, despite the importance of the particular gifts being discussed, there is actually huge diversity of gifting, just as the body has a huge diversity of parts and functions.

Even if a whole group of people were exhibiting a particular form of gifting, e.g. prophesy ['I desire that you would all prophesy...'], and even if all were sensing the same message or instruction from the Lord, they would each express that message in a different way. They would use different forms of words, possibly from a different perspective or angle, some in prose and some in verse, some in logical argument and some in picture language, some concisely and some at length, some with emotion and some in a calm and controlled manner.

The body analogy needs to be re-thought because the closer you look, the more intricate and complex and diverse are its attributes. The unifying factor, for David in Psalm 139 and Paul in 1 Corinthians 12, is the Spirit who both weaves in and distributes gifts variously – different kinds of service and different kinds of power, but the same Lord – instructing and inspiring each part to operate correctly, in accordance with His will.

He has put a sense of 'specialness' in the heart of man and a yearning to express it

Our ability to imagine ourselves in a different role or context

Another thing that John Medina explains in 'Brain Rules' is that humans have traits that separate us from every other creature. One of the most interesting is 'symbolic reasoning' – our ability to see an object or a shape as real all by itself and yet, simultaneously, also representing something else – in fact, it could be multiple other somethings. We have the ability to attribute characteristics and meanings to things that don't actually possess them – we can make things up that aren't actually there.

Children learn to do this from the age of two or three and it has benefits not just for the development of imagination but also for learning. Take my granddaughter for example – she was four at time of writing this and, unlike her older brother who seems to respond very quickly and easily to words and logical argument, and seems to remember most of what is said to him, she doesn't seem to focus so much on words but responds much more readily to sound and movement and pictures.

She can watch someone on television and imitate their movements, even remembering a sequence of dance steps the next day, with the ability to demonstrate and develop them.

However, she has had difficulty recognizing some numbers, among them, bizarrely, the number 8. Until, that is, she saw a number 8 lying on its side and said, 'that looks like binoculars' [which is impressive because I'm pretty sure I didn't know what binoculars were at the age of four]! Now, whenever she looks at an '8', she thinks 'binoculars' and she knows what it is.

We are human because our brains can perform all sorts of amazing contortions and we can fantasize. It gives us the ability to plan and to adapt and to imagine things that have yet to be.

I am not claiming that this is directly and inextricably linked to a person's yearning to be doing something different or more meaningful but, as humans, we also have an ability to appreciate our own personal characteristics and to imagine their use in different contexts. We can project ourselves, in our imagination, into situations that don't yet exist. Further than that, we take delight in the times when aptitude and passion collide and, conversely, we are painfully aware of when there is no resonance at all between what we are doing and what we yearn to do.

Our predisposition to yearn

I would propose that the idea of 'calling' is close to the surface in a great many people. The logic was laid out earlier in this chapter – the fact that He has given every one of us a set of unique characteristics, along with a sense of awareness that, as an individual, we are unique and, in some way, 'special' (by which I mean that we have a sense of being earmarked for something that only we can do), leads to us yearn to fulfil our potential.

Most of those whom I have sought to engage in conversation on the topic have shown no reticence in offering personal opinions and have done so with very little prompting. The conversation very rarely remains at the intellectual level – it quickly becomes personal and inevitably points either towards something that the person is doing (in fulfilment of some kind of call) or, more frequently, towards something they have felt stirred about but are not doing and yet wish they were.

A high proportion of the people to whom I have put questions about career and fulfilment have (unprompted by me) recounted a time when they felt either there was something special they ought to be doing with their life or something different about them, compared to those around them. In most cases, they then go on to express dissatisfaction with the outcome so far.

Our sense of a purpose to be fulfilled

Proverbs 20:5 says, 'The purpose in a man's heart is like deep water, but a man of understanding will draw it out.' This is pointing to an underlying thing that is there in a person's heart and which persists. It is identifiable and, presumably, can be articulated.

Purpose seems to be linked to the desire of a person's heart, as it says in the verse immediately preceding the one above, 'May He grant you according to your heart's desire and fulfil all your purpose.' So, it's that deep-seated thing that drives you on to a desired end goal or outcome. A person will not usually have a single purpose in life but will feel driven to accomplish different things at different points and each of those accomplishments will be pursued to some kind of conclusion over varying periods of time.

As such, purpose is not vague. It starts to take on form and to gain clarity as someone begins to understand what they have to do. They may not, at that stage, know how they are going to accomplish this thing and they may have significant doubts as to their own ability but they know that something is brewing.

Proverbs 19:21 says, 'Many are the plans in the mind of a man but it is the purpose of the Lord that will stand.' The plans indicated here are linked to the purpose spoken of in Proverbs 20:5 above and God is drawing a distinction between the two. In so far as we, as human beings, can either concentrate on our own purposes (live by our own instincts and pursue things of our own making and design) or seek to be involved in God's purposes, these verses are conveying two truths: firstly, in working out His overall purpose, God also has a specific purpose for each one whose participation He invites; and secondly, there is frequently a difference between what seems to us to be a good idea and what is actually the Lord's will.

God's purpose is enduring and He articulates aspects of it clearly to those who are sensitive to Him and will listen. There is a sort of inevitability about the overall outcome but there may be some variability in terms of the personnel He is able to engage. God is deliberate about who He invites and what He wants them to be part of. For each person, to accept the invite and be caught up in the divine purpose will always be beneficial, even if the experience is also painful, but to shun it will be detrimental.

So, although we must concentrate mainly on the positive outworking of God's purpose, as a result of men and women embracing His calls on their lives, we should also sound a cautionary note: In Luke 7, when talking to the crowds about John the Baptist, Jesus states that John was purposely sent ahead, as a herald, to make way for His own coming, and He confers greatness upon John for his obedience and faithfulness. But Luke then makes a telling comment about the intended benefits of John's ministry – 'All the common people that heard him, and the tax collectors as well, acknowledged the justice of God's ways by allowing themselves to be baptized with John's baptism; *while the Pharisees and the experts in the law, in refusing to be baptized by him, frustrated the purpose God had had for them*' verse 29,30. (Cassirer, 1989)

The baptism offered by John was intended by God as a 'way in' or a 'means of grace' for many to appreciate His overall purpose, be caught up into it and then to discover His specific purpose for them as individuals. If God wants men and women to be engaged in His work and if He tailor-makes tasks for us and calls us to fulfil them and if we, in turn, hear those calls, He becomes the author of the purpose that takes shape in our hearts. 'Purpose' then becomes the impetus to fulfil a call or a commission.

Here are three biblical examples of people in whom a special 'purpose' took root. They knew that God had called or commissioned them and each had a desire to fulfil the resulting sense of purpose. Each was different and together they show something of the uniqueness of different callings: in the first case they were able to go ahead and do it; in the second case they had to wait a very long time before they saw the fulfilment, but it did come about; in the third case God said it was not for them personally to see it through but they were able to prepare for it and to instruct someone else about how it should be done.

Case 1: The people who made the tabernacle – When the nation of Israel had come out of Egypt, the first big construction project was the building of the tabernacle and creation of utensils and garments for those who would minister. Exodus 35:21 says, 'Then everyone came whose heart was stirred, and everyone whose spirit was willing, and they brought the Lord's offering for the work of the tabernacle of meeting, for all its service, and for the holy garments.' Exodus 36:2 goes on to say, 'Then Moses called Bezalel and Oholiab, and every gifted artisan (craftsman) in whose heart the Lord had put wisdom (skill), everyone whose heart was stirred, to come and do the work.' The key phrase is 'everyone whose heart was stirred' – they had seen and appreciated that something special had to be done and they had a desire to be involved.

Case 2: Simeon and Anna – in Luke 2 it tells us first of all that Simeon 'was righteous and devout, waiting for the consolation of Israel, and the Holy Spirit was upon him' and secondly that Anna 'was a prophetess... advanced in years and... didn't depart from the temple, worshipping with fasting and prayer night and day'. These two were eagerly waiting for God to do something – Simeon had been told he would set eyes on the Lord's Christ before he died and Anna likewise was looking for His sign of redemption – they were actively pursuing a fulfilment of what God had planted within them. They were not disappointed.

Case 3: King David and a house for God - In 2Samuel 7:2,3, King David, having rest from his enemies, tells Nathan the prophet of his desire to build a house for God because 'the ark of God (still) dwells in a tent'. Nathan says, 'Go, do all that is in your heart, for the Lord is with you.' Later, the Lord speaks to Nathan and tells him to pass a message to David, part of which is, in verses 11-13, 'I will give you rest from all your enemies. Moreover, the Lord declares to you that the Lord will make you a house. When your days are fulfilled and you lie down with your fathers, I will raise up your offspring after you, who shall come from your body, and I will establish his kingdom. He shall build a house for my name.'

David's heart has been stirred up to build God a house but God, though pleased with David's desire, has a better plan. We know from 1Chronicles 28:3 that God said to David, 'You may not build a house for my name, for you are a man of war and have shed blood.' However, that did not stop David, before he died, from gathering much of the building material and precious metals that would be necessary for the project and from drawing up the plans, all of which he presented to Solomon. 1Chronicles 28 gives us the details and it is particularly interesting that David says to his son, in verse 19, 'All this the Lord made me understand in writing, by His hand upon me, all the works of these plans.' [NKJV] So, we see that, rather than overstepping the mark and dabbling in things that were not his to specify, David had had detailed discussions with God on the matter. God let him be involved after all and had confided to this man, of whom He says in Acts 13:22, 'I have found David the son of Jesse, a man after my own heart, who will do all my will', all the details of what He wanted.

Footnote concerning uniqueness:

In January 2020, some six months after I first drafted this chapter, a filmed interview with some of the founders of the Vineyard Movement was shown at the Vineyard National Leaders Conference in Nottingham, UK.

The film features Carol Wimber, former wife of the late John Wimber, and John & Penny Fulton. It was made in 2019 and uploaded to YouTube by Vineyard UK in April 2020. The whole interview is well worth watching but the following are some of Carol Wimber's words, said towards the end of the conversation:

He needs us in our place for what is coming... I am not exactly sure what is coming, but I know that it is coming. I know it is soon and I know it is huge. It's going to be the whole thing, like nothing we've ever seen before. That's kind of scary and wonderful to think about.

You need to get in your place for what God has called you to and do it with all your heart, because it's so very, very important, because no one else has been designed to do it like you will do it, and you are the one He has called. No one else will ever be able to do what you are called to do because we really are unique, each one of us. Unique. Designed for our place.

It's coming and it's going to be so big and so huge and wonderful, but terrible too. We need to be in our place, so we can handle the influx, because masses of people are going to be brought in, this last harvest.

[Legacy // https://www.youtube.com/watch?v=97dOO3vlFJc (Vineyard, 2019)]

Chapter 7

Modelling God's Character – Culture and Gender

God's calls cut across the expectations of society and culture

A culture establishes ingrained norms and a society, although shifting and adapting, tends to support and promote a certain set of attitudes and behaviours at a particular point in time. The Bible tends to use the phrase 'the world' to indicate the fallen nature of where we live and John makes a clear statement about it in 1John 2:15-17: 'Do not love the world or the things in the world. If anyone loves the world, the love of the Father is not in him. For all that is in the world – the desires of the flesh and the desires of the eyes and pride of life (or pride in possessions) – is not from the Father but is from the world. And the world is passing away along with its desires, but whoever does the will of God abides forever.'

So, it is no surprise that God frequently called people to stand against the world's values and to act in countercultural ways and He is still doing it. Insofar as those who shape society do so contrary to God's ways, He leads individuals and groups to stand against those changes and to act in an opposite spirit, thus demonstrating His alternatives.

We will briefly consider examples of it in the Bible: in one-off events involving ordinary individuals and families, during the normal course of life; repeatedly in the words and actions of men and women called out to be prophets; in the establishing of a new nation of Israel, as it was called out of Egypt; and in the Church as the 'Holy Nation' of 'called-out people' after the resurrection.

Ordinary individuals

Every time a righteous person is surrounded either by a standard of behaviour that is not acceptable or cultural norms that run counter to what God has put in his/her heart, there is the potential for acting in the opposite spirit.

This is what Lot determined to do in Genesis 18 and 19, when he had to be rescued by angels from Sodom before the city was destroyed. We see Lot's conduct towards the angels (whom he thought to be just men at the time) in seeking to protect them, and at potential cost to himself and his family. And we then read commentary about him in 2Peter 2:7,8: 'He rescued righteous Lot, greatly distressed by the sensual conduct of the wicked (for as that righteous man lived among them day after day, he was tormenting his righteous soul over their lawless deeds that he saw and heard).'

In Acts 10 we read about Cornelius, a Roman centurion, calling for Peter to come and speak to all those gathered in his home in Caesarea, and how the Holy Spirit fell for the first time on Gentiles. Cornelius had received a call from God to do something quite unusual – in fact, in keeping with what we have already said, when establishing the framework of calling in Chapter 3, he had already been building some unusual, yet persistent attributes into his life and was therefore already doing 'counter cultural' things in the period leading up to this event.

Cornelius was subject to the military culture of the invading forces which had subjugated the nation of Israel. However, he not only feared the Jewish God, which was not a 'Roman' thing to do, but he was also practising his religion with an open and generous heart, more in tune with the ways of Jesus' followers than according to the prevailing Jewish religious culture.

He had made two cultural shifts and was not behaving like a Roman centurion would have been expected to behave – firstly he 'prayed continually' and secondly, he 'gave alms generously to the people' and his whole household shared his faith. He then had a visit from an angel, who gave him instructions (commissioned him) to call for Peter, thus setting in motion a complex train of events that altered everybody's understanding of the Church and the kingdom... Jesus had apparently died for Gentiles as well and they were to be welcomed into the body of Christ alongside the Jews.

The prophets

Several of the prophets were asked by God not just to speak out against the behaviours and attitudes prevalent at the time but also to act out illustrations of those behaviours, their inevitable outcome and the word that God wished to bring.

We are not focusing on the fact that symbolic acts featured in God's message, because it was relatively common for a prophet to use this method of communication, but rather drawing attention to the *nature* of some of those acts. These demonstrations ran counter to the 'acceptable' behaviours of the day and would be frowned upon in Christian circles today, illustrating that God's calls cut across cultural norms – it was definitely a case of 'don't try this at home' or, if you do, be very sure that it's God who is instructing you:

Isaiah – As a sign that the Assyrians would take the people of Egypt and Cush captive and lead them away naked, God said to Isaiah, "'Go and loose the sackcloth from your waist and take off the sandals from your feet" and he did so, walking about naked and barefoot [for three years]' Isaiah 20:2.

Jeremiah – With the Babylonian invasion imminent and Israel still defiant that God would not let it happen, at a time when envoys had come to Zedekiah, the king of Judah, from the independent, neighbouring states of Edom, Moab, Ammon, Tyre and Sidon, the Lord said to him, 'Make yourself straps and yoke-bars and put them on your neck. Send (back) word, by these envoys... to their masters: "Thus says the Lord of hosts, the God of Israel: It is I who by my great power and my outstretched arm have made the earth, with the men and animals that are on the earth, and I give it to whomever it seems right to me. Now I have given all these lands into the hand of Nebuchadnezzar, the king of Babylon, my servant. All the nations shall serve him..."' Jeremiah 27:2-7. Jeremiah was being instructed by God to crash the king's party and deliver His message because this word was to be spoken not just to Judah but to all the rest of Israel, including the territories represented by the envoys.

Ezekiel – In chapters 4 and 5 of his prophecy, Ezekiel recounts a whole series of very strange instructions that he received from the Lord, all of which illustrated various aspects of the forthcoming siege of Jerusalem and its inevitable destruction. These included lying, bound with ropes, on his left side for 390 days and then on his right side for 40 days; adopting a highly restricted and weight-limited diet, that included items forbidden by the law; shaving his head, weighing the hair and then burning some of it. Then, if that were not enough, in chapter 12:3-6, he is told to pack an 'exile's baggage', to carry it from place to place and then to dig through the wall and take it out at dusk with his face covered.

Hosea – The first few chapters of Hosea graphically illustrate God's judgment on Israel for forsaking Him. He instructs Hosea to marry a prostitute [a wife of whoredom] and the resulting children were then given symbolic names, describing God's intended judgmental actions. Hosea lets her go – she is said to be loved by another man – and then he buys her back again [redeems her]. All of which could be regarded as above and beyond the call of duty but it shows what God was prepared to do, to convince Israel of its apostasy and the consequences that would follow.

John the Baptist – We are including John because, in one sense, he was the last of the Old Testament prophets and he is likened by Jesus to Elijah. Like Elijah, God called John to make his home in the wilderness and Matthew 3 tells us that he dressed in animal skins, fed on locusts and wild honey and proclaimed a radical message that demanded repentance from any who came out to hear him. This was not 'normal' behaviour, it was striking and evocative and, after 400 years of near silence, once again challenged the establishment figures in Jewish society to listen to God.

Israel and the Church

Both the post-Exodus nation of Israel and the post-Pentecost Church are examples of God initiating wholesale cultural revolutions.

The nation of Israel that came out of Egypt was handed a completely new set of laws and customs that covered all of the social, economic, political and religious aspects of life. Although the people complained and hankered after certain, selected aspects of Egyptian life, the new practices marked them out as different from all the surrounding nations and, if followed, those practices would also protect them from and give them dominance over the surrounding nations.

This wasn't so much a call to act in a contrary way to the surrounding culture, it was a challenge to their whole way of life and a call to 'holiness' in its most fundamental sense – to be consecrated to God and separated for Him. To be purified from their own sin and that of the other nations around them.

A Holy Nation of 'called-out' people – after the Holy Spirit fell on the apostles and other disciples at Pentecost, an altogether new way of living was established among the community of believers. Acts Chapters 2-6 in particular detail just how radical was the shift and just how much the presence of the Holy Spirit among them mirrored the presence of God among the Exodus people. For example, it brought about:

- **societal change** in having everything in common, hospitality, frequent healings and deliverance;
- **economic change** in the selling of properties, redistribution of wealth, and care for the poor and needy;
- **governmental and structural change** in the emergence of strong apostolic leadership who had the power to enforce, on God's behalf, a new standard of holiness and to release others into effective leadership;
- **religious change** in recalling, recording and establishing both the teaching of Jesus and the first-hand experience of living with the Saviour; and giving new form and new content to their meetings together.

The new 'nation', thus established, soon received an even more radical call from God that required them to submit to what was previously unheard of. They had to lay aside their historic prejudices and to open their doors to

Gentiles, who were to become part of the same community and to receive the same Holy Spirit.

God's calls cut across the expectations of gender

Gender is a fraught issue in our society today and many have felt that even expressing an opinion on the subject is now discouraged. Nevertheless, we need to ask the question whether callings issued to men and women tend to follow common stereotypes or whether God appears to have a different way.

Completeness and teamwork

From a biblical point of view, the important fact is that God created both man and woman 'in His image'. His reasoning in Genesis 2:18 was that it was 'not good for Adam to be alone' – He knew that Adam lacked certain essential characteristics and so He created Eve, as 'a helper fit for [or 'corresponding to'] him'. This was the way God determined to provide completeness and it achieved three essential goals: firstly, providing the companionship of equals; secondly, creating the means of procreation that requires the participation of both genders and thirdly, introducing complementarity and therefore teamwork.

In other words, it was His deliberate strategy to make them different but that *together* they would have all the essential characteristics and God clearly intended that they learn to operate *together*. There is no biblical basis for saying that one gender – one member of the team – is more valuable than the other but they are clearly different from each other and each is intended to bring different capabilities to the team. God provided a solution to the incompleteness of Adam but introduced a profound challenge – if a team is going to work together, they each need to recognize both their own and the other's skills and limitations and they need to learn how to make the right decisions *together*.

Marriage and parenthood

Having established gender as an integral part of being human, two other concepts then follow on right behind – *committed relationship* and *parenthood*. Both are inherent to God's character and therefore fundamental to the character of those made in His image:

- Marriage/man & wife (Genesis 2:24) – God created woman and immediately described her as a 'wife' for the man, who would leave his own father and mother in order to 'hold fast' to her. It is the language of a committed, faithful and lasting relationship. The faithfulness and commitment of this relationship is reinforced in many other places, not least of which is God's description of His own relationship with the nation of Israel and His distress and anger at their unfaithfulness to Him:

- o Isaiah 54:5 says, 'For your maker is your husband, the Lord of hosts is his name.'
- o Jeremiah 3:20 says, 'Surely, as a treacherous wife leaves her husband, so have you been treacherous to me, O house of Israel, declares the Lord.'
- o Jeremiah 31:32 says, 'The covenant that I made with [your] fathers on the day when I took them by the hand to bring them out of the land of Egypt, my covenant that they broke, though I was their husband, declares the Lord.'

Then, the same terminology is used in His declaration that Jesus is the 'bridegroom' and the Church is to be 'the bride of Christ':

- o Matthew 9:15 says, 'And Jesus said to them, [in response to the disciples of John the Baptist, on the subject of fasting, alluding to His own departure from the world] "Can the friends of the bridegroom mourn as long as the bridegroom is with them? But the days will come when the bridegroom will be taken away from them, and then they will fast."'
- o Revelation 21:2 says, 'Then I, John, saw the holy city, New Jerusalem, coming down out of heaven from God, prepared as a bride adorned for her husband.'
- o Revelation 22:17 says, 'And the Spirit and the bride say, "Come!" And let him who hears say, "Come!" And let him who thirsts come. Whoever desires, let him take the water of life freely.'

- • Fatherhood & motherhood – Adam called his wife's name Eve, which sounds like the Hebrew for 'life-giver', 'because she was the mother of all living' Genesis 3:22. The word 'father' first occurs in Genesis 2:24, as quoted above, and thence is used of each successive male person who begets or 'fathers' a child. God then refers to himself as 'Father' in numerous places across both the Old and New Testaments and, more than that, *acts towards us as a father would*:

- o Proverbs 3:12 says, 'for the Lord reproves him whom he loves, as a father the son in whom he delights.'
- o Psalm 103:13 says, 'As a father shows compassion to his children, so the Lord shows compassion to those who fear him.'

As with all such concepts in the Bible, it doesn't mean that we each must be able to assume the exact role – husband/wife or father/mother – in order to experience the benefit. It does not mean that meaningful things can only happen in that actual human context. Some people will not be married and some will never have children of their own. Nevertheless, God wants us to grasp something of these relationships, to understand why they are at the heart of His dealings with men and women and to act accordingly.

We are fallen but not irretrievably so. Our own human relationships may be badly broken and our own parents may not have demonstrated much if anything of God's ways but we are not without hope. He wants to speak into our brokenness, adopt us as His sons and daughters and progressively apply His grace to develop the attributes of son- or daughter-ship with a father. As He does so, we will gain an understanding of what He means by committed relationship and what are the true characteristics of fatherhood and motherhood and it will inform how we operate.

Part of the Holy Spirit's work in us is to make the Fatherhood of God tangible – Jesus said to his disciples, in John 14:6,7,23, 'No one comes to the Father except through me. If you had known me, you would have known my Father also. From now on you do know him and have seen him... If anyone loves me, he will keep my word, and my Father will love him, and we will come to him and make our home with him.' The parenthood of God administers strength and tenderness, wrath and mercy, exaltation and condescension, surpassing wisdom and patient guidance, all in perfect balance.

When Paul is talking to the Ephesians about the ultimate goal of oneness in Christ – the breaking down of walls of hostility and all having 'access in one Spirit to the Father, through Christ' – he says, 'For this reason I bow my knees before the Father, from whom *every family* in heaven and on earth is named...' The Greek word he uses here for 'family' is 'patria' and it is closely related to the word for 'Father'. The best rendition of the verse therefore is 'from whom all *fatherhood* in heaven and on earth is named' 3:14,15.

Psalm 68:5,6 says, 'Father of the fatherless and protector of the widows is God in his holy habitation. God settles the solitary in a home [in families – NKJV]; he leads out the prisoners to prosperity, but the rebellious dwell in a parched land.' His intention is that, as people submit to him, He will minister to them and set them free from their orphaned state and their widowhood. The truth is that every one of us has only ever known in part what committed relationship and parenthood is about – we all need the Father to take us into His family and to reveal it to us. Otherwise we won't be able to exhibit those characteristics properly when we undertake our God-given tasks.

There are many things we could say to develop this argument further, such as the New Testament's insistence that the acid test, in the world's eyes, of us truly being disciples is whether we love one another; that the Church is supposed to operate as a collection of cooperatively-functioning, mutually beneficial parts of a 'body'; that 'status', as the world sees it, is not applicable for the 'called-out' people of God and those who consider themselves the greatest will be brought low; that we are each to take hold of the kingdom of God as a child would; and that the Holy Spirit's intention is always to arrange gifting in order to confer honour on the least honourable part. All of these reinforce the notion that God calls us to operate instinctively according to His own nature.

Gender and calling

So, how are we to consider how gender affects 'calling'? Are men and women called to different things that reflect the differences between the sexes or is it less about male and female and more about uniqueness, complementarity and teamwork?

As you might infer from the way in which that question is phrased, I think we have to look past gender and start to understand how and why God has chosen not to put all the necessary characteristics, skills, abilities and experience for the task at hand into each person whom He calls, but rather to leave each with limitations and the consequent need to associate and collaborate with others in order to achieve the desired outcomes.

It would be wrong not to state that there are differences between the sexes and that much scientific research has tried to characterize those differences. Not all such research is helpful and none of it should lead to us adopting stereotypes. We can make observations about what is generally the case but God frequently seems to overturn our expectations.

In preparation for writing this book it was clear to me that both men and women are commissioned and called by God. But, my own experience suggests that women seem to need more prompting to talk about 'calling' in relation to 'what one does or feels compelled to do with one's life' or to 'finding one's vocation'. It might be because, in general, women give a higher priority to talking about 'real, personal issues' than men do. Men would usually opt to talk about 'what they do' rather than 'who they are', preferring to focus on deeds and activities and to keep their personal feelings hidden.

Although a man's preferred mode of conversation might have him arrive at the topic of vocation more quickly, he is nevertheless naturally more reluctant to divulge his hopes and fears. However, whenever the talk turns to dreams and aspirations; to what someone enjoys doing and has done well, to the tasks and activities they would consider 'characterize them', and to what someone has a heart to accomplish in the future, both men and women tend to 'come alive'. As long as they know and understand that the person conducting the conversation is genuinely interested in hearing what they have to say, most people become extremely articulate in expressing who they believe themselves to be.

Scientific research continues to report on differences and, in terms of 'vocation' and what an individual might naturally choose to pursue, there is evidence that we each will tend to pursue the things that interest us. Accordingly, women's areas of interest are, in general, shown to be more 'people oriented' and men's interest areas tend to be more 'thing oriented', with predictable results (Men and Things, Women and People: A Meta-Analysis of Sex differences in Interests, 2009).

Abstract: Psychological Bulletin 2009, Vol 135, No.6, 859-884
The study suggests that interests may play a critical role in gendered occupational choices and gender disparity in e.g. the STEM fields. We know intuitively that there are differences between men and women in terms of the vocation they might instinctively choose to pursue. This study points to such vocation choice based on differences in interest inventories.

If God has engineered the differences between the sexes, are those differences therefore born out in the types of calling He bestows on men and women?

Men are generally physically stronger than women. That strength may lend itself better to military service and warfare and also to the building trades – it is harder to imagine a woman going out at the head of the army and then pursuing the enemy for days or casting huge bronze utensils for Solomon's Temple than for those roles to be taken by a man. However, women are more emotionally astute than men and can often perceive things more quickly and clearly – it is therefore harder to imagine a man breaking a jar of costly ointment and anointing Jesus in preparation for his burial.

Although there are some tasks that God could only give to a woman, especially relating to the bearing and raising of children, to focus on what one person can do more easily than another is to miss the point. God is sovereign in His choices and more interested in teamwork than individual glory. The angel Gabriel had to come to Mary, not Joseph, because the Holy Spirit was to overshadow her and she was the one who would bear the Son of God. God respects the individual and speaks directly to each one whom He calls – He would never have sent Gabriel to tell Joseph what was going to happen and then ask him to tell Mary! Mary had a unique calling but God also had a vital job for Joseph to do and instructed him accordingly.

Despite Joseph's desire to break off the marriage and to save Mary from as much shame as possible, instead he learned that he too had been carefully chosen and his candidacy was confirmed by important facts – that he was directly descended from David and his home town was Bethlehem. His priceless calling was to 'stand with' Mary, to protect and watch over both her and the child and, in responding to a dream and then the call for census and then to more dreams, to be the facilitator for several ancient prophecies to be fulfilled. What a team they made – she could not have done it without him and the infant Jesus needed them both.

We tend to get hung up on questions of gender and the Bible has often been accused of favouring male over female but in truth it does not. We are therefore going to consider three things in the next few pages:

- Biblical examples of people, including Jesus, called by God to exhibit traits that would normally be associated with the other gender;
- How Jesus, as a man, living in a culture that placed many restrictions on women, viewed and treated women;
- Some examples, in what is often regarded as a male-dominated book, of God calling women and using them to achieve His purpose.

Moses and Jesus both demonstrated male and female traits

God embodies all our human characteristics. He created us male and female and there are good reasons why they are not the same – not least being His desire for complementarity and teamwork to characterize the way we operate. There are therefore times when God speaks to one sex in terms you might think are reserved for the other and appoints one to a task that might be thought more appropriate for the other. However, He does not make mistakes.

We have already considered an example of that complementarity and teamwork when He chose Deborah to be prophet, judge and anointed leader in Israel. We saw how He needed someone to be 'a mother to Israel', how she then confirmed God's call on Barak to command the army and declared to him the strategy and then how they together went up to wage battle against Sisera.

If we look at a time slightly earlier in the nation's history, just after the commandments had been given at Sinai and they were on the move again in the wilderness, we find the people of Israel complaining to Moses that they were sick of manna and needed meat. Numbers 11:10 says, 'Moses heard the people weeping throughout their clans, everyone at the door of his tent. And the anger of the Lord blazed hotly, and Moses was displeased.' What follows is Moses' dialogue with God about the nature of the calling that had been laid upon him.

Numbers 11:12-13 says, 'Did I conceive all this people? Did I give them birth, that you should say to me, "Carry them in your bosom, as a nurse carries a nursing child," to the land you swore to give to their fathers? Where am I to get meat to give to all this people?... I am not able to carry all this people alone; the burden is too heavy for me.' This is remarkable language because it indicates that the burden given to Moses to carry was that of being a 'wet nurse' to the people of Israel.

A wet nurse is a woman who breast feeds and cares for another's child. Wet nurses are employed if the mother dies, or if she is unable or elects not to nurse the child herself. Moses regarded himself as having been called to carry God's children for Him, to bring them nourishment and to deliver them safely to their destination and he is reminding God of the impossibility of accomplishing such a task. God appointed Moses as leader of His people, with part of the responsibility requiring him to act as stand-in parent. Again, a key aspect to the task was to be 'a mother to Israel' and, in this case, He gave the job to a man.

There is a great deal that Jesus did that you would characterize as 'masculine' but, at other times, you would have to say that some of his words and actions are more characteristic of his 'feminine side'. For example, in Luke 13 Jesus laments over Jerusalem – it happens when some Pharisees come to warn him of Herod's intention to kill him. Jesus is quite scathing about Herod, making clear that His work will not be hindered by such threats, and then says, 'O Jerusalem, Jerusalem, the city that kills the prophets and stones those who are sent to it! How often would I have gathered your children together as a hen gathers her brood under her wings, and you were not willing!' It's a simile that almost edges over into metaphor because it is expressed as a mother would say it – you can almost see Him miming the actions to what He is describing.

How Jesus viewed and treated women

The attitude of Jesus to women is enlightening. He treated them very much as equals, counter to the prevailing culture and expectations, as the following examples show:

- Jesus addressed women directly, in public, in a manner that was most unusual in His day – in John 4, when his disciples returned to the well at Sychar they 'marvelled that He was talking with a woman'. He spoke freely with the woman taken in adultery (John 8); with the widow of Nain (Luke 7); and again, with the woman who had the bleeding disorder, calling her 'daughter' (Luke 8; Matt 9; Mark 5). He addressed a woman bent over for 18 years and called her 'a daughter of Abraham', which conferred on her a spiritual status equal with a man (Luke 13). He also spoke with a group of women en-route to the cross (Luke 23).
- In Luke 10:38-42, Jesus is at the home of Mary and Martha. Martha is cooking and Mary has chosen to sit and listen. Martha asks Jesus to redirect Mary to the serving duties but Jesus takes the opposite view – saying, 'one thing is necessary. Mary has chosen the good portion, which will not be taken away from her.' This is not what anybody present would have expected – He went against the cultural stereotype and affirmed Mary's right to learn.

- In both Luke 24 and John 20, in the midst of the mad scramble on the morning of the resurrection, when people were running backwards and forwards between their homes and the tomb, Mary Magdalene (in John) and a group of the women (in Luke) found themselves outside the tomb, with no men around, and they encountered angels, who spoke to them. In Luke, the angels gave the women clear information about the resurrection and the fulfilment of Jesus' word. In John's account, Mary receives the information from the risen Jesus himself. Both Gospels report that they went back to relate what had happened to the disciples and others who were gathered. In neither gospel account were the women believed. It was not just stress and natural incredulity that led to that disbelief, it was also the fact that, in the culture of the day, important information was not communicated to or by a woman. Nevertheless, God had deliberately vouchsafed critical information to those women – He trusted them to be the bearers of the news.

Examples of women whom God called and/or commissioned

Although there are not really any examples of women being called to or commended for the practical trades, they certainly didn't just bear children and support their husbands. There are instances of women prophesying, leading, overcoming enemies, exercising wisdom & discretion, being courageous & politically astute, taking an honourable position and showing loyalty, responding to life-changing instructions from God and leading in the Church and it is worth looking briefly at a few. In the examples given below, there was a point in time when each person took stock of the situation and came to a clear decision about what God was requiring of them and therefore the action they had to take:

Sarah was barren and lived the majority of her life with Abraham unable to have the child that had been promised. Abraham tends to get most of the good press and Sarah is often remembered more for her errors than for what she got right e.g. presumptuously giving her servant to Abraham as a concubine, in Genesis 16, and then laughing when the Lord later appeared to them and declared that she would have a son the following year, in Genesis 18. Actually, Abraham made his own series of mistakes, such as trying to pass his wife off as his sister on several occasions, out of fear for his own life, and agreeing to take Sarah's servant as concubine. However, we are told in Hebrews 11:11, 'By faith Sarah herself received power to conceive, even when she was past the age, since she considered him faithful who had promised.' They were a team and, in order to fulfil God's call, each had to recognize it and respond in faith to that call.

Rahab was a prostitute who took in and hid the two spies whom Joshua sent to spy out Jericho. She did that because she had heard how Israel had escaped Egypt, had gone across the Red Sea on dry land, and had then destroyed the kings across the Jordan before coming across into Canaan. In Joshua 2:11 she says, 'There was no spirit left in any man because of you, for the Lord your God, he is God in the heavens above and on the earth beneath.' She therefore sensed in that moment what she had to do and threw herself on the mercy of the God of heaven and earth, committing herself and her family to Israel. She was spared and God honoured her in a remarkable way – she married Salmon, a man of Israel, and her son was Boaz, who later married Ruth, the Moabitess. Rahab is therefore named in Matthew 1, in the direct line to Jesus and she gets a mention in Hebrews 11:30,31, 'the walls of Jericho fell down… [and] By faith Rahab the prostitute did not perish with those who were disobedient, because she had given a friendly welcome to the spies.' A remarkable woman.

Deborah, who was a prophetess and judged Israel, has already been considered at length in Chapter 6. Her story is set out in Judges 4 & 5.

Jael, whom Deborah prophesied about, is the woman into whose hands Sisera fell. Judges 4:17-22 relates how she duped the exhausted commander of Jabin's army and then killed him as he slept. She was cunning, ruthless and courageous – every bit as valiant and committed as anyone in Barak's army.

Ruth, the Moabitess, was widowed but would not leave her mother-in-law Naomi's side and returned with her to Bethlehem. By faith, she sought out Naomi's relative, Boaz, and married him when he agreed to perform his duty as 'kinsman redeemer'. Ruth thereby became the mother of Obed, who was grandfather of King David. The decisive moment in Ruth's life came when Naomi, whose husband and two sons had all died, determined to return from Moab to Bethlehem and told her daughters-in-law to turn back and remain with their own people. Ruth said to her, 'Do not urge me to leave you or to return from following you. For where you go I will go, and where you lodge I will lodge. Your people shall be my people, and your God my God. Where you die I will die, and there I will be buried. May the Lord do so to me and more also if anything but death parts me from you', Ruth 1:16,17. As such, this decision was very similar to that made by Rahab – both women recognized the need to forsake their own people and to declare their allegiance to the God of Israel. In doing so, they both became an integral part of the story of redemption.

Hannah, the mother of Samuel, was barren but begged God for many years for a child. In 1Samuel 1:10 she says to God, 'O Lord of hosts, if you will indeed look on the affliction of your servant and remember me and not forget your servant, but will give to your servant a son, then I will give him to the Lord all the days of his life, and no razor shall touch his head.' God heard her, she claimed the prize for her faith and perseverance and then she gave him away in fulfilment of her vow. Samuel became one of the Old Testament's greatest prophets and, although she did not know it when she let Samuel go, 1Samuel 2:21 tells us that God gave Hannah three more sons and two daughters.

Abigail, wife of Nabal, as 1Samuel 25 tells us, 'was discerning (or good in discretion) and beautiful but the man was harsh and badly behaved.' David was still being pursued by Saul and in need. He sent his young men, who had been courteous and accommodating in the area where Nabal's shearers had been working and had offered them protection, to ask Nabal for some food. Nabal was rude and boorish and refused any assistance. This behaviour would have been disastrous for Nabal and his entire household were it not for the quick thinking of his astute wife. Nabal's own men knew that he was 'a worthless man' and Abigail knew what she had to do. She duly got provisions together and set out to meet David. When she found him, she is reported as saying, 'On me alone, my lord, be the guilt. Please let your servant speak in your ears, and hear the words of your servant. Let not my lord regard this worthless fellow, Nabal, for as his name is, so is he.' [Nabal means 'fool' whilst Abigail means 'father's joy'] verses 24,25. She went on to prophesy of David's success and the care that would be afforded to him by the Lord his God. Her wisdom overturned David's anger and he said to her, 'Blessed be the Lord who sent you this day to meet me! Blessed be your discretion, and blessed be you...' verses 32,33. When Nabal heard what had happened, he died and, in due course, David invited Abigail to be his wife.

Esther was the Jewish girl brought up and tutored by her cousin Mordechai in Susa (capital of the kingdom of the Medes and Persians) who, by faith, became queen to Ahasuerus and subsequently, because she found special favour with the king, was able to foil the plot by Haman to destroy all the Jews. Mordechai, a Jew, refused to bow down and pay homage to the king's chief official, Haman, and hence was despised. In his pride, Haman determined not just to kill Mordechai but to do away with the entire Jewish race. When Haman's plans became known and Esther made a way for Mordechai to pass messages to her, Mordechai said, 'Do not think to yourself that in the king's palace you will escape any more than all the other Jews. For if you keep silent at this time, relief and deliverance will rise for the Jews from another place, but you and your father's house will perish. And who knows whether you have not come to the kingdom for such a time as this?' Esther 4:13,14. Esther accepted the task, even though it was extremely hazardous, and exhibited both courage and great political awareness in luring Haman into a trap. God's sovereign intervention during the night before the decisive meeting, called by Esther, caused the king to examine the chronicles of past deeds and to discover how Mordechai had frustrated a plot to assassinate the king himself but had never been honoured for his loyalty. Haman duly walked into a trap of God's devising but which had required Esther to play a decisive part.

Mary received possibly the most famous calling of anyone in all of the Bible and hence she is referenced, for different reasons, in several other places in this book. We know the manner in which her calling happened and her gracious response to the overwhelming news. We also know that, in several places, when things are said and done that reveal aspects of Jesus person and ministry, she is said to 'treasure up these things in her heart'. She clearly formed a deep appreciation of the Father's purpose for His son as she watched it all unfold. Her relationship with Jesus was obviously unique and we get a glimpse of that specialness in John 2:1-12. They were in Cana at a wedding and the wine ran out. We are not told why Mary took it upon herself to champion the cause of the wedding party but she did and the conversation between her and Jesus is fascinating – she says, 'They have no wine.' And he says to her, 'Woman, what does this have to do with me? My hour has not yet come.' She then says to the servants, 'Do whatever he tells you.' You could infer that Jesus' response was a 'push back' but I think it must have been said with a slight smile and a knowing look in the eyes, an expression that perhaps only Mary was able to interpret.

Anna was an old woman of eighty-four and, according to Luke 2:36-38, she was a prophetess who was widowed only seven years after having married as a young girl. For more than sixty years she had worshipped the God of Israel, with fasting and praying, and was all but resident in the temple courts. Like Simeon, she came up at the very hour Mary and Joseph brought Jesus for dedication, eight days after his birth. She too recognized the Messiah and knew that it was he who would bring about 'the redemption of Jerusalem'. She therefore spoke of him to everyone she met.

Priscilla, and her husband Aquila, moved from Italy to Corinth a short time before Paul arrived there. Acts 18 tells us that their trade was tentmaking, the same as Paul's, and so he stayed with them and worked. After trouble arose on account of Paul's message, he and they set sail together and eventually came to Ephesus, where Paul left them. Aquila and Priscilla were a good team – among other things, they corrected the theology of Apollos, when he too arrived in Ephesus, so that he was better equipped to preach the gospel. When Paul returned to Ephesus, for a more prolonged period, they were there to support him. 1Corinthians 16:19 tells us that they had a church in their house and in Romans 16:3 Paul calls them his 'fellow workers in Christ Jesus'. What is particularly telling is a reference in 2Timothy 4:19, at the end of what was probably the last letter Paul ever wrote, probably from a Roman prison cell in

AD67, the year he died. Timothy had been ministering in Ephesus for at least four years and Priscilla and Aquila were still there. Paul says, 'Greet Prisca and Aquila and the household of Onesiphorus.' His use here of the respectful form of her name (Priscilla is the diminutive form of Prisca) conveys how much Paul valued her and the fact that he puts her name ahead of that of Aquila suggests she was the driving force in the work of the gospel – a church leader of real standing.

Personal reflections on relationship and parenthood

It is ironic that God has had to point out to me the critical importance of committed relationship and parenthood in the outworking of all that we do and especially our callings. Ironic because those are the two things that I have felt, throughout my whole life, least capable of achieving and exhibiting.

I've always known that something failed to connect during the early years of my life. Bringing up children is difficult and so I don't blame my parents, but I've always felt an emotional detachment from them and always had difficulty forming close relationships. It didn't crystallise for me until somewhat later in life when I was looking, with my wife, at a series of old family photos, taken when I was young.

We lived in quite a large house in Manchester where my grandparents occupied the ground floor and we, my parents and my sister and brother, had the upper two floors. The first clue showed up clearly in several family groupings where I am seen to be a little separated from the others and slightly turned away. A second indicator concerned my grandfather – I could always have told you that I had been close to him and spent a lot of time with him but, in one shot, the camera caught everyone having a picnic in the garden and me coming to join the party hand in hand with my grandfather. In and of itself it isn't proof of anything but the reaction in me as I looked at that particular photo told me all I needed to know – I felt a deep loss and, not having consciously thought about him for a long while, I suddenly missed him terribly.

I think the most significant parts of my relational development must have happened in interaction with him, although I cannot tell you exactly why I took every opportunity to go and try to find him rather than stay with my mother and father. He died when I was nine years old and I then somehow closed up in a way that took the Fatherhood of God decades to penetrate.

When I married Dawn in 1982, I did so because I really wanted to and because both of us believed wholeheartedly that it was the right thing to do. Great intentions are one thing but I now know that I didn't really have a clue how to love someone and almost immediately after the ceremony I was struck with panic. Here was someone I was now committed to, someone I had accepted responsibility for and who had promised always to be there and I had the uncomfortable realization that I didn't know how to relate to a constant companion.

Four years later we had our first child, Joy, and I was traumatised by the whole process! Again, as we brought her home from the hospital, I panicked. Here was someone who would always be around and I didn't have the first clue about how to meet her needs. The first few weeks were not good – I now know, having looked it all up, that I was probably suffering from PTSD... the symptoms and the experience, as I recall it, all match those associated with that condition.

The panic faded as I grew more used to being a father and better able to interpret needs. However, I was not as much use to the children, as they grew up, as I should have been. I was never absent – I was there and I participated and I read stories and I tried to give advice and exercise appropriate discipline and I stood for interminable hours on the touchline for football and hockey etc. However, though not absent, there were many times when I was not 'present'.

I have since learned what 'presence' is all about – my friend, Nick Isbister, of the Listening Partnership, patiently explained it to me as part of the training and coaching input that has been so important to me in recent years. (I talk more about the value of his input in my reflections at the end of Chapters 3 & 11).

Nick is fond of quoting Darya Funches on this subject – 'We cannot be "present"... when we are preoccupied with how we are being seen or experienced, or with determining the "right thing to do". We can be "present" only when we are in touch with our feelings, thoughts and intuitions "in the moment". The gift of presence gives [leaders and parents] access to an arena of "creative indifference", enabling them to work with others without predetermining how things *should* be and what they *should* do.' Peter Senge also says, 'We first thought of "presence" as being fully conscious and aware in the present moment. Then we began to appreciate "presence" as deep listening... [as] letting go of old identities and the need to control...' (Isbister, et al., 2016)

I realize I have been a sad case for much of my life but I now understand that people will intuitively know whether or not you are 'present' with them. I am guilty of not really listening to my wife or to my children or to my friends on many occasions because I was subconsciously worried about how I was relating, what they might be thinking of me and how I could take back control of the situation. I now consciously practice being 'present'.

God is very good to us – He gives us second chances and with the advent of grandchildren I was granted a new lease of life. It was different right from the beginning of their lives because I had learned quite a lot and repented of a fair few things since the time my own children were born. But there was an 'epiphany' moment when the first grandchild, Anna, was about nine months old – I was actually ironing shirts and she had been propped up on the settee, in a corner, with some toys, and was watching me. She wasn't even crawling at the time and so it was a relatively easy task to supervise her. I was having a bit of difficulty with one of the shirts and made an involuntary 'uh oh' sort of noise, whereupon Anna promptly mimicked it. So, I made a slightly different noise and she mimicked that too. We proceeded to have a conversation that didn't involve any intelligible words and something I cannot explain happened to me – in my head and in my spirit – in those moments.

After that, I found that I didn't just tolerate children any more, it was as if I could understand a little bit of how they were thinking and could be sympathetic to their needs. I found that I could be 'present' with a child – not predetermining the outcome and not trying to control the situation and not worried about what they thought of me.

Our God wants to be 'present' with us and He will be, whenever we let Him. We are His children and His desire is that our daily lives and interactions should exhibit evidences of His essential nature. The way in which He passes those on, and they become part of the fabric of our lives, will be slightly different for each person because we are all unique, but He cannot be other than our parent and He cannot do other than develop lasting relationship with us.

The exercise of parenthood does not have to involve control or a predetermined outcome and that's why it's not incongruous to say that committed relationship and parenthood are both at the core of how God wants us to undertake our callings and both essential to the teamwork that will be necessary for their outworking.

It is worth saying that, despite my relational disabilities and all the pain I caused to Dawn, especially over the first twenty years of our marriage, we are still together, which is testament to her sainthood rather than my ability to change. She is outgoing, interested in people and always seems to know what question to ask and she helps me greatly in almost any social situation.

It is not all plain sailing – I regularly have to move from 'not present' to 'present' either to start a conversation or mid-conversation. If we have people visiting us, even family, and I am left alone with one person in a room, often a frisson of panic will pass over me and I will have to offer up a prayer that I'll be able to communicate effectively with no one to give me prompts!

Chapter 8

Modelling God's Character – Watchmen and 'Standing With'

God as watchman and companion

Please bear with me as I try to explain two functions or activities that are important for the successful outworking of your and my calling and for the callings of other people who are known to us. These functions are integral to the way God works and are given as vital roles for us to play. To ignore their importance may mean either our own or another's call does not find fulfilment:

The first of these roles (that of a watchman) is essentially about prayer – a very particular kind of prayer that many of us may not have practised very often. It is also about 'being there' for someone and exercising faith for the safe and successful outworking of God's purpose. The second role (that of one who 'stands with' another) also involves prayer for a successful outcome but it is much more about physically coming alongside and participating in (i.e. taking an active role in) what someone else is called to accomplish.

The Old Testament prophets show God, in His plurality, declaring His purpose for Israel and then being posted as a *watchman*; looking out and never sleeping, calling for the realizing of that purpose. They depict Him ready to warn His people and to safeguard them but also to 'see' evidence, even a long way off, of the promise realized and the call fulfilled. Those same prophetic passages indicate that He is passing on the role of watchman to various of us who are, in turn, given responsibility to recognize what we and others have been 'called to' and to *watch out* and *intercede* until we see its fulfilment.

Then, there are the many examples of God's constant companionship with His people – His constant willingness to 'stand with us'. It is illustrated by His 'walking in the garden in the cool of the day', back in Genesis, and His being visible in the pillars of cloud and fire in the wilderness and then, via prophets and kings, having a presence by proxy until the revealing of Jesus, the 'Anointed One'. Jesus, after His departure, bequeathed to us the Holy Spirit, who is described variously as Counsellor, Helper and Truth-giver, but the best rendering is 'He who will stand by your side', John 16:7,13 (Cassirer, 1989). Likewise, God is looking for our willingness to *stand with* people as they seek to fulfil His purpose for their lives, those who are acting out their own calling and who are calling on Him to make good on His promises. We need to do it for others and we need others to do it for us.

Being a watchman

Praying guardians

There are many references to 'watchmen' in the Bible. They are most often appointed to keep an eye out for physical threats (e.g. 2Kings 9:17) or to safeguard fields during harvest (see ref. to a tower in Isaiah 5:1,2 and Matthew 21:33) or to announce the morning (e.g. Psalm 130:6). Various of the prophets are also referred to as 'watchmen' over the people, in a spiritual sense (e.g. Ezekiel 33:7 and Hosea 9:8), which was often a thankless task!

The sense in which I want to talk about watchmen, in the context of 'calling', is slightly different to these more common usages and, in order to explain it, I will need to plunder the wisdom of the late Alec Motyer, from his Devotional Translation of Isaiah (Motyer, 2011):

In Isaiah 62:1-7 God is speaking about the deliverance and the new purpose He is going to bring to the nation of Israel and to their land. Alec points out that this is part of a series of poems about the Anointed One and he translates verse 1 as, 'For the sake of Zion I will not be quiet, and for the sake of Jerusalem I will not be still. Until its righteousness issues out like a flash of light, and its salvation burns like a torch.' His commentary on the phrase 'I will not be quiet' is as follows: 'The verb (chasah) applies as much to inactivity as to silence. Combined with 'to be still' (shaqat) it describes the Anointed One as ceaseless in intercession and action.'

The last two verses of this passage, 6 & 7, are rendered, 'Upon your walls, Jerusalem, I have appointed guardians (watchmen). Every day and every night, continually, they will not be quiet. You who keep Yahweh mindful, have no rest yourselves! Give him no rest, until He establishes – until He makes Jerusalem a praise in the earth.' Alec entitles this little section, 'The praying guardians' and says, 'This is parallel with verses 1-3 in which the Anointed One commits himself to prayer until the full reality of salvation is consummated, and here he appoints intercessors (the watchmen or guardians) to the same ministry.'

So, we see that, in this passage, a 'watchman' is likened to 'a praying guardian' and his role is to cry out to God day and night for the fulfilling of His word – you could say the watchman role is to make a nuisance of himself for the sake of God's people and their land, that the full outworking of God's purpose be seen. As Alec says, the role is taken first by the Anointed One and then given to other appointees to play.

The prophecy of the coming of an Anointed One, who would pray unceasingly for His people, was fulfilled in the coming of Jesus and He is described as such in the words of Hebrews 7:25, 'Consequently, He (Jesus) is able to save to the uttermost those who draw near to God through him, since He always lives to make intercession for them.' The importance of us, in turn, taking up the role of intercessor is stated by Paul in 1Thessalonians 5:16-18, 'Rejoice always, pray without ceasing, give thanks in all circumstances; for this is the will of God in Christ Jesus for you.'

A new name

Okay, but what has this got to do with 'calling'? It is linked to the concept of calling because of what we find in the middle of the Isaiah 62 passage we were discussing above; in verses 2-4 God relates how He had formerly 'called' His people and their land by certain names but would now change those names. He says, 'You shall be called by a new name that the mouth of the Lord will give. You shall be a crown of beauty in the hand of the Lord, a royal diadem in the hand of your God. You shall no more be termed Forsaken [Heb. "Azubah"], and your land shall no more be termed Desolate [Heb. "Shemamah"], but you shall be called My Delight is in Her [Heb. "Hephzibah"], and your land Married [Heb. "Beulah"]; for the Lord delights in you, and your land shall be married.' ESV

God is using names to describe His people's current and future states – what they are now and what He intends for them to represent or to become. As is usual with God's calls, it is about both the now and the not yet.

Why does He need to do this? Because He had named them back in the time of Jacob but they decided to rebel against His purpose and to ignore His many warnings about the inevitable consequence. He would execute judgment on them and send them into exile. He would withdraw a significant measure of His providential care, forsake them, give them over to an enemy and leave their land desolate. Through Isaiah, He is putting on record, prior to the event, what will happen and how His actions will be viewed by all the surrounding nations – they will say of Israel that God has 'forsaken' His people and 'desolated' their land. It will be as if they are no longer 'Israel'.

Now, In Isaiah 62, He is giving notice, through the prophet, that He will reverse that process and restore the people, in whom He delights, to their land – it will be a restatement of their calling and it will have a whole new dimension: from them will come an 'Anointed One', whose actions, words and intercessions will cause 'the nations [to] see your righteousness', verse 2, and 'make Jerusalem a praise in the earth', verse 7.

Reminding God of his commitments

All of which is intended to show that God is appointing watchmen, whose responsibility it is to remind Him continually of the work that He is committed to undertake. They are to be engaged and involved in the process, looking out for progress or delay, volubly cheering Him on to victory when things are going well and persistently petitioning Him for action when progress is opposed.

This is a particular kind of prayer that we, especially those of us who are British, might find uncomfortable – we are being bidden to importune God as if He were reluctant to act. In other words, we are to harass Him persistently to do something. We see it repeatedly demonstrated in the Bible.

[The term He uses for Israel in this passage is 'Zion', which is a synonym in the Old Testament for Jerusalem and in the New Testament for The New Jerusalem. Zion was the mountain of the Lord and sometimes the word indicates the whole of the land of Israel. It is the place where He has chosen to dwell and the people among whom He has chosen to dwell. Exodus 29:46 says, 'And they shall know that I am the Lord their God, who brought them out of the land of Egypt that I might dwell among them.' And Psalm 132:13 says, 'For the Lord has chosen Zion; He has desired it for His dwelling place.' For our purposes, we could define Zion as 'the gathering of His faithful people in the place of His choosing'.]

People who 'importuned God'

Here are a few random examples of people who made a nuisance of themselves because either they believed something was too important to set aside or they were hanging on for justice to be done:

Abraham – in Genesis 18 is his famous conversation with God, over the imminent destruction of Sodom, where he intercedes for the few righteous within the city. Six times he begs God for their deliverance, saying things like, *'Far be it from you to do such a thing*, to put the righteous to death with the wicked... shall not the Judge of all the earth do what is just? ...Oh, *let not the Lord be angry, and I will speak again* but this once. Suppose only ten are found there.' And God hears him.

David – in many of the Psalms he is being pursued by enemies too strong for him, who are threatening not just himself but his kingship and the people whom God had anointed him to lead. He does not hold back, he is insistent. So, we read in Psalm 28, 'To you, O Lord, I call; my rock, *be not deaf to me*, lest, if you be silent to me, I become like those who go down to the pit. *Hear the voice of my pleas* for mercy, when I cry to you for help, when I lift my hands toward your most holy sanctuary.'

Mary – In John 2, at the wedding at Cana, she was the one who, having realized that the wine had run out, went to Jesus and told Him. His first reaction was, 'Woman, what does this have to do with me?' but she knew exactly what she was doing and that she was on firm ground and so she prevailed upon Him.

Jairus – Luke 8 says that 'Jairus, who was a ruler of the synagogue... falling at Jesus' feet, *implored him* to come to his house... for his daughter was dying.' On the way, Jesus is delayed by the woman who has had a discharge of blood for twelve years and whose faith in touching Jesus' garment makes her well. By the time He has finished speaking to the woman, a messenger from Jairus' house comes to tell him that the child has died, saying 'Do not trouble the Teacher anymore.' We are not told what then passes between Jairus and Jesus at that moment but Jesus has come to this position because Jairus has *implored Him* and He says, 'Do not fear, only believe, and she will be well.'

Two blind men - the men were sitting by the roadside and Matthew 20 says, 'when they heard that Jesus was passing by, *they cried out, "Lord, have mercy on us*, Son of David!" The crowd rebuked them, telling them to be silent, but *they cried out all the more*... and stopping, Jesus called to them and said, "What do you want me to do for you?"'

Without wanting to labour the point, it is instructive to read Jesus' parable in Luke 11 about the friend who comes at midnight to borrow bread, 'yet because of his impudence (or persistence) he will rise and give him whatever he needs'.

God wants to be Importuned!

God himself is described as looking out to check if there are those who have seen or appreciated the state of affairs around them and been moved to intercede. Isaiah 59:14-21 is one such passage: 'The Lord saw it, and it displeased Him that there was no justice. He saw that there was no man, and wondered that there was no one to intercede; then His own arm brought Him salvation, and His righteousness upheld Him.' It is as though He is saying, 'Is there nobody willing to stand up for my word and my ways and my righteousness?'

God is looking for intercessors to partner with and would work with those who share His mind. What He is seeking is a commitment, on the part of all who understand what 'calling' means, not just to talk to Him about problems and difficulties that may arise but rather to take 'by the scruff of the neck' each God-given enterprise that stirs them and to lay hold on Him for a successful outcome, as if they were a watchman patrolling the walls and looking out for news.

Standing with someone

Partnership and support

Coming alongside someone in order to support them, identifying with that person's mission and committing to giving them encouragement and, where necessary, physical help is an easier concept to grasp than being a watchman. There are also a greater number of ready examples we could use.

However, there is a link between those who intercede and those who 'stand with' someone in support. Paul uses 'partnership' language when he is writing to the Philippians – he says in 4:14-16, 'It was kind of you to share my trouble. And you Philippians yourselves know that in the beginning of the gospel, when I left Macedonia, no church entered into partnership with me in giving and receiving, except you only. Even in Thessalonica you sent me help for my needs once and again.'

He is talking to a group (a plural 'you') and saying, 'nobody stood with me, except you guys'. Paul's expectation was clearly that more could or should have shown willingness to 'be there for him'. Equally clearly, not everybody in the group could physically 'stand with' him but they did send him practical help and they would have been interceding for the work he was doing and, presumably, passing on messages of encouragement.

Supporting roles essential to a successful outcome

Let's look at a few examples which all describe a supporting role, played either by a human person or by God himself, that turns out to be vital to somebody's call having a successful outcome:

Aaron with Moses – In Exodus 4, as has been described previously, Moses' confidence failed him and he would not accept God's call unless there was someone else alongside to help. God duly appointed Aaron to 'stand with' him and to be the mouthpiece.

The elders with Moses – Later in the Exodus, when Moses is overwhelmed by the need to adjudicate in matters of dispute across the nation, a group of elders is appointed to help him. The Lord says to Moses, in Numbers 11:16,17, 'Gather for me seventy men of the elders of Israel, whom you know to be elders of the people and officers over them, and bring them to the tent of meeting, and let them *take their stand there with you*. And I will come down and talk with you there. And I will take some of the Spirit that is on you and put it on them, and they shall bear the burden of the people with you, so that you may not bear it yourself alone.'

Ruth with Naomi - In Ruth 1, after Naomi's two sons have died and she elects to return home to Bethlehem, her daughter-in-law, Ruth, although a Moabitess, pledges to return with her saying, 'where you go I will go, and where you lodge I will lodge. Your people shall be my people, and your God my God.' Ruth commits herself to 'stand with' Naomi, to look after her 'among a people that she did not know before' and to 'take refuge under the wings of the God of Israel', Ruth 2:11,12.

'A Son of the Gods' with Shadrach, Meshach and Abednego – In Daniel 3: 24,25, when Daniel's three companions refuse to fall down before Nebuchadnezzar's golden statue, they are condemned to be thrown into a fiery furnace. They say to the king, 'our God whom we serve is able to deliver us from the burning fiery furnace... But if not, be it known that we will not serve your gods or worship the golden image that you have set up.' Having bound them and thrown them in, the king is then astounded by what he sees. He says, 'But I see four men unbound, walking in the midst of the fire, and they are not hurt; and the appearance of the fourth is like a son of the gods.' When there was no human who could do the job, God sent His messenger to 'stand with' them and to deliver them.

Jonathan and his armour-bearer – In 1Samuel 13 & 14 Saul has been king in Israel for two years and he is not doing well. He has goaded the Philistines, who have massed all their forces against him and Saul's army has panicked and is scattering. He calls a sacrifice, to seek the favour of God, in whose name they are supposed to be fighting, and then fails to wait for Samuel to arrive. In offering the sacrifice himself, he transgresses the law in a big way and is rightly condemned by Samuel.

To make matters worse, there is no blacksmith in all of Israel – Saul has made the strategic blunder of allowing them all to be in Philistine territory. Consequently, none of his forces, apart from himself and his son Jonathan, has a sharp sword or a spear! The position is desperate and the king, who has been disowned by God's prophet, is incapable of exercising the necessary leadership.

It is a situation crying out for a person of faith to hear what God has to say and to take control. Jonathan is that man... he says to his armour-bearer in 1Samuel 14:6, 'Come, let us go over to the garrison of these uncircumcised. It may be that the Lord will work for us, for nothing can hinder the Lord from saving by many or by few.'

This is not a whim or a foolish act of presumption; they are the words of a man of faith. Jonathan proposes this action based on unshakeable confidence in the God of Israel, knowing that victory will always be dependent on Him, irrespective of how many fighting men Israel might have. The armour-bearer, instead of focusing on the overwhelming odds against them, recognizes the source of Jonathan's faith and says in verse 7, 'Do all that is in your heart. Do as you wish. Behold, I am with you heart and soul.'

Jonathan not only knows *what* he has to do but he also knows *how* to go about it and outlines the plan in verses 8-10. His heart has been stirred by God to undertake an 'impossible' task and he has sensed the way it should be undertaken, but he also knows he cannot accomplish it alone – he needs someone to stand with him. The armour-bearer is that someone and commits himself gladly to 'stand with' Jonathan.

The 'standing-with' has its hazards and its challenges and it requires not only accompanying and giving encouragement but also active participation – we read, 'Then Jonathan climbed up (a rocky crag) on his hands and feet, and his armour-bearer after him. And they (the Philistines) fell before Jonathan, and his armour-bearer killed them after him. And that first strike, which Jonathan and his armour-bearer made, killed about twenty men within as it were half a furrow's length in an acre of land. And there was panic in the camp...'

Joseph with Mary – Matthew 1&2. In the last chapter we talked briefly about how God spoke different things, distinctly and clearly, to both Mary and Joseph because their roles were obviously to be different in the outworking of God's master plan to bring the Anointed One into the world.

In spite of the upheaval that the angel Gabriel's message caused, Joseph honoured his betrothal to Mary and elected to 'stand with' her in Nazareth, then on to Bethlehem, then to Egypt and then back to Nazareth, where they set up home. Although they had other children, He faithfully played the supporting role in Jesus' life beyond the time of His emergence into adulthood and passed on to Him the trade of carpentry. Joseph is one of the giants of the New Testament!

The Lord with Paul – In what is probably his last letter, written from Rome, Paul says to Timothy, 'At my first defence no one came to *stand by me*, but all deserted me. May it not be charged against them! But the Lord *stood by me* and strengthened me, so that through me the message might be fully proclaimed and all the Gentiles might hear it. So, I was rescued from the lion's mouth' 2Timothy 4:16,17. The same terminology is found in Acts 23:11, when Paul has had to stand before the council and there is violent unrest concerning his testimony – Luke says, 'The following night the Lord *stood by him* and said, "Take courage, for as you have testified to the facts about me in Jerusalem, so you must testify also in Rome".'

Paul's language here, to Timothy, is cautionary. It implies that he expected one or more of his co-workers or friends to stand with him through the ordeal. He saw it as a responsibility and to abdicate that responsibility was desertion.

Does my call or someone else's have priority?

There is no conflict between, on the one hand, our need to find and pursue our own 'calling' and, on the other, the responsibility we have to support or stand with others as they pursue theirs.

The nature of 'the Body', as it is set out in Paul's letters, is that each individual part is there by necessity but all the parts need to learn to operate together. We are individuals before God, having to take responsibility for our own lives and not abdicating that by leaving others to make decisions or determine direction for us. However, we are also together with others – one flesh with a spouse, if we are married; bound in relationship with family; and part of the same 'body' alongside the rest of God's 'called-out' people.

Everything we get involved in and which makes demands on our time, skill set, energies and resources, be it a personal project or involvement in someone else's, must be referred back to the God who 'calls'. If we defer to Him we will find that He is clever – He knows what we need to learn; He knows how our relationship with Him needs to be developed; He knows how our human relationships with those around us need to be developed; He knows where He is taking us and what succession of involvements will best fit His intentions. Above all, He understands our uniqueness and that our individual contribution needs somehow to be integrated with that of others. He knows that 'uniqueness' means what it says – it doesn't restrict us to a superficial treatment of 1Corinthians and choosing from a list of nine gifts!

All of the biblical examples used in these chapters, of people who heard and followed their own calling and of people who supported others in the pursuit of a call, show that God is able to synchronise effort wherever men and women are willing to listen.

We will be talking later about what to do *after* we receive a calling and two necessary actions are: firstly, to determine whether complementary skills will be required in the outworking of that calling; and secondly, to identify confidantes to whom we can tell our story and who will be able to offer wise counsel and encouragement along the way. What that means is that everyone to whom God issues a call or gives a commission may need help to see it through.

The underlying principles, in determining God's intention for what we should each focus on, would appear to be that God issues calls or gives commissions to most, if not all, individuals, and we need to heed them (more about that in the next chapter). However, He doesn't much like either 'prima donnas', who think theirs must be the most important cause to espouse, or 'hangers-on', who are always chasing after somebody else's call.

Prima donnas always tout for support from others but rarely are they to be found 'standing with' others, or even coming alongside. Hangers-on are always on the lookout for something exciting that's going on 'over there' and then wandering off to look so that, if possible, they can either muscle in on/help with it or bask in the glow of it.

By contrast, those who genuinely listen out for God's word and humbly go about their Father's business are most likely to be found both working on their own projects (with or without assistance from others) and giving active support and encouragement to others.

Bio #4 - RJ

In 1924, a few days after he had resigned from his job, RJ, as he was known to his friends and colleagues, is reported to have had a conversation with his wife, Diana. It happened in the kitchen of their home in Hampshire. Diana was upset and RJ was despondent, knowing that he had now to contemplate the possibility of a job that didn't involve designing aeroplanes.

He is alleged to have said, 'I feel I would be giving up something I was meant to do. I feel it very strongly – if I give it up, it's almost as if I would be doing something wrong.' He went on to tell Diana, 'I wouldn't say it to anybody but you.'

RJ was twenty-nine years old at the time. He had been appointed Chief Designer at Supermarine Aviation Works at the age of twenty-four and then Chief Engineer a year later. He had tremendous powers of concentration and, when looking at an engineering drawing, an innate sense of the rightness or otherwise of a design. In 1923, the company had entered one of his designs in the Schneider Trophy – an air race for sea planes, usually contested by some combination of the UK, the USA, France and Italy – and they had been beaten by the Americans. RJ then produced a revolutionary new design of seaplane which, instead of being a 'conventional' bi-plane with two wings (one over the other), both attached to the fuselage via struts, it had a single wing that was integral with the fuselage. The plane also had a whole host of proposed engineering features that had never before been employed on an aircraft. He was chasing more speed and greater manoeuvrability and believed that this was the design of the future.

The Board of Supermarine, on the other hand, thought they knew better and had disagreed, refusing to sanction the spend. Reginald Joseph Mitchell, knowing he was unwilling to spend his time fabricating the past and believing wholeheartedly in what he saw as the only way forward, resigned. He was not a man of faith but he had had an epiphany or two, of sorts; knowing that he was supposed to spend his life making planes and having been inspired to produce a scarily radical new design.

However, RJ did have an ally – Supermarine's managing director, Commander James Bird, who worked on the other board members and persuaded them that there was only one sensible option... to trust RJ and to let him build his new aircraft.

The new design was very fast but it crashed just before the 1925 Schneider

Trophy race and RJ was given only one more chance to make it work. In 1927 the race was held in Italy, just as Mussolini's fascist state was making itself heard, and Supermarine entered two aircraft. They came first and second, achieving record speeds. That same year, RJ was appointed Technical Director.

In early 1928, Supermarine was bought by Vickers, who were committed to investing in the future of aviation, but the purchase was made on the condition that RJ remain with the company for five years. RJ continued to improve his seaplane designs and, in 1929, his entry won the Schneider Trophy again, at a new record speed.

The 1931 race, to take place in the UK, was under threat of cancellation because Parliament was unwilling to pay the £100k that staging it was due to cost. The money, to allow it to happen, came from a private source – a philanthropist, political activist and suffragette called Lady Lucy Houston – who had met RJ a couple of years previously and who was becoming greatly concerned by the rise of fascism in Europe.

The Supermarine entry won the race for the third time, at another record speed, which meant that the Schneider Trophy was to remain permanently in the UK. RJ was given the CBE for his efforts but felt that he had achieved the ultimate with his seaplane design. He continued to work on various projects but without much inspiration. He was also getting sick with what we now know to be bowel cancer.

In 1933, RJ underwent a colostomy and, whilst recuperating, took a holiday in Germany. During the course of that trip he had an epiphany – it became clear to him that the formation of the fascist state, the rise of Adolf Hitler and the production of armaments for war on land and sea and in the air, in contravention of the Versailles Treaty, was extremely dangerous. He came back with a conviction that he needed to design and build a fighter aircraft and that it needed to be the best in the world.

With renewed purpose he began work, seeking funding from the Air Ministry and securing the promise of a new, yet-to-be-manufactured, but destined to be more powerful, engine from Sir Henry Royce. In one new aircraft RJ incorporated his own innovation plus a whole series of technical advances that had been made or proposed by other people, in other places. His genius was to bring it all together, in a coherent way, and to create what the RAF still calls today the most beautiful and significant fighter plane ever built.

The first prototype Spitfire flew in March 1936, by which time RJ's cancer had returned. He lived long enough to see some of the repeated testing of the aircraft and to know that the RAF had ordered hundreds of Spitfires to be manufactured.

R J Mitchell died in June 1937, at the age of forty-two, having fulfilled what was clearly a calling on his life, the effect of which was to provide a vital tool for the dismantling of Hitler's war machine. Even though RJ was not a man of faith, did God have a hand in it all? Most definitely – the outstanding skill, the sense of purpose and the unstoppable enterprise, maturing as they did at exactly the right time, in a man who could do none other than follow through on his deep convictions, points to a God holding his hand and making it happen. There wasn't anybody else who could have planned and pulled off that rescue mission – in a way, it was like what God did with Cyrus many centuries before.

Sources:

R. J. Mitchell: Schooldays to Spitfire, by Gordon Mitchell in association with the Imperial War Museum. Published by Tempus. (Mitchell, 2006)

The First of the Few, a Film Directed and Produced by Leslie Howard and Starring Leslie Howard & David Niven. (Howard, 1942)

Chapter 9

Can Everyone Receive Calls or Commissions from God?

This is a fundamental question. Although I have effectively answered it in the affirmative several times in previous chapters, we need to prove it or at least leave very little room for doubt.

My surety is built upon the conviction that God actively wishes to communicate with us, naturally and directly, on a daily basis and, in keeping with the many people we read about in the Bible, He delights to reproduce His character in us and partner with us in activity.

Put simply, I believe the main reasons why many people do not receive and act on calls and commissions are because:

1. They are not able to 'hear' what God is trying to say to them, either because they have no expectation of God wanting to speak to them or, even if they believe that to be something He does, they have no track record of knowing for certain what He may have said and nobody to help them with the discernment process;
2. They do 'hear' and may even develop a clear sense of what they think God is saying but either the pressing circumstances of life or the opinion and advice of those around them convince them to drop the notion or at least postpone consideration of it.

In order to justify my assertion, that calls and commissions should be commonplace, it is necessary first of all to reaffirm God's desire both to speak to us and to 'employ' us.

He is speaking and hearing Him is about expectation and practice

Hearing God is a vital skill. It is undeniable that, from Genesis to Revelation, God is engaged in conversation with creation, that He is interested in individuals and that He gives individuals specific, strategically important tasks to do.

Is He still speaking? Definitely – without any shadow of doubt. But I'm distressed by the number of Christians who seem to have no expectation of a personal dialogue with God. I'm also distressed by the comparative lack of teaching on it in our churches. A personal relationship with Jesus, which is the heart of the gospel, has to be about knowing and being known. It has to be about doing His will – not vaguely but specifically – and it therefore has to be about daily, two-way communication.

We need to practice hearing what God may be saying to us and testing what we think we've heard so as to build expectation. Jesus, in John 10, suggests that 'hearing' and 'following' should be a simple and extremely natural process – 'The sheep hear his (the shepherd's) voice, and he calls his sheep by name and leads them out... He goes before them, and the sheep follow him, for they know his voice. A stranger they will not follow, but they will flee from him, for they do not know the voice of strangers.'

Douglas J Schuurman, in his book *Vocation*, says 'Many Christians fail to see most of their lives in terms of vocation. Many also assume that "hearing" God's call is an extraordinary, miraculous event, and so fail to discern God's callings in their lives... They never heard God speaking from a burning bush, or from the heavenly courtroom, resonant with echoes of cherubim. God does sometimes call in such extraordinary ways, but for the vast majority of Christians God's callings are discerned quietly, when the heart of faith joins [with] opportunities and [when] gifts [join] with the needs of others.' (Schuurman, 2004)

His final statement here closely echoes the benchmark of Reformation ethics: 'Faith active in love through one's callings'. Faith is not a nebulous thing: it is anchored in what God has said and what God has done. It's about discerning His voice – separating it out from the other voices that clamour for attention – and then obeying Him. What we must embark on, if it is not already part of our experience, is a daily walk with Jesus that develops a heart of faith and quietly discerns His callings. He will give us the gifts necessary and help us to acquire the skills to meet the needs.

Does God speak to everyone who believes in Him and turns to Him? Yes. Does He also sometimes speak to people who haven't turned to Him? Yes, and sometimes, as with Cyrus and Artaxerxes, we can see evidence of them having acted decisively to fulfil His purposes, rather than their own.

Jesus promised to send the Holy Spirit to lead us into all truth

When Jesus returned to heaven, He promised that the Holy Spirit would come 'to stand beside' all those who believe – John 16:7 says, 'I tell you the truth: it is to your advantage that I go away, for if I do not go away, the Helper will not come to you. But if I go, I will send Him to you.' Jesus also stated that He only ever did those things that He saw the Father doing and He told the disciples that, 'he who believes in Me, the works that I do he will do also; and greater works than these he will do because I go to My Father', John 14:12. He went on to say, 'If anyone loves Me, he will keep my word; and My Father will love him, and We will come to him and make Our home with him.' John 14:23.

The inference is clear – He wants us to be accompanied by the Holy Spirit and He wants us to be engaged 'on our Father's business'. If that is the case, we need to discern for ourselves what that business is – presumably by means of communication from God.

The evidence of the Bible, in which no two people are described as performing the same tasks in exactly the same way, is overwhelmingly in favour of the outworking of His will for my life being different to His plans for you. We may both be believers in the same God and we may be working for the furtherance of the same kingdom and we may even, for a time, be engaged on the same project but you will not be doing exactly what I'm doing and how you do what you do will not be the same as my 'how'. You are different to me – you have different skills and capabilities; you express the 'sense of purpose' for your life in different words to mine and you get excited about different aspects of the work to me.

It is therefore incumbent upon you to hear God for yourself – I cannot take on your responsibility and hear Him for you. I can listen to Him and He might, as encouragement, use me to confirm what He is saying to you but He will not by-pass you. Neither can you rely on your church leaders, or a 'mentor' or what you are told from the pulpit or the advice of friends to shape what you do – that isn't how a personal relationship with God is supposed to work. Neither should you be afraid that embarking on a quest to 'hear God' puts you on a slippery slope to some intense, unbalanced, over-spiritualised and therefore abnormal existence. Jesus calls you by name and leads you and you are supposed to recognize His voice *for yourself*, as a natural and normal part of everyday life.

The Father's desire is to give people useful things to do (however late in the day)

In Matthew 20:1-16, Jesus tells the story of 'Labourers in the Vineyard' where a master of a house goes out five times in a day to hire labourers. It is an oft misunderstood passage because some claim that it was not fair of the master to pay the late arrivals the same wages as those who had been hired early in the day. However, the master negotiated the deal with those who were first hired and he committed to paying the later arrivals 'whatever is right'. David

Pawson, in a talk you can probably still get hold of and listen to, calls the master's actions 'more than fair'.

The purpose of the parable is to illustrate what Jesus said, in the previous chapter, concerning worldly riches and the sacrifices that are required in order to follow Him. The final verse of chapter 19 says, 'But many who are first will be last, and the last first'. Then to emphasise His point, Jesus' final statement of this parable is, 'So the last will be first, and the first last'. In the context of God's 'callings', there are two important points to draw out of the story:

1. The worker's reward is given for a willingness to seek work, to respond to the invitation and to go and undertake useful work. It is *not* related to the length of time he/she works for or how hard the work is;
2. The master goes to extraordinary and exhaustive lengths to find useful work for people to do. He went out early, then at the third hour, then at the sixth hour, then at the ninth hour and then again at the eleventh hour, looking for and, without discriminating, engaging with those he found.

Let it never be said that God is uninterested in us doing something useful or that He puts no effort into the recruiting process. If it is the beginning of the day or around the third hour for you, look out for His coming, talk to Him about what He wants you to do and accept the invitation quickly and gladly.

Many of us, however, may feel that we are at the ninth, or even approaching the eleventh, hour of our lives. Some of us may feel that we blew it by not accepting an invite back at the third hour. Don't despair – He will hire you if you make yourself available and He will do so personally.

A warning about trying to follow another person's calling rather than listen for our own

As we have already established, God wants to speak to *you* and He wants to allocate a task or create a role that is designed around *you,* so that you can get on with it (in the event that it is a 'solo task') or, quite possibly, participate with others who have complementary skills. The primary focus should not therefore be on what God may be saying to everybody else but, too frequently, we find Christians trying to piggy-back on what God has said to another person or group.

I can sort of understand the thinking that says, 'There seems to be evidence that God is working over there, let's go and see what is actually happening', especially if we are personally going through some wilderness experience where nothing seems to be happening in our neck of the woods. Even so, what are we expecting if we travel to see this other thing? Do we think that it might rub off on us or transfer itself or kick-start us in some way and that we'll come back a different person?

There have been historic revivals that have been 'caught' by those who came close and who, by proximity or association, similarly experienced the Holy Spirit's presence, but this has generally been a work of salvation where those individuals have come under conviction of sin and been moved to repent and believe. If, on the other hand, the excursion we make is to witness some phenomenon or to observe someone else's 'success' we need to be honest about whether we are doing so out of idle curiosity or just 'because it is there' or because we know God is clearly leading us to explore it.

I don't want to stand against people's search for God or their desire to see Him work BUT, if we hear of a move of God's Spirit in another location, among another group of people, there is a very strong likelihood that those people have, for some time, been crying out for Him to visit them and have probably received some specific instruction from Him about what they ought to do. In other words, they have heard a call and responded and whatever is now happening is an outcome of that response.

What therefore should we be doing? We should not be blinkered to what is happening in other parts of the body but we should be crying out to God ourselves for what He wants to do with *us*, either here in our part of the world, among our group of people or in a place of His sovereign choosing. We should be seeking our own mandate, commissioning us to serve Him in the unique way in which He has gifted us.

There are many in the Christian world who have initiated a great work, not because they happen to be a phenomenally talented superstar but, rather, it has come about through dogged prayer, simple obedience, not a little hardship and periodic acts of great courage. As I write this, I can think of some well-known names who heard from God and obeyed the call despite almost all those around them being opposed to it. In not a few cases that opposition came from people in senior ministry positions, who should have known better and should have taken time to listen to what God was actually saying. They subsequently had to bite their tongues and miraculously then became enthusiastic advocates of the work!

I also know, from listening to candid testimony, that one of the most difficult things for those at the centre of a work is knowing how to handle the constant stream of individuals and groups wanting to 'come alongside them' and 'learn'. How much better would it be and how much more 'kingdom work' would get done if all of those individuals and groups were instead to seek the Lord and receive their own mandate and get on with obeying it?

One of the messages of this book is that the fulfilment of a 'calling' will take courage and determination and patience. There is no 'hind's feet on high places' without a willingness to count the cost and Chapters 12 and 13, dealing with what happens *after* a call is received, are therefore two of the most important for the reader to understand. To maintain a balanced and realistic view, we must read and re-read what Paul says in Philippians 3:9,10 – a letter in which he talks more about *rejoicing* than in anything else he wrote: '...righteousness from God depends on *faith* – that I may know Him and the power of His resurrection, and may share His *sufferings*, becoming like Him in his death.'

The Bible is full of examples of people being called by God to do stuff

There is a primary 'calling', to follow God and to be shaped by Him, and there are secondary 'callings' to specific tasks. As to the specific tasks, we have divided those into short-term 'commissions' and long-term 'callings' or 'vocations'. The latter term describes being called to fulfil a role or occupy a position or take up a profession or exercise a specific set of skills for the majority of one's working life, and this notion has been rehabilitated as a concept since the Reformation.

A couple of writers on this subject have argued that there are only approximately one hundred people in the Bible to whom God unequivocally speaks a word of instruction about their vocation and they therefore conclude that such guidance is 'rare' and certainly not for everyone.

I would actually classify some of those one hundred people as having received instruction about a significant 'commission', rather than their life's work. But, in spite of that revised classification, my conclusion is still completely opposite to the naysayers – the very fact that there are many examples of God leading individuals to embrace a vocation or commission of His calling indicates clearly that it is something He is in the habit of doing!

So, will every person be 'called' to something? Yes, I think they will – and, even if their vocation is unclear, I definitely think God has specific (shorter term) tasks for them to do. We are going to look at a few examples – people who heard from God at a very early age, receiving either clues or an unequivocal statement about what He wanted them to do; people for whom the decisive word came much later in life; and whole groups of people whom God dedicated to a particular purpose. A key point to grasp is that, even in the case of corporate callings, God always respects the individual and preserves his/her uniqueness. Each person's contribution is different.

Calls to individuals received at an early age

Certain people in scripture knew from an early age that God had singled them out for something special because God told them and/or gave them tasks to do from early in life. However, with the exception of Jesus, none knew exactly how it was going to work out. It is instructive to look at some examples of the first indication, either from God or from an individual about their sense of calling:

Joseph (17 years) – Genesis 37v:5-11, 'Joseph had a dream and... told it to his brothers... we were binding sheaves in the field and... your sheaves bowed down to my sheaf... and his brothers said to him, "Are you indeed to reign over us?"'

Samuel (according to the historian Josephus, about 11 years) – 1 Samuel 3, 'Now the boy Samuel was ministering to the Lord in the presence of Eli... Then the Lord called Samuel... And Samuel said, "Speak, for your servant hears."'

David (teenage) – 1 Samuel 16:1, 11-13, 'And the LORD said, "Arise, anoint him, for this is he." Then Samuel took the horn of oil and anointed David... and the Spirit of the Lord rushed upon him...'

Jeremiah (about 17 years) – Jeremiah 1, 'Now the word of the Lord came to me, saying, "Before I formed you in the womb I knew you and... I appointed you a prophet to the nations." And the Lord said to me, "Behold, I have put my words in your mouth. See, I have set you this day over nations and over kingdoms, to pluck up and to break down, to destroy and to overthrow, to build and to plant."'

Mary (teenage) – Luke 1:26-38, 'Do not be afraid, Mary, for you have found favour with God. And behold, you will conceive and bear a son, and you shall call his name Jesus...'

Jesus (12 years) – Luke 2:49-52, 'Did you not realize that I must be about my Father's business?'

Peter/John & other apostles (early twenties) – Mark 1:7, 'And Jesus said to them, "Follow me and I will make you become fishers of men."'; Matthew 28:16-20 'Jesus said to them, "Go therefore and make disciples of all nations..."'

The process that led to fullness of expression of each one's calling was radically different in each case and in most cases involved all sorts of delays and setbacks. The individuals concerned made mistakes; they had to be resolute; some experienced injustice; and all had to endure difficulty in order to see it through, but each could also testify to God intervening on their behalf during the process.

Calls to individuals received a little later in life

Others received their calling a little later in life but were left in no doubt about what God wanted of them. For example:

Noah (500 years) – Genesis 6:5-14, 'The Lord saw that the wickedness of man was great in the earth and… The Lord said, "I will blot out man whom I created…" But Noah found favour in the eyes of the Lord… And God said to Noah… "make yourself an ark."' [See also the section on short-term commissions below]

Abram (about 75 years) – Genesis 12, 'Now the Lord said to Abram, "Go from your country and your kindred and your father's house to the land that I will show you. And I will make of you a great nation, and I will bless you and make your name great, so that you will be a blessing… and in you all the families of the earth shall be blessed."'

Moses (80 years) – Exodus 3, '…God called to him out of the (burning) bush, "Moses… I am the God of your father, the God of Abraham, the God of Isaac, and the God of Jacob… and I have surely seen the affliction of my people who are in Egypt…"'

Nehemiah (probably thirties) – Nehemiah 1:1-4, 'I asked (certain men from Judah) concerning the Jews… who had survived the exile… and they said, "…the wall of Jerusalem is broken down"… As soon as I heard… I sat down and wept and mourned for days.'

Isaiah (unknown) – Isaiah 6, 'In the year that King Uzziah died I saw the Lord… And I heard the voice of the Lord saying, "Whom shall I send, and who will go for us." Then I said, "Here I am! Send me."'

Ezekiel (30) – Ezekiel 1v1, 'In the thirtieth year… as I was among the exiles… the heavens were opened and I saw visions of God.'

Saul/Paul (probably 28–31 years) – Romans 1:1; Galatians 1:15, 'Paul, a servant of Christ Jesus, called to be an apostle'. We deal with Paul's calling in a little more detail in the next Chapter because we need to illustrate how it led to the shaping of a new identity for him.

Every one of these people (with the obvious exception of Jesus) was extremely ordinary. Do not therefore disqualify yourself on the basis of unworthiness or lack of social status or shortage of money or absence of education.

Calls to large numbers of people together - corporate callings

When God calls people, it is not only as individuals – sometimes He calls a whole group of people to a particular form of service or to undertake a task or ministry. It does not necessarily mean, however, that there can be no variation among members of the group, as to their own individual expression.

Israel – this is the most obvious example of a call to many, rather than to one person. In Deuteronomy 7:6 God says of the whole nation of Israel, 'For you are a holy people to the Lord your God; the Lord your God has chosen you to be a people for Himself, a special treasure above all the peoples on the face of the earth.'

The nation knew that there were special things for them to do because God continually spelled it out to them, from the time when they were slaves in Egypt and on throughout their history.

The Levites – this was a call to many, but to a lesser number than the whole nation. The book of Numbers explains how the tribe of Levi was to be set aside for a special purpose – 'The Levites were not listed along with them (the rest of the nation), by their ancestral tribe... the Lord said, "you shall not take a census of them... but appoint the Levites over the tabernacle of the testimony and over all its furnishings, and over all that belongs to it... And if any outsider comes near, he shall be put to death".' Numbers 1:47-51. And then God says, 'Behold I have taken the Levites from among the people of Israel instead of every firstborn who opens the womb among the people of Israel. The Levites shall be mine...' Numbers 3:11-13.

Aaron was of course a Levite and in 1Chronicles 23:13 we are reminded that, 'Aaron was set apart, he and his sons forever, that he should sanctify the most holy things, to burn incense before the Lord, to minister to Him, and to give the blessing in His name forever.'

The Disciples – Jesus called the twelve, as a group, to become 'Fishers of men' e.g. Matthew 4:19.

The Church – The Church is that universal body of believers who have given their hearts to Jesus Christ and it was born on the Day of Pentecost. After the Holy Spirit was poured out on approximately 120 persons (the Disciples, their relatives and others who had known and followed Jesus), Peter stood up and preached his first sermon. Acts 2 then tells us that about 3000 people received his word and were baptized. The Acts of the Apostles goes on to relate how the Church grew, how it prospered and how it was persecuted, how the Gentiles were admitted alongside the Jews and how the whole organism, in its diversity of expression, sought to fulfil Jesus' Great Commission.

As to there being freedom for personal calls and individual expression, in spite of being part of a larger group that is set apart for a purpose, it is obvious that, although the nation of Israel was called 'out of the world' to be a people special to God and to be governed by His laws, that did not mean God failed to recognize individual uniqueness and to issue personal calls appropriately.

We can also see with the disciples that there were distinct differences in gifting – they were not cloned from each other but undertook different ministries: the preaching and pioneering of Peter; the caring and pastoral heart of John; the writing, historical awareness and keen ear for prophecy of Matthew.

The same argument might be thought more difficult to make where the Levites are concerned, given the particular nature of their duties and responsibilities, but it is not so – if we look carefully we can find members of that tribe with a wide range of skills:

Asahel, in 1Chronicles 17, was commissioned by Jehoshaphat to teach the Law to Judah;

Ahijah, in 1Chronicles 26, was the treasurer in the tabernacle;

Elkanah, in 1Chronicles 12, was a mighty man in David's army, skilled with a bow and with slinging stones;

Heman [great name], in 1Chronicles 6,15 & 16, is 'The Singer' and clearly a consummate musician;

Joah, Jahath and Obadiah and others, in 2Chronicles 34, had building skills for repairing the house of the Lord;

Barnabas, in Acts, was known as 'Son of Encouragement' and, along with his great generosity, had evangelistic and apostolic skills.

Short-term commissions given to individuals

Virtually everyone in the Bible, who is recorded as following God, did things that played a part in the overall story. Whether big or small, long or short, those things were significant and, in many cases, there is a record both of how they came to do them (the trigger, the motivation, the instruction etc.) and the circumstances surrounding their words or actions.

Let's take a step back from 'Vocation', which is God guiding someone towards a life's work that is matched to 'who they are', and focus for a while on 'commission', which is God guiding someone to do something specific – a set of actions or a project – that occupies them for a period of time. The commission may be characteristic of 'who they are' but it might equally be something to be obeyed as a stepping stone to something bigger.

God tends to entrust little things to us, to prove our faithfulness and to train us in obedience, before vouchsafing the big things. It is more likely that we will heed the 'call' to a vocation if we are already practised at hearing the lesser calls. In the biblical examples we often see a progression – lesser calls that prepare and develop someone in appropriate ways, such as Joseph having his own dreams as a teenager, then interpreting the dreams of the cup-bearer and the baker in prison, in preparation for interpreting Pharaoh's dreams at a later date and his vocation being revealed.

All of the following people swam against the tide – they were compelled by God to act in a contrary way to those around them in order to accomplish His purpose:

Noah & the Ark – Genesis 6-9 – some will disagree with this decision but I have put Noah in the commissions list because he was 500 years old before God told him to build an ark. It took him one hundred years to construct and then for one year it kept him and his family safe. He then lived for another 350 years. So, this was not his life's work but you absolutely know that his life up to the age of 500 was preparing him for this major commission – he was THE righteous man on the planet whom God determined to save from the flood. It emphasises the critical importance of Point 4A in the Os Guinness framework: God calls us primarily to a quality of life that is characterized by certain persistent attributes, before we are given important but secondary things to do. Noah's identity was established in his relationship with God over 500 years, not by his building of an ark.

Gideon – Judges 6-8 – like Moses, here is a reluctant character, called in adverse circumstances to free his own people from oppression. Like Moses, he objected and wanted various proofs of God's good intentions. Gideon fulfilled the initial commission but, unlike Moses, went on to make a series of poor choices. God had given him a sphere of influence but he ventured beyond it to the detriment of both his own family and the nation.

Hiram – 2Samuel 5 [1Chronicles 14] & 1Kings 5-10 [2Chronicles 2-8] – here is an interesting case of someone who we are told, 'blessed the Lord' and 'always loved David', even though he himself was king of Tyre. In what was seen as a sign that God had established David as king over Israel and that his kingdom was highly exalted, Hiram took inspired action to build David a house. Then, because David's desire to build a house for God was deferred by God to the next generation, Hiram's further involvement also had to await the time of Solomon. But, at the right time, Solomon 'sent word to Hiram…: "As you dealt with David my father and sent him cedar to build himself a house to dwell in, so deal with me."' And thus, the enormous project to build both the Temple and Solomon's royal palace began, along with a successful business association, trading in precious metals and other commodities. These examples highlight, once again, God's love of craftsmanship.

Simeon and Anna – Luke 2:22-38 – these two were each waiting for the Messiah and had grasped something, in the Spirit, that the others around them had not. Consequently, they recognized Him and, in the shortest of encounters, blessed Him and his parents, testifying to His deity and to God's purpose. Both Simeon and Anna 'had to do' what they did – Simeon had had a revelation about the Lord's Christ and Anna was a prophetess and they were both walking in obedience to the Spirit. They each fulfilled their commission and were satisfied.

The Woman & the Alabaster Flask of Ointment – Matthew 26:8 – this act of anointing for burial stands out because, when everyone else failed to appreciate the enormity of what Jesus was about to do, she perceived it and knew the duty she had to perform. Jesus' acknowledgement and His gratitude were a clear endorsement of the rightness of her action.
Joseph of Arimathea – Matthew 27:57 – at a moment when all the other disciples were overcome with grief and unable to comprehend what had happened, Joseph acted decisively. He was uniquely equipped – a disciple of Jesus, rich, possessing a new tomb very close by. Like the woman above, he knew what he had to do.

Multi-threaded callings

God might give you a life's work, as you learn to listen, but He is as likely to give you a series of stepping stones that are satisfying in and of themselves but also prepare you for something bigger.

It is also important to state that God will not necessarily limit someone to a single 'thread of calling' in their life – think of David who had a wide skill set and who could be said to have had multiple callings to: war-craft; worship & music; leadership & motivation; kingship; organization & management, etc.

This was something that God did deliberately – it says in Isaiah 55:3,4 'Incline your ear and come to me; hear, that your soul may live; and I will make with you an everlasting covenant, my steadfast, sure love for David. Behold, I made him a witness to the peoples, a leader and commander for the peoples.' God knew what was needed and who He would use and He purposely made David both a witness *to the peoples* and a leader and commander *for the peoples*.

Does God revoke a calling if it is not taken up?

The short answer is, 'No, not most of the time'. However, the hardness of heart of the person(s) called will sometimes lead to the answer being, 'Yes'.

Calls generally persist

His word is always now

At the time when Moses was being called by God to lead the people of Israel out of Egypt, he inquired of God what he should say to the people of Israel, after he had declared to them that, 'The God of your fathers has sent me to you' and they then asked him, 'What is his name?' So, God said to Moses, 'I AM WHO I AM'. 'Say this to them, I AM has sent me to you.' God then went on to tell Moses that, 'This is my name forever, and thus I am to be remembered throughout all generations.' Exodus 3:13-15

The same thought is expressed in the first letter of Peter, echoing the words of Isaiah 40: 'All flesh is like grass and all its glory like the flower of grass. The grass withers, and the flower falls, but the word of the Lord remains forever.' 1 Peter 1:24,25

Calls persist because the word that God speaks is always 'Present', always 'Now', always 'Today', and it carries with it a sense of immediacy. In the book of Hebrews, where the writer is comparing and contrasting Moses with Jesus, it says, 'Consider Jesus, the apostle and high priest of our confession, who was faithful (as a Son) to him who appointed him, just as Moses was faithful (as a servant) in all God's house.' It goes on to say, 'And we are his house if indeed we hold fast our confidence and our boasting in our hope. Therefore, as the Holy Spirit says, '*Today*, when you hear his voice, do not harden your hearts...' Hebrews 3:1-8

The present tense language that God uses to describe himself and His word means that, even if His calls to us do not last for ever, they are at least enduring of mishap, disobedience and wrong turns. In Joshua 14 we read about Caleb, one of the original team sent by Moses to spy out the Promised Land. Caleb had wanted, with all his heart, to enter that land but had had to endure forty years of wandering in the desert, through no fault of his own. He finally did enter it, participated in the battles to possess it and emerged, at the age of eighty-five, having wholly followed the Lord, still as strong as he was at forty, ready for war and for 'going and coming'. He was ready to take up his inheritance and to fulfil his calling and says to Joshua, 'So now give me this hill country of which the Lord spoke on that day (45 years previously). It may be that the Lord will be with me, and I shall drive them out just as the Lord said.' ['them' are the Anakim – giants that had terrified Israel all those years before.]

Caleb's expression of faith and his dialogue with Joshua, at the point where the Promised Land had been subdued, attest to God's call to him enduring and being as 'present and active in him' after forty-five years of waiting as it was that first day.

His purposes persist – both for the individual and the corporate

Not only is the word that God speaks to us always 'present' but it carries with it a tangible sense of purpose – almost 'yearning' – a sense that persists until the word has been completed. It was not just Caleb's physical capabilities that had been preserved intact for forty-five years, it was also a deep sense of purpose both for himself as an individual and for his family.

It is important to note that in both the Exodus and Hebrews passages, quoted above, God is 'calling' a corporate body – firstly the nation of Israel and secondly the ecclesia or 'called-out' people. Having rescued us, both physically and spiritually, from slavery, God goes on to declare His purpose for each individual and His purpose for the national and transnational bodies. He is committed to fulfilling those purposes against all odds and despite repeated opposition – I need to emphasise that He will fulfil *all* of His purpose, both for the individual and for the corporate, however entangled or even conflicted those callings might seem to us and however long it takes.

The New Testament verse which, more than any other, conveys a sense of persistence and longevity for God's calls is Romans 11:29 and it occurs towards the end of a group of three chapters that many find hard to interpret. So, I must be very careful not to take it out of context.

The outworking of a call on an individual's life may be problematic but God's will and purpose for corporate bodies rarely finds peaceful acceptance among us. Unfortunately, disagreement over (and sometimes outright opposition to) His plans often comes from among the very people whom He calls. This is illustrated clearly in the Old Testament in interactions between the nation of Israel and the Gentiles, and in the New Testament between what is termed 'Israel' and the largely Gentile Church. Such disagreement has continued on to the present day:

- In the Old Testament, deliberate provision was made for those not descended from Israel to be welcomed among His covenant people, as stated in Genesis 17; Exodus 12; Numbers 9; and Deuteronomy 16. If God had not done this, the spirit of exclusivism among the Jews would have kept them out;
- In the New Testament, soon after Pentecost, with the tendency to exclusivism still prevalent, God poured out His Spirit on the Gentiles, leading to a crisis in the early Church. He had to radically re-align the apostles' theology – see Acts 10&11 where Peter receives a vision, preaches at Cornelius' house and then has to report back to the apostles in Jerusalem. See also Acts 15 where 'The Council at Jerusalem' has to debate the question of circumcision;
- Then, in Rome, after the Jews had been expelled by Claudius in AD49 and were subsequently allowed to return by Nero in AD55, what was

now a wholly Gentile Church said it did not want the Jewish believers back and declared them unnecessary to God's purpose. Paul, writing to the Romans in about AD56-58, uses 'calling language' in chapters 9-11 to explain how God has not forgotten or revoked his covenants; that Israel is still vital to His plans and that the Church must be 'one';

- Today there is still a tendency to downgrade Israel and to doubt that God can convince substantial numbers of the Jews to embrace their Messiah. It is not often acknowledged that the desire of the Gentile Church in Rome, in AD55, to exclude Jews, was a key reason why Paul wrote his letter. Most Christians love most of Romans but chapters 9-11 are rarely properly expounded in our churches. Perhaps that's because they cast doubt on the widely held notion that the Church has somehow 'replaced' the nation of Israel in God's purposes.

I do not subscribe to 'replacement theology' but some aspects are not clear cut – for example, Paul's definition of 'Israel' bears investigation: in Romans 2:28,29, Paul says, 'No one is a Jew who is merely one outwardly... but a Jew is one inwardly, and circumcision is a matter of the heart, by the Spirit'. Then, in Romans 9:6-11, Paul says, 'not all who are descended from Israel belong to Israel'. He is drawing a distinction between 'the children of the flesh' and 'the children of the promise' and the difference is that those of the promise (those who are truly 'Israel') are the offspring of 'faith' – the true descendants of Abraham, who heard and believed 'Him who calls'.

The use of the term 'Israel' may not therefore be entirely synonymous with 'the Jewish nation' but reading these chapters is strongly recommended because the whole tenor of Paul's argument throughout Romans is that God has not forgotten His chosen people and clearly has plans for the outworking of their call.

We do not know how He will work it out and we should not fall out with each other over what we don't fully understand. What *is* clear is that God has long-term plans and global intentions. He asserts that the full complement of the Gentiles will come in and then all who are truly 'Israel' will be saved because, *'the gifts and the callings of God are irrevocable'*, Romans 11:25 & 29. It is a magnificent verse and the word 'irrevocable' makes the point but the translation of this that I like the most is from the Jewish professor of philosophy whom I talked about earlier – he puts it thus: 'There is no such thing as God's coming to regret the gracious gifts which he bestows or the calls which he sends out.' (Cassirer, 1989)

Recall what we said in Chapter 2; firstly, about the need to sacrifice our lives on God's altar of service (dedicating whatever we do to Him, so that those sacrifices are a natural consequence of our response to His call) and secondly, about God administering personal doses of grace to us, wisely and prudently (how His far-sighted judgment calls are intended to make us into what we have not yet become and His intention is that we find 'shalom' in the performance of good works). It is my belief that, because of the irrevocable nature of God's purposes, once He has issued a call He will honour our obedience to it even if: we fail to heed it initially; or are prevented from following through by circumstances beyond our control; or we first need to take time out to learn a pile of lessons to prevent us messing it all up.

It's not just that God makes a clinical, administrative decision with respect to our salvation and to the individual path of obedience for each follower, but rather He is *invested in* that decision – He *wants* to be gracious; His calls are 'bestowed', not imposed; He wants us to succeed.

Biblical examples of the persistence of God's callings

Caleb – as already stated, he was steadfast in yearning for the word of the Lord to be fulfilled, having recognized a calling many years previously, and was not disappointed.

Moses – he, on the other hand, having been strategically placed and brought up in the palace of Pharaoh, an observer at first hand of the slavery of his own people, until he was forty, only received a calling to set Israel free at the age of eighty. At that age, although seemingly content with more mundane pursuits, he had undergone a further forty years of God's character development. The burning bush shook him from his passivity and God had to engage in some serious persuasion before Moses agreed to obey the call.

Jonah – he received a very specific call from God and, instead of obeying, ran off in the opposite direction. After attempting to evade responsibility, there was a divinely appointed misadventure with the storm and the 'big fish'. He learned a critical lesson and then discovered that God's call had not gone away but was enduring. At the second time of asking, he (reluctantly) fulfilled it.

A dynamic conversation

The conversation between God and me, throughout my life, is a dynamic thing and my interaction with Him is intended to change me, bit by bit, into the likeness of His son. Hence, a call of God that comes to me at age twenty, after which I make various errors and take several wrong turns before God reiterates His call to me at age fifty, may be the same in essence but will not be quite the same in the way it is out-worked because I am then a different person.

If, from the age of twenty, I took a different path to the one that God was calling me to and, as a result, I acquired skills and abilities that would not originally have been part of His intended outcome, He is nevertheless able to weave that experience into His leading of me now. He is uniquely capable of bringing the conversation around again to what He asked of me all those years ago and if, this time, I am listening more intently, with a commitment to obey and to follow, He can imbue the outworking of His calling with maybe different (but perhaps even greater) richness than it would have had back then.

We have used Caleb as a prime example – he was reunited with his calling after an interval of about forty-five years but the delay was not because he himself took a wrong turn. It was the fault of his compatriots, who were unwilling to exercise faith for the taking of the land of Canaan. As a result, Caleb, although much older, was the same person as he was before and God had taken care to preserve him so that the fulfilment would not be impaired. There are, however, other examples of people whose return to an earlier call finds them 'altered' in important ways.

Sometimes calls can be lost

After dramatically being called to be prince and leader over his people Israel, being anointed by Samuel, being 'given another heart', prophesying with the prophets, being proclaimed king, defeating the Ammonites and seeing the kingdom renewed, Saul failed to fulfil his calling. He got impatient, disobeyed Samuel's instructions and sacrificed to the Lord unlawfully. He then made a rash vow that nearly cost him his son and, when given another chance, he failed to heed the instruction to destroy the Amalekites and he took some of the spoil for himself – 1 Samuel 10-15.

As a consequence, Samuel had to tell him, 'Because you have rejected the word of the Lord, he has also rejected you from being king' and 'The Lord has torn the kingdom of Israel from you this day and has given it to a neighbour of yours, who is better than you.' – 1 Samuel 15:23, 28. We are told that God's Spirit departed from Saul and the kingship was passed to David. Saul did not know God's guidance for the rest of his life.

In the next chapter, we will be talking about permissions and spheres of influence. Saul's loss of his calling came about through actively disobeying the instructions he was given, doing what he did not have permission for and deliberately overstepping his allotted sphere of influence.

Jesus' parable of the talents, in Matthew 25, is also salutary. It is never a good idea to bury what God has given us. We need to pray for courage to use what we have, even if we are afraid and even if we don't think we have sufficient resource for what has to be done. The same God that gave the resource will help us to use it wisely, if we ask Him, and we will find that it multiplies. But if we insist on burying what we've been given, we are likely to find that it is taken off us and given to another.

Personal reflections on my own commissions

Do I believe I have a calling? Yes, and it is going to be worked out in what would otherwise have been my retirement years. Someone told me a few years ago that there is no word for 'retirement' in Hebrew, for which I'm most grateful – it always struck me as a deeply flawed concept.

However, rather than talk about *the big thing* I thought it might be helpful to relate a few of the occasions on which I have sensed God telling me to do smaller, short-term things. Please understand that nothing of this kind, big or small, short or long, seems 'small' at the time – each episode involves a growing sense that a role or activity or project may be important, then there is a decision-making process and then the outworking of that decision.

Nothing, however small, if it is an instruction from God that He wants us to obey, will prove unimportant in the long run. He knows what He is doing and each episode is meant for our good, to build in the necessary attributes and to develop the required character. The following examples come from various different aspects of life – home, church and work:

Helping a friend to find a new job and to realize his calling

Just in case my comments, earlier in the book, about God approving of a lot more than calls to mission and ministry, left you feeling I have something against either or both of those, this is offered as redress.

A long time ago, before I ever began to think seriously about the concept of 'calling', I saw that a friend of mine was becoming increasingly stressed about his work, to the extent that his health had begun to deteriorate. I was genuinely concerned but, more than that, felt God was challenging me to commit to 'standing with him' and, if possible, helping him to a new place.

He was a partner in a solicitor's practice, performing well but starting to become fearful of making errors. He was losing confidence in his own abilities and getting panic attacks. However, he also led worship in church, was clearly gifted and, by contrast, seemed relaxed in that role. And, when he preached it was as though he had been liberated – he was like two different people.

I discovered that he had had a calling to the ministry from the age of seventeen but had fought it off and not told anyone because he was afraid both of what his father might think and of not being able to earn enough. Money now had quite a hold on him and his status in the community was all important.

In the end it took nearly two years for him to be helped out of his 'career post' and into his calling. He wanted to get there but couldn't manage it on his own – he needed encouragement and counsel to keep on track, as resolve ebbed and flowed. He came out of partnership, undertook part-time theological study and his health began to improve.

God intervened on two separate occasions to enable him to leave the law firm and become established in Ministerial training. When he began to face a problem with money, he sold some things that he should never have bought in the first place and he gradually came to understand his status before God.

Many years later, he is still in ministry and has also been able to use his legal training in part-time roles in order to supplement his income.

Pastor of a church

The Baptist church that I attended, prior to and for a number of years after I got married, went through a period of dramatic growth. Its membership increased from about 150 to 450 in five years. It planted two other churches, first to the west and then to the east, as increasing numbers of people from various outlying communities began to attend. I became the pastor of the second such plant and did the job for three years, whilst remaining in full-time employment.

This is an example of an initiative that I knew was going to happen but which I did not intend to have personal involvement in. I was happy where I was. I had to drive either past or through these communities, out to the east, in order to get to work in the morning, and then back through at the end of the day. I didn't like the area and didn't feel any 'connection' with it. I was, however, very interested in how this new initiative would pan out – having previously been a little apprehensive about the whole process of church-planting, I now felt I understood a bit about it and was looking forward to seeing how it would happen.

Then, one weekend, when my wife and I were driving home from visiting my parents, road works diverted us through the area and past the community hall where the new church was due to be located. Quite suddenly, I knew, whereas I had not known up to that moment, that we needed to be involved in this place and with these people. She and I had a conversation about it and agreed that it seemed as though God was directing us. So, I said to her, 'I feel we should be here but I'm not going to say anything to the pastor or the other leaders of the "mother church". They will have to come to me, if they want me to be involved, and that will be the confirmation.'

It was difficult to keep quiet because I was part of a leadership group responsible for a number of aspects of church business and we regularly discussed the planting initiatives. But this was a time for praying and waiting. Then, about a month later, the senior pastor came back from a conference and said that he had been in a lecture but not really concentrating on it and just knew he should ask me how I felt about being involved in the new church plant. I was then able to tell him our own thought processes.

The three years that followed were a time of team-building, learning new skills, making and rectifying errors, building community and modest growth. When I left it was because my wife and I knew that it was time for a new start, in a new job, in a completely different part of the country.

A Football Association coaching course

When my son was young it became clear that he was extremely good at various sports, including football. He played for various club sides, over the years, back in the day when even seven-year-olds played 11v11 each week on a full-size pitch! Some of the people who took on managing a kids' team, and had responsibility for coaching, were very good. But, some of them were awful. The bad ones had no idea about warm-up or cool-down, no knowledge or imagination when it came to fitness regimes, no ability to develop skills and their only advice seemed to be to 'run faster', 'tackle harder' or 'put more effort in'. Children grow at different rates and it affects their athleticism. If you push a kid too hard, for too long, or at the 'wrong' phase of growth, they can develop over-use injuries and it curtails any chance they might have of enjoying the sport into adulthood.

When he was about eleven or twelve, as was my habit, I had been accompanying my son to training sessions and matches but, for several months, had been uneasy and felt that he was 'at risk'. However, I didn't have a solution and was complaining about it one evening to my wife when I got the uncomfortable feeling that I needed to go and get training as a football coach, which was most definitely not the solution I was looking for.

You have to understand that, although I could kick a ball, knew all the rules and had been as a spectator to many professional football matches, I had no experience of playing football competitively. I had gone to a school where we played Rugby Union and football was called 'the round ball game' – if you were seen with a football you were immediately given an after-school detention! However, the sense of it being right, to pursue a coaching qualification, persisted and I went ahead and enrolled on an FA course that was way above my capability. There were actually only two alternatives – one beginner's course that addressed hardly any of the questions I was asking and one really 'grown-up' course that dealt with everything that concerned me, and more.

Today it is not possible to jump in at such advanced level, from a standing start. The FA has thankfully closed that loophole because, among other things, it means people are less likely to risk embarrassment and ridicule every week for six months because their personal skills don't allow them to put the theory into practice! Nevertheless, although it was painful, I knew it was the right thing to do and the course instructors knew and understood the dilemma about my son. Even before the course had finished, we were able to 'save' him from being very poorly coached and to get him into a football academy.

I didn't pass the course (only three out of twenty-one participants actually did) but I met some great people and I learned a massive amount. It totally changed the way I watch the game – I can see patterns of play, appreciate both subtle and obvious skills and see where even professionals are failing to do the simple things correctly.

Redesigning a software system, used daily by many thousands of professionals

Let's be clear, from the outset, that I am emphatically not the best designer of software user interfaces but, whilst director of a software distributor, selling a product designed and built on the other side of the world, we found ourselves in trouble. We were having to sell a functionally rich system that had a very poor user experience. We were being beaten to the majority of sales by two other competitor systems and were deeply worried that the company would not survive.

My wife and I prayed earnestly about what should be done and then my fellow director and I scheduled a crisis meeting. Within minutes of sitting down to discuss the situation, it suddenly became clear to both of us what had to be done – we somehow had to redesign the way the whole system looked, at our own expense, and to present a new, integrated and coherent user experience to the parent company for consideration.

For me, it was a kind of revelation – one minute I didn't know and the next, I did. I instantly attributed it, in my own mind, to God but what made it even more unusual was that the other person in the room, who was definitely not in the habit of asking God for answers, had the same understanding, at the same time. However, although we knew what we had to do, I knew I'd never done anything like it before. What upped the stakes for me was that I was nominated as the one to give maximum effort to this initiative whilst my colleague got on with running the company. I was apprehensive because I didn't believe I was up to the task and so my wife and I once again did the only thing you can do at a time like that – we prayed.

My colleague and I contacted a gifted web designer, who also understood database systems, with whom we had associated in a small way previously, and agreed a price for a chunk of his time over the following few weeks. I began to sketch what I wanted the screens to look like, what information should be presented on each page, where the links needed to be, what should happen whenever someone pressed a button etc. etc. I sent emails and had long telephone conversations with my new 'techie friend' and, within a day or two, something I had not expected began to happen.

I have used the word 'resonance' in several places previously and I can't describe it any other way – there was a strange, progressive amplification of our meagre efforts and the project 'took off'. The experience was quite exhilarating – almost as though we were operating at a heightened level of consciousness where the air was cleaner and we could think more clearly.

Within four weeks we had created a fully functional working model of what we wanted the system to look like – it was stand-alone but it contained carefully chosen examples of real data and it looked just like the real thing. Like a real system, it was multi-layered, making it possible in certain places to keep on clicking through to deeper and deeper levels. It illustrated almost everything of importance that the real software could do but, during the course of design, we had also introduced approx. a dozen major new features. I cannot tell you where those new features actually came from, except to say that they all seemed 'obvious' – it's as if we just knew (or were being told) what people might want to do in the future and I do not deserve credit for any of it.

Having created the 'new' system, we loaded it on a laptop and I wrote a demo script to illustrate its features. I then flew across the world and presented it to the people who ran the parent company. The new UI was adopted within twenty-four hours of my first demonstration and first shown as part of the real system about six months later. It was a huge success and completely reversed the trend in sales. It saved the company and showed me that God is interested in our work, 'secular' though it may be, to an astonishing degree. He is a craftsman and, if we ask His help, He delights to participate in our projects and to pass on His craftsmanship to us.

This was one of only a few occasions in my working life so far when I have genuinely been 'in my element'. In Chapter 11 we examine this concept more closely. A characteristic of doing something you love and where your aptitudes match the task is that your senses seem heightened. When I look back over my working life, to that four weeks of design effort, it stands out as a time when I had an ability to concentrate and to be creative beyond almost any other period. I know it was God who did it – He can and will gift us for what needs to be done.

Chapter 10

Callings and Your Personal identity

How would you describe yourself?

If you were given just a few minutes in which to introduce yourself to a group of people and to explain who you are... if you want to be entirely truthful, to really 'own' what you say about yourself, so that those who hear you properly understand you, what would you say?

Would you talk about nationality; where you were born and about your family? Would you list educational achievements and your professional experience? What about your skills and abilities? Would you talk about some of the things you have accomplished, that you've done well and enjoyed? Would you mention significant difficulties and how you overcame them or perhaps try to give an understanding of the challenges you currently face?

The question of personal identity is a sensitive subject – people fiercely defend who they believe themselves to be and, consequently, what they believe are their rights. As you contemplate your answers to the questions posed, would you say you are happy with, or even proud of, who you are? Or do you feel ashamed of or disappointed in who you are?

Most definitions of personality and identity suggest that they are 'bio-socially determined', in other words both are genetically pre-defined and socially reshaped. Psychologists suggest that self-identity is the combination of qualities, beliefs, personality, looks and/or expressions that make a person. It is further said that personal identity allows an individual to appear unique through a specific combination of personality characteristics, abilities, interests, physical attributes and biography. The Cambridge English Dictionary defines identity as, 'who a person is, or the qualities of a person or group that make them different from others'.

It is then suggested that interpersonal identity development comes about through an individual questioning and examining various personality elements such as ideas, beliefs and behaviours. The actions and thoughts of others create social influences that change an individual. This process would allow for someone's identity to evolve over the course of one's life.

The appearance of words like 'unique' and 'different' in the definitions given above is a relief because reading some sociological studies might lead you to believe that all our key characteristics are determined by social influences and, furthermore, some psychometric testing tries to divide human personality into just sixteen types! Our secular society would essentially have us believe that a person, starting from their genetically pre-defined position, becomes who they are largely through their own efforts and the influence of those around them.

The biblical picture, however, is somewhat different – God is presented as the author of life and the agent of creation; He sets the standards, rescues the fallen, redeems the lost and forgives the repentant; He reveals himself as Father, restores hope and gives purpose. Those who embrace His fatherhood, He can mould, change, develop & sanctify, until, 'we who have been saved are presented blameless before the presence of His glory with great joy', Jude 24. How different is that to the haphazard and chancy outcomes presented by secular society?

Although there may be things about us that are genetically pre-defined and although we may have been heavily influenced and shaped by family and the society around us, looking at identity from a biblical standpoint means that genetics, family and society are not the things that define us.

Although we may not have had the privileges or opportunities that others have enjoyed and although we may have been prevented from taking chances due to ill health or lack of available resource, looking at identity from a biblical standpoint means that privilege, health and wealth are not limiting factors in who or what we are able to be.

Identity comes from someone, not from the somethings that we do

As was said much earlier, salvation is a personal transaction between you and Jesus – your response to His call. Ephesians 1:4 says, 'He chose us in him (Jesus) before the foundation of the world, that we should be holy and blameless before him' – his intention being that we should be 'adopted as sons' (verse 5). It is a process, a journey that he has put into motion and, just as no two children are exactly alike, our adoption is meant to lead us as individuals from our unholy state, by degrees, to maturity.

So, the central character is Jesus. He is the only one who has pleased the Father and He is therefore the only one on whom we can depend. He only ever did what the Father told him and He wholly demonstrated to us what the Father is like. He bore all the attributes of God, in human form, and completely fulfilled his unique calling. In fulfilling his calling, He made it possible for us to fulfil ours.

The purpose of our sanctification is that, whatever our starting point, when we first knew that we needed Jesus, we are set to become more like Jesus – 'He (the Father) predestined (us) to be conformed to the image of his Son, in order that he (Jesus) might be the firstborn among many *brothers*.' Romans 8:29. 'He has granted to us his precious and very great promises, so that through them you (we) may become partakers of the divine nature, having escaped from the corruption that is in the world because of sinful desire.' 2 Peter 1:4.

Sanctification does not kill uniqueness

Now, we have already said this once but it bears repeating because there is a common misconception that needs to be cleared up – when we read about us all becoming more like Jesus, as we submit to God's cajoling, mending, moulding change process, it does *not* mean we all end up alike. So, nobody needs to be afraid that the 'ecclesia' is intended to be a set of clones. If that is what's happening in your church, you can be sure that people are not engaging in the process I'm describing here. Sanctification does not kill uniqueness.

God made every person different to the next because He has a unique purpose for each one and because he wants to be the Father of each one. Just as we who have children take delight in each one's individuality, and long for them each to fulfil their potential, God's process of sanctification makes us into who we were always intended to be.

Getting there, however, is not quite as easy as walking hand in hand into the sunset. Some of the changes that God wants and needs to make to us are fundamental and will require courage on our part for the change process.

So, if we want to 'get there', there is first of all a requirement to take our identity package – the way we have decided to describe ourselves to the assembled audience; our best and most honest guess at the truth of who we are – and to give it to Him. We are submitting both ourselves and the many *somethings* that we do, to the *someone* who created us and has our best end in view.

In doing so, we are acknowledging that the secular solution is just not good enough – we don't want to be dependent on our own efforts or submitted to the influence of those around us. We are allowing Him to scrutinise the package and to be prudent, asking Him to speak to us about how He wishes to administer His doses of grace. We are expecting Him to work on our identity package and, progressively, to make us different.

Some kind of different

What kind of 'different'? Well, think back to the calling framework set out in Chapter 3 – we said that, having called people to be followers of Christ, God then issues a call:

- To live according to Kingdom principles;

- To undertake specific tasks.

We went on to say that, in order for us not to mess up the specific tasks, we need first of all to establish a quality of life in Christ that is characterized by certain persistent attributes. Only God knows the degree to which that foundational life in Christ needs to be worked on, before He chooses to entrust us with specific tasks, because only He knows the starting point with each person and only He knows the nature of the tasks He intends to give us.

It is not possible to predict how long that process will take or the route that God will have each one travel but the mechanism He employs is likely to involve a repetition of the following sequence...

- Us *actively* listening for instruction;
- Him *speaking* to us by various different means;
- Us *hearing* what He says and *discerning* it to be Him;
- Us *obeying* what He has said.

What He speaks each time will be a *call to action*, of some kind, and our response will be an act of faith. We are never required to have faith in a vacuum – as Paul says to the Romans, 'Faith, then, comes through what is heard, and what is heard has its source in its having been spoken by Christ.' Romans 10:17 (Cassirer, 1989). Again, to the Galatians, he says 'Let me ask you only this: Did you receive the Spirit by works of the law or *by hearing with faith*?' and 'Does he who supplies the Spirit to you and works miracles among you do so by works of the law or by *hearing with faith*?' Galatians 3:2,5.

I hope the preceding paragraphs have not discouraged you – I am not trying to give the impression that there's an interminable sequence of hard lessons to learn before we can get to enjoy the 'good works prepared beforehand'. Finding our element, or even a measure of it, is not a pipedream. But it is important that we are honest before God about who we are because the good works are *His* works, not ours, and the outcome of doing them should have lasting qualities. He does not want us to mess them up and, furthermore, we too should be determined not to let that happen.

Far from being discouraging, the sequence of hearing and doing should actually be quite exciting because He will be working on our identity to do all of the following: to alter our understanding because 'His ways are not our ways'; to shape our firmly-held beliefs because the core values that we hold to are of vital importance; to instil the missing foundational qualities and persistent attributes; to develop our sense of purpose; to reveal our aptitudes and motivated abilities; to enhance our skill set; and to move us to a place where natural aptitude meets personal passion.

Let's look at an example from the Bible of someone who's identity got altered when he encountered the some*one* who questioned the some*things* he was doing.

Paul's identity and calling

Paul was called to be an apostle – Romans 1:1 says, 'Paul, a servant of Christ Jesus, called to be an apostle, set apart for the gospel of God...' But, more than that, he was called to be an apostle *to the Gentiles* – Gal 1:15 says, '...when he who had set me apart before I was born, and who called me by his grace, was pleased to reveal his Son to me, in order that I might preach him among the Gentiles...' See also: Acts 13:44-48; 18:6; 22:21; and 26:17,18.

As was stated in Chapter 3, Paul's description to the Philippians of his own identity was a list of his impeccable credentials – 'If anyone else thinks he has reason for confidence in the flesh, I have more: circumcised on the eighth day, of the people of Israel, of the tribe of Benjamin, a Hebrew of Hebrews; as to the law, a Pharisee; as to zeal, a persecutor of the Church; as to righteousness under the law, blameless', Philippians 3:4-6. But, he then goes on to say, 'whatever gain I had, I counted as loss for the sake of Christ. Indeed, I count everything as loss because of the surpassing worth of knowing Christ Jesus my Lord.' Philippians 3:7-8

Paul's primary identity was 'in Christ' and he had renounced the carefully nurtured identity as a Pharisee. He is now straining towards faith in Christ, a participation in His sufferings and knowing the power of His resurrection and, in doing so, is prepared to lose everything else.

Actually, his identity overhaul was even more radical. He had previously built up an impressive set of human credentials for acceptance, and those credentials clearly identified him to his *own* people – a Jew, of the tribe of Benjamin, circumcised, an educated Hebrew, a Pharisee, zealous, a persecutor of the Church, righteous under the law.

But, after he was converted on the road to Damascus, he relinquished everything that he had become over many years of hard work, that had made him implacably opposed to Christ's Church, because his primary allegiance was now to Jesus. He submitted everything to Jesus in order to *become* an apostle. Then, because the unthinkable was happening – the God of the Hebrews was not only saving Hebrews, He had extended the gospel of grace to the Gentiles and was pouring out His Holy Spirit on them – he had to submit it all again.

It is almost as though Paul was required to give up his identity twice – the human credentials were laid down and his identity remade in order to do the works of an apostle and then the new apostolic calling was also submitted, otherwise he could never have been a minister to the Gentiles.

The same must be true of us, in principle. The calling to salvation means that whatever we believe our identity to be, it must be submitted to Christ.

What He has for us to do cannot be done apart from Him and He may have to shift our understanding in some radical way for us to appreciate what He's asking of us. Do not underestimate the change that might be required – the reworking of our identity – in order for us to occupy the sphere of influence that He intends.

We must all grow into the somethings that we do

Look again at Romans 1:1-5 – when Paul says that he was 'called to be(come) an apostle', he means that he was not an apostle at the time of the call and he didn't know how to be one until God showed him.

In verse 5 he says that '(through Jesus Christ our Lord) we received grace and apostleship'. In other words, in keeping with the prudent applications of grace in Ephesians 1, and the acquisition of skill in Exodus 28-34, Paul is testifying to the call being followed by a necessary process of change.

Saul had to learn to be an apostle and we get some clues about that process in Galatians 1 & 2: 'When he who had set me apart before I was born, was pleased to reveal his son to me, in order that I might preach Him among the Gentiles, I did not immediately consult with anyone …. I went away into Arabia, and returned again to Damascus… then after three years I went up to Jerusalem to visit Cephas, but I saw none of the other apostles apart from James… then I went to Syria and Cilicia and I was still unknown in person to the churches… then after fourteen years I went up again to Jerusalem…'

Saul had a selection of skills and a wealth of experience at the time of his call but if he had plunged straight in he would have messed it all up. He had to be transformed, step by step, into the person God intended, by constant application of grace, by understanding the truth and by learning new skills. It's a principle that he passed on to others – as he says to Timothy in 1Timothy 4:14,15, 'Do not neglect the gift you have, which was given you by prophecy when the council of elders laid their hands on you. Practice these things, immerse yourself in them, so that all may see your progress.'

The One who calls also grants permissions and allows spheres of influence

When you read both the Acts of the Apostles and Paul's letters it is clear that Paul sought only to do what God specifically gave him permission to do:

- Acts 16:6-10 – '(Paul and Silas and Timothy) went through the region of Phrygia and Galatia, having been forbidden by the Holy Spirit to speak the word in Asia. And when they had come up to Mysia, they attempted to go into Bithynia, but the Spirit of Jesus did not allow them. So, passing by Mysia, they went down to Troas. And a vision appeared to Paul in

168

the night: a man… urging him to… come over to Macedonia and help us… When Paul had seen the vision, he concluded that God had called us to preach the gospel to them…'

- 1 Corinthians 16:7 – 'For I do not want to see you now just in passing. I hope to spend some time with you, if the Lord permits.'
- 2 Corinthians 10:13-16 – 'But we will not boast beyond limits, but will boast only with regard to the area of influence God assigned to us, to reach even to you. For we are not overextending ourselves as though we did not reach you… But our hope is that as your faith increases, our area of influence among you may be greatly enlarged, so that we may preach the gospel in lands beyond you, without boasting of work already done in another's area of influence.'

In a verse that we have quoted previously, from John 3, we also see John the Baptist's clear understanding of his own permissions and limits – speaking about his calling, he says 'There is nothing a man can receive except what has been granted to him by heaven.'

The callings of God for an individual have boundaries of permission and authority beyond which we are not permitted to go and it would appear that we must be careful to limit ourselves to the sphere of influence granted to us. We need to be willing to step into that pool of light (even if it is some distance from where we are currently standing) and then, once in it, stay alert to its position and remain within it.

True identity

So, what is the link between identity and calling? God determined, from before we were born, to adopt us as sons and daughters and He also determined the pathway to sonship. We are all different and although called, as individuals, to a variety of interesting vocations, we are first and foremost called to salvation. Our salvation unlocks a dynamic relationship with God through which He reveals to us our true identity. Our true calling is the outworking of an identity shaped by Christ – the specific things that God gives us to do because of who we are.

I use the terms 'true identity' and 'true calling' because there are many, both believers and unbelievers, who discover at least a measure of their natural aptitudes coinciding with their personal passion. Often that coinciding comes about almost by accident – not through any conscious process of hearing God and acting in faith. I would therefore suggest that there is a qualitative difference in the outcomes – getting there by accident, where faith is not involved, may benefit the individual but it's less likely to result in God's good works getting done and having lasting benefit for the 'kingdom'.

Consequently, what I am advocating is our willingness to partner with God, to entrust to Him our identity package and to let Him mould us. I am claiming that, if we do so, He cannot do other than reveal our calling because it's an inevitable consequence of His Fatherhood towards us. In doing so, there is a double benefit – He calls us to the good works that fulfil His purposes and we are most likely find our element in the doing of them.

Personal reflections on identity

This is a difficult one – it has taken a long time for what I'd call my true identity to begin to form. At this later stage of my life, describing myself and really 'owning' those words is more of a challenge than ever, not because there's nothing meaningful to say but because I am learning and changing faster now than at almost any previous stage and whatever is written here might need updating before too long. But that is a good thing.

As the story at the end of Chapter 4 tells, I am an 'Iain' [meaning 'God is gracious'] who is aspiring to be a 'Benjamin' [meaning 'Son of my right hand']. I believe God has given me a job to do, which is to find and to recruit 'craftsmen' for Him, giving each of them the necessary encouragement to hear their individual calling from God and then to begin to realize it. Nevertheless, I am having to grow into the thing that God requires to be done.

I have a bunch of skills, honed over many years, which include business development and operational management; recruitment; career development and team-building; methodologies for describing personality traits; coaching of individuals and leadership groups; church leadership and Bible teaching. None of this really qualifies me for what God is asking me to do but all the experience and the lessons learned along the way have come through the application of His grace and because of His patience and it has created a toolkit to choose from as and when necessary.

But, as important as skills and experience undoubtedly are, character-building and values development and taking on the attributes of God's nature matter more. This is the territory where the most fundamental shifts in identity, to mould it into something God can use, have to take place. In my case, it has taken a long time because I have been weak in the area of relationships and it is in learning to relate that many of the sharp corners of our nature are either sanded down or knocked off. God has been patient and relentless, requiring me to relate to Him directly and then to those whom He has put around me, who also love Him.

I don't have many friends because, like a lot of men, I'm not very good at getting beyond the acquaintance stage, but the ones that I do have I value very highly. As well as providing comradeship, they are quite effective at issuing timely challenges, but it is my wife and family who have been largely responsible for the human factor in driving identity development. Dawn, to whom I've been married for thirty-eight years, is relationally skilled, gives wise, God-inspired advice and, mercifully, has somewhat more patience than me. Our children, likewise, are pursuing God with vigour and I now have no hesitation in going to them for counsel.

God's wisdom is beyond our understanding and His ways of orchestrating our sanctification cannot be nailed down but, if I had to try to define the most common mechanisms He has employed, in my case, to initiate periods of effective learning and to drive identity development, two in particular come to mind:

- Either, He brings an interesting/challenging/potentially exciting project or task to my attention and then, when I'm contemplating, investigating and discussing with others what my involvement might require, He speaks a word that brings me face to face with my inadequacy and redirects my focus;
- Or, He allows a difficulty/business downturn/disappointment/ relationship crisis, or the like to happen and then, when I'm vulnerable and thrown back on Him, He speaks a word that brings me face to face with a) my part in the failure and b) His desired outcome and re-orients my mind.

The first method is frequently His means of issuing a 'call' or giving a 'commission'. The feeling of inadequacy is a common initial reaction in me but the new focus leads to acquiring new skills, finding others with complementary skills and a profitable leaning on the One who gifts.

The second method tends to make me question myself and to re-evaluate one or more of the things I'm involved in. The renewed vision that His word has brought, plus the reality of my state, brings a desire in me for change or development and thereby leads back to the first method because He tends to respond by finding ways to dangle new possibilities in front of me.

Chapter 11

Callings and 'Being in your Element'

A tantalising but elusive place

The Bible tells us that very early in mankind's history, we fell from a state of innocent obedience to a state of guilty disobedience, prior to which God gave the man and his wife creative and useful tasks to do (Genesis 2:18-25). He participated with them and talked to them regularly (Genesis 3:8). After 'the fall', we read of people having a bewildering variety of capabilities – people to whom God gave 'a spirit of skill' and whose hearts He stirred to be involved in projects requiring great precision and excellence of execution (Exodus 28:3; 35:35).

Not only was excellence celebrated, but we are told that the coming together of such skills sparked joy (1Chronicles 12:40). In the New Testament we see people being directed by the Holy Spirit to apply their skills and resources in particular ways and, in the Church era, a principle is articulated of God having prepared good works for people, the outworking of which is intended to bring an experience of 'shalom' (Ephesians 2:10).

Whenever God himself does something, He could be said to be 'in His element'. He has no shortage of creativity, no hesitation about rightness or timeliness, no worry that His skill set is lacking and no doubt about the outcome. Furthermore, He takes delight in the doing and, having completed the task, His oft recorded response is, 'It is good'.

In a perfect world, therefore, it would surely be normal for each of us to find useful ways to express our unique personhood and skill set and equally normal for that activity to be fulfilling and the results enduring. It is possible to imagine heaven as a place where we return to such normality but, right now, we are caught up in an imperfect and deeply challenging environment where even our best intentions to listen to and obey God are prone to compromise and where failure seems more likely than success.

How wonderful then that, in the midst of this present mayhem, people still have moments of epiphany when it is as if everything aligns correctly and, in the course of a project or activity or task, we say to ourselves, 'this is *me* – I feel as if I was made to do this'. Such an experience of 'shalom' (however fleeting) is a powerful indicator of God's love and governance and, to me at least, a proof that we have been made in His image. Why? – because, when that happens, it is as though we are free from constraint, compromise and fear, able to operate 'normally' again and to know that 'it is good'.

His declared desire is that we cohabit with Him (John 14:23), share His joy (John 17:13) and become 'one with Him' (John 17:20,21). This suggests that, rather than it only ever being fleeting, we might aspire to more prolonged and meaningful periods of 'shalom' in what we do but He knows that, in this present darkness, there are only certain ways that this can happen and it will require from us both patience and focus.

For those reasons, we have been careful to place the concept of 'callings' in their proper biblical context – namely, that God first of all attracts our attention and then invites us by name into relationship with Him, then opens a way for us to exhibit a variety of aspects of His character and only then does He give us useful things to do.

He is trying to impress upon us what are the keys both to success and enjoyment: the tasks that He gives us are all somehow 'relational' and cannot be undertaken or completed otherwise; our skill set will always be inadequate but is to be enhanced and enriched in the doing; it is His work, not ours – we are just the apprentice or participant who has been granted a role to play; and an enduring outcome depends on whose glory or reputation we are working to enhance.

So, having established the foregoing, let's remind ourselves of the definition of being 'in our element' that has been stated several times in the previous chapters and was coined by Sir Ken Robinson. It is said to be 'the place where natural aptitude (the things that we are naturally capable of, and indeed gifted at) meets personal passion (what we not only *can* do but *love* doing)'.

It is a highly desirable place, that only God's creative genius makes possible, and testimonial evidence from a whole host of people suggests that, from that position, we will really enjoy what we are doing most of the time; feel motivated to learn and to practice and to achieve; and be less prone to stress-related conditions. But, how reasonable is it to expect that kind of experience this side of heaven, and, if reasonable, should it be the thing we want above all else?

We will explore alternative ways to get there but, desirable as it may be, I would caution against that destination being seen as the ultimate prize. It may describe matching the way someone is ideally set up to operate, and what they are uniquely gifted for, with an appropriate or even ideal set of activities, or way of life, but oneness with Jesus is truly the ultimate prize and we are told to seek first His kingdom (Matthew 6:33).

Nevertheless, a real place

All the biblical evidence suggests that God creates, prepares and moulds people to fulfil both their potential and His purposes:

He designed us… David says in Psalm 139, 'I am fearfully and wonderfully made [the word 'made' means 'set apart']… your eyes saw my unformed substance; in your book were written all the days that were formed for me, when as yet there was none of them.'

He calls us… God says to Moses in Exodus 31, 'I have *called by name* Bezalel and… filled him with… ability and intelligence, with knowledge and all craftsmanship… and behold I have appointed him to…' Paul says of himself, in Galatians 1, 'he who had *set me apart* before I was born, and who *called* me by his grace, was pleased to reveal his Son to me, in order that I might preach Him among the Gentiles'. And again, in Romans 1, 'Paul, a servant of Christ Jesus, *called* to be an apostle'.

He has prepared tasks for us to do… Paul says to the church in Ephesus, 'For we are God's handiwork [workmanship], created as men who have their being in Christ Jesus, in order that we should give ourselves up to good works which God has prepared beforehand, so that we might enjoy our lives in the doing of them.' We are to be 'zealous for those good works', Titus 2:4, and 'careful to devote ourselves to them', Titus 3:8.

I have already alluded to the fact that 'being in one's element' is a concept that is also under discussion in the secular world. Ken Robinson said this in his book 'The Element', '*I've lost track of the numbers of people I've met who have no real sense of what their individual talents and passions are. They don't enjoy what they are doing now but they have no idea what actually would fulfil them. On the other hand, I also meet people who've been highly successful in all kinds of fields, who are passionate about what they do and couldn't imagine doing anything else.*' (Robinson, 2010)

Ken dedicated himself to addressing failures in the education system and the mismatch between what people are doing now (often as a direct result of the narrowness of their education) and what those same people actually have the innate skill and passion and potential to become. He went on to say, '*My aim in writing is to offer a richer vision of human ability and creativity and of the benefits to us all of connecting properly with our individual talents and passions. (These are) issues that are of fundamental importance in our lives and in the lives of our children, our students, and the people we work with. I use the term "the element" to describe the place where the things we love to do and the things we are good at come together. I believe it is essential that each of us find his or her Element, not simply because it will make us more fulfilled but because, as the world evolves, the very future of our communities and institutions will depend on it.*

'*Those in their element are doing the thing they love, and in doing it they feel like their most authentic selves. They find that time passes differently and that they are more alive, more centred, more vibrant than at any other times. When people are in their Element, they connect with something fundamental to their sense of identity, purpose and well-being. Being there provides a sense of self-revelation, of defining who they really are and what they're really meant to be doing with their lives. Many describe finding their Element as an epiphany.*' (Robinson, 2010)

Ken was a highly respected and hugely experienced and engaging educationalist. He was a disruptive influence, challenging the status quo, willing to confront entrenched attitudes and he was speaking the truth. But, he was not openly acknowledging the agency of the God who both made us and knows each one of us inside out. Having said that, he described 'The Element' in pseudo-spiritual terms as 'a hymn to the breath-taking diversity of human talent and passion and to our extraordinary potential for growth and development.'

The fact that Ken's approach did not describe or acknowledge a spiritual agency or seek testimony from people who express an active faith in God, but nevertheless finds incontrovertible evidence of people in their element and was then able to celebrate each one's uniqueness, confirms that this is a real phenomenon.

The doctrine of 'common grace' would say that because God has created us in His image, and has given each individual a unique set of attributes, it consequently means that the range of human achievement we can expect to witness around us will be staggering, despite this being a 'fallen' world where the majority of people choose to follow their own life-plan and to take no notice of the God who made them. How much more desirable then to acknowledge God's deliberate agency and explore the possibility of His leading us to our 'element' by giving us appropriate outlets for our gifting, that provide the sought-for fulfilment and also achieve His purposes.

Most people can recall examples of undertaking a project or performing some duties or rising to a challenge or going on an adventure which, when they look back on the experience, they can say it was enjoyable, it was successful and it had a positive payoff (satisfying/character building/ developed them as a person). In short, they were 'in their element', or close to it.

As already stated, it is common for people to describe the feeling of such experiences as 'doing what I was made for', so common in fact that it's the sort of thing that should prompt investigation, to see if it is anchored in biblical principle and therefore a legitimate hope. Commonality and a feeling of 'rightness' are not enough – many have been and are deceived by only applying those tests – we must look not only into its reality but ask whether God intends it to be normative.

Although it may seem elusive, I do believe it to be a legitimate hope. It is also entirely reasonable that we should ask God to help us find that 'sweet spot'.

Two ways to get there

So, how do you find it and, if you happen to arrive there, how should you then conduct yourself? There are two main ways to get there:

The first way is more, as we say, 'hit and miss'. You might just happen upon a set of activities where you feel 'in your element', either by following your heart or doing more of what you like or, possibly, by someone observing you and discerning that you are gifted at certain things. Ken Robinson interviewed a number of people who have 'got there' and they all did so via this fairly 'haphazard' and 'secular' means but this is not meant to detract from the reality of the destination they each reached. Our examination of the concept here is in the light of what God has revealed to us both about His nature and man's purpose but, having said that, people of faith might equally happen upon the destination, or somewhere close to it, by a combination of innate purposefulness, enterprise and a growing knowledge of the stuff they like doing.

The second way to 'get there' is more calculated and carries a greater degree of certainty and it is to follow God's calls. As we have already said, receiving a 'calling' has to do with embarking on something of kingdom purpose because callings only ever come by revelation. Callings are given both to those (the few) who might already have found, or at least have a good idea about, 'their element' and to the ones (the majority) who haven't a clue about 'their element'.

The key point, that applies to all categories of person, is this: God's purpose for an individual is to issue callings and to work them through to a conclusion in a way that is tailored to that person's uniqueness and, when He does that, a natural consequence is likely to be that they will find themselves 'in their element'. Hence, to follow a 'calling' is not the same thing as 'being in your element' (and vice-versa) but doing the former is the surest way to discovering the latter.

We have to introduce a disclaimer at this juncture – even though you may come to a place where you feel the 'rightness', the 'fit' and the 'timeliness' of what you are doing and even though you may think or know that you are 'in your element', it does not mean that everything will be easy. There will, of course, be difficulties, setbacks and frustrations but the sense of calling and the rightness of what you are doing will bring joy, build stamina and create a determination to push through.

Having got there, various qualities of outcome

There is no doubt that finding your element is a significant prize, since those who get there enjoy much of what they do to a greater degree, in the here and now, than those who have not found it. But, the prize of enjoyment in what you do, although desirable, does not, in and of itself, constitute 'success'. True success is about the value that can be attributed to the results of using those skills and applying that passion. Are you going to fritter the prize away or use it to build a lasting legacy?

The Bible suggests that there will be measurable, qualitative differences, in terms of the fulfilment gained and the outcomes achieved. Furthermore, the extent of those differences will depend on whether someone makes God the foundation of their work, how well they listen to His guidance and instruction and the degree to which their work is then done for His benefit rather than for their own. Whatever method someone uses to find their element, we can expect God to apply the same tests to the results as He does for all human activity.

There is another, fairly subtle point to make here; because calls come to those of the 'called-out' people, by revelation, either by discerning a word from God at the outset or by discovering His approval of and directing hand on the activity over a period of time, the decision-making process needs to discern between having a good idea (it matches what I'm good at and it's something God would approve of) and responding to what He is actually saying.

Waiting for surety on the latter may be tiresome but it will prevent us from finding compelling reasons to do exactly what *we* want to do, rather than what *He* wants us to do. Obedience is different to following one's heart.

'Successful' work

As to outcomes for the one who does not acknowledge God – God said to Jeroboam, just before taking the kingdom out of the hands of Solomon, 'If you heed all that I command you, walk in my ways, and do what is right in my sight, to keep my statutes and my commandments, as my servant David did, then I will be with you and build for you an *enduring house*, as I built for David', 1Kings 11:38. As it happened, although Jeroboam became king and despite God's promise being real, he did not listen to God's word and there was consequently nothing enduring about his legacy – he was not 'successful' by any measure.

And as to outcomes for the believer – Paul said to the church at Corinth, 'No one can lay a foundation other than that which is laid, which is Jesus Christ. Now if anyone builds on the foundation with gold, silver, precious stones, wood, hay, straw – each one's work will become manifest, for the Day will disclose it, because it will be revealed by fire, and the fire will test what sort of work each one has done. If the work survives (*endures*), he will receive a reward. If anyone's work is burned up, he will suffer loss, though he himself will be saved, but only as through fire', 1 Corinthians 3:11-15. This confirms what we already know intuitively – God's value judgments are not the same as ours and He will ultimately apply His criteria to our work.

Callings are an explicit offer, on God's part, to have us partner with Him in His work and therefore they present an opportunity for us to engage in useful activity and to achieve results that will survive.

Fulfilling work

We can also point to qualitative differences in terms of fulfilment. For the unbeliever, who does not acknowledge a spiritual dimension and does not seek to engage with the God whose genius endowed them with skills, doing what they love to do can only provide a 'temporal' reward, in both the worldly and the time-related sense of the word.

For the believer, who is taking this journey in faith, the fulfilment I'm talking about is not just a combination of human emotions, it has a profoundly spiritual sense to it as well. As such, it goes some way beyond the experience that the subjects in Ken Robinson's research were testifying to. Indeed, an appropriate word for us to employ at this juncture might be 'joy'. Joy is robust, rooted in the character of God and able to display resilience in the face of difficulty, whereas 'happiness' is fleeting by comparison and, having its root in human emotion, is fickle and evaporates when faced with difficulty.

Fulfilment for the believer would appear to have at least two aspects to it which are additional to that experienced by the non-believer:

Resonance – the heightening or amplification of our spiritual senses...

In Exodus, the narrative about building the tabernacle talked about 'everyone whose heart stirred him/her up to come to do the work'. The quotation from Ephesians, that we have cited many times, talks about 'good works which God has prepared beforehand, so that we might enjoy our lives in the doing of them'.

This is describing a work of the Holy Spirit, who confirms and establishes something by witnessing to its 'rightness' and 'fitted-ness', and it is His activity that triggers the amplifying of the senses when we enter into something for which we were intended all along. It is a lifting of the spirits and a confirmation of 'destiny' that goes beyond the human emotions and touches something divine.

Joy results from being obedient to what God tells us to do – a principle that is confirmed by Jesus' words to His disciples in John 15:10,11, 'If you keep my commandments, you will abide in my love... These things I have spoken to you, that my joy may be in you, and that your joy may be full.'

Holistic involvement – the conscious engagement of all aspects of the human condition; physical, mental, emotional and spiritual...

In Matthew 22 and Mark 12 we have a lawyer being sent from the Pharisees to test Jesus by asking, 'Which is the great commandment in the Law?' This is not just any old question, it is *the question* – the burning question of Jesus' age: What is the one abiding principle of the Torah? Jesus' response was to quote not just one passage, which would be expected, but two. He knew the Pharisees, hypocrites that they were, usually allowed the two to conflict to suit their own purposes, so that they could choose which to be seen to obey.

He quotes from Deuteronomy 6:4,5, 'Hear, O Israel: The Lord our God, the Lord is one. You shall love the Lord your God with all your heart and with all your soul and with all your mind and with all your strength.' And then He gives them just the part of Leviticus 19:18 that is here underlined, 'You shall not take vengeance or bear a grudge against the sons of your own people, but you shall love your neighbour as yourself: I am the Lord.'

To digress for just a minute; the Pharisees would have known the whole verse by heart and, as the answer was relayed back to them, would not have been able to stop rehearsing the whole thing in their minds. Jesus deliberately wanted them to know which bits He was *not* saying. He was being provocative – not only did the Pharisees deliberately ignore their responsibilities towards family and their fellow Jewish brethren, in favour of an outward show of commitment to God, but He knew they were planning vengeance against Him and He was again stating His lordship. [This characteristic of Jesus' teaching method is best expounded in Ann Spangler and Lois Tverberg's book, *Sitting at the Feet of Rabbi Jesus* (Spangler, et al., 2017)]

In articulating this, the greatest commandment, Jesus is declaring the possibility that we might be awakened to an understanding of and a love for the God who made us, such that we are caught up in Him and wholly focussed. There is debate as to whether English translations of the Bible have rendered the original language correctly but, leaving that for others to resolve, 'heart, soul, mind and strength' is meant to indicate everything about us and therefore covers, at the very least, our desires, affections, purposes, imagination, will, feelings, character, thoughts and behaviours i.e. the real 'us' in all its entirety.

One can imagine this kind of involvement from time to time in worship but it is more difficult in the course of daily work. Nevertheless, Jesus is opening the way for it to be part of our experience, for us to focus on our callings so 'holistically' that not only are we fulfilled in the doing but love for 'our neighbour' follows on and our work spills over into ministry and mission.

Obeying His callings means that we can know we are in the place of His choosing; that our activity is 'for Him'; that our time, skills and creative energies are in a real sense 'dedicated to Him'; and, if possible, in the course of applying our whole selves to the work He gives us, we may also find our aptitudes fully engaged on a task that we are passionate about.

This last condition is the 'element condition' but, although it would make the task more rewarding, I am forced to conclude that it does not necessarily need to be met in order for us to please God and do lasting work. It is eclipsed by the need simply to pursue relationship with Jesus to want to fulfil the greatest command.

The temptation is always to take our eyes off Him and to focus on ourselves and our personal reward but we must resist that and look instead for those 'resonant' moments where our hearts are stirred up to do His work. As we keep our attention on Him, He can be depended upon to walk with us, to apply His grace to our efforts and to reward our obedience by giving us joy.

This is really only a restatement of the age-old injunction from Psalm 37:4, 'Delight yourself in the Lord, and He will give you the desires of your heart.' And again, Jesus' familiar words in Matthew 6:33 express the same truth, 'But seek first the kingdom of God and his righteousness, and all these things [that you are anxious about] will be added to you.' So, we need not worry about the tantalising goal of 'finding our element' because our obedience will inevitably bring us closer to it – let's instead regard it as the 'icing on the cake'.

Someone who did lasting work and found their element

There are many examples in the Bible of people who did vital and lasting work, who have become household names and any mention of them brings to mind one or more of the things they accomplished. If we had to talk about someone who pleased God and successfully followed their calling, we could choose from a long list of names.

However, when you look for documentary evidence that someone not only responded to God's calls, applied themselves obediently to His instructions, learned and developed their skills as they fulfilled the tasks, saw the work safely through to God's intended outcome *and* also absolutely loved the job they did, the list is a lot shorter. Let's be clear, it is not necessarily the case that the others *didn't* enjoy their calling it's just that we are not told that they had icing on their cake.

So, who to choose? My pick is not someone I thought of myself, he is someone my daughter suggested because she has a more agile brain than me and she uncovered what is probably the key fact about his cake that has the word 'icing' written all over it. It is Ezra.

For the Jews, the two people who have touched more lives for good than anyone else, over the past 2.5 millennia, are Moses and Ezra. In terms of historical impact, the two at the top of the list would probably be David and

181

Ezra. Moses' and David's contributions are known, even by those who are not well versed in biblical history, but Ezra's much less so. However, his position at the top of the list is well justified because he is responsible for devising the concept of the Jewish Synagogue (as a house of study as well as a centre of worship), for formalising the annual schedule of readings that the Jews still follow to this day and for copying all of what we know as the Old Testament scriptures into the Hebrew language.

Ezra was a scribe and a priest and a close relative of Joshua, the first high priest of what is known as the Second Temple – the one that was built in Jerusalem after the exile to Babylon. Ezra led a group of exiles, predominantly Levites, back to Jerusalem from Persia (Babylonia), with the blessing of King Artaxerxes, around 457BC. Ezra 7:9,10 says, 'He came to Jerusalem, for the good hand of the Lord was on him. For Ezra had set his heart to study the Law of the Lord, and to do it and to teach His statutes and rules in Israel'.

These verses make clear both his expertise and his motivation and they confirm that he was responding to the call of God. He was the most highly respected scholar in all of Babylon and, when he arrived 'back home', he duly introduced and established observance of the Torah among a people who had forgotten God's pattern of life for their nation. He was then ably assisted by Nehemiah, who returned from Persia a few years later, intent on rebuilding the walls of Jerusalem.

Ezra is author of the book of Ezra-Nehemiah, which was originally one scroll not two and, when it was first divided, was known as first and second Ezra. He was skilled in both Aramaic and Hebrew, being credited with creating the square letters that today are a standard part of the Hebrew script, and he was meticulous when it came to the recording of facts and figures. Jewish tradition, supported by other Bible scholars, also makes him the writer of probably 1 but definitely 2 Chronicles, along with parts of Kings and perhaps even a part of Jeremiah.

If you read Ezra-Nehemiah it is impossible not to appreciate Ezra's skill as a scribe, his attention to detail and his obvious passion for the Law of the Lord. If you read Chronicles it is also clear that he was a gifted historian. But is it enough to conclude that, in undertaking these important projects, he was not only working out his callings in obedience and in relationship with his God but had, in addition, found his element? Where is the evidence of 'icing'?

The fact that, for me, tips the balance and convinces me that Ezra had indeed been employed on tasks where his natural aptitudes had well and truly meshed with his personal passion, is that he also wrote Psalm 119.

This is the longest chapter in the Bible, a wisdom poem and passionate song of the heart, expressing love for the word of God. It is also an acrostic, with each of the twenty-two letters of the Hebrew alphabet beginning a section of eight verses, and, overall, eight different words being used for God's law, with one appearing in each of the 176 verses. In one of the sections of eight verses (verses 17-24) scholars see allusions to life in exile. God is mentioned in every verse but the writer refers to himself no less than 325 times, such is his complete identification with the law that he had committed himself to study and to pass on to his fellow Jews.

Ezra was entrusted by God with some absolutely vital tasks, which he executed zealously and with precision, the results of which were lasting, enduring up to and no doubt way beyond the present day. God knew that Ezra's focus was assured and that he had no intention of stealing the limelight and so He graciously gifted him with lots of icing on his cake.

Personal reflections on being in my element

When I sit and think about it, there have been several – maybe five or six – occasions in my life when I have genuinely felt as though I was in my element. Whilst I'm happy that there have been such experiences, all but one (or, at a push, two) of them happened outside of my regular employment. Moreover, that kind of testimony is relatively common – most people pay the bills, put food on the table and take the occasional holiday with the proceeds of paid work that they don't really enjoy.

In my case, as I have testified elsewhere, one instance of feeling 'in my element' came at a time when work was not productive or satisfying and when the company I was working for was not performing very well. I had always been interested in the concept of finding a match between a person's job and their capabilities and almost by accident, over a period of weeks in the early '90s, I was introduced to, and fell in love with, what I will call 'the antidote to psychometric testing'.

The technique in question, rather than have you answer a series of multiple-choice Qs, tick a few boxes and then turn a handle, involved taking time to compile meaningful personal data, about real happenings, across my whole life. Better still, it concentrated on those things that I had enjoyed doing and which had had a positive payoff. Having written them up, I was then interviewed and got to talk in more detail about some of the examples I'd provided. The interview was transcribed and then analysed and conclusions drawn from it.

As such it was a very data intensive exercise and obviously time-consuming for the analyst. Nevertheless, at the end of it, the results were, for me, mind-blowing. It felt as though, at long last, someone had discovered who I really am. Decades later, I still have that report and I am still that person.

Given that this technique appeared to offer the possibility of plugging people into more meaningful job roles, following my stint as guinea pig I studied the methodology further. Having discussed it with the experts, I was offered the chance to train as an analyst/consultant. This was a priceless opportunity to change career and to do something I would enjoy but I had a young family at the time and, even though the daily grind was just that, I let the cost of the training and the natural uncertainty of the change process get the better of me and I turned it down.

I am relating this for at least two reasons: firstly, to say that, like me, most people are change-averse. We are naturally reluctant to give up a regular salary, for doing something we think we understand, and accept a new and untested opportunity, to do something we don't yet understand and for which we might need a few additional skills. The second reason is because God is always around on these occasions and, if He grants an interlude where I 'mesh' with what I am doing and a little explosion goes off in my head, He won't then let a bit of fear, uncertainty, and doubt carry the day.

There were other 'element' moments in the years that followed, each providing a slightly different resonance but together giving a better picture of what I feel called to do. Then, after a long time, during which I learned a lot about the ups and downs of doing business in both the UK and the US, I ran into Nick Isbister, the person who had originally introduced me to the 'antidote to psychometric testing' and we connected as though there had been no time in between. He is a clever guy and, in the meantime, he and his wife (Jude Elliman) had developed the technology in very interesting ways. Once again, I became a guinea pig and studied the methodologies and this time, when the opportunity for training arose, I did not let it slip through my fingers.

I can be glad that it happened this way because I am approaching it differently to how it would have been back then. Nothing is wasted in God's economy and, in the interim, I have become better at listening to God and have had to face many things about myself – bad attitudes, emotional and relational disability, selfish ambitions and 'blindness' in various forms – about which I have had to repent and from which I have experienced a measure of healing. I think I am now more interested in what God wants than what I want and, as a result, have a clearer understanding of what He wants me to do.

For a number of years, whilst still in employment and now looking beyond that, the focus of my attention has not been on finding tasks where I can be 'in my element' but on asking God to give me His choice of 'useful' things to do.

An oft repeated prayer has been that I will be like those described in Psalm 92:12-15, 'The righteous... still bear fruit in old age; they are ever full of sap and green, to declare that the Lord is upright'. Using Jesus' terminology from the parable, in Matthew 20 – as the clock ticks round to a late hour of the day, we should not fall into the trap of thinking that the master has finished recruiting 'labourers for his vineyard'.

Bio #5 - Elizabeth

Those who were close to her – both members of her immediate family and some former colleagues – have variously described Elizabeth as 'enterprising', 'determined', 'focussed', 'intrepid', 'a strong personality' and sometimes even 'hard to live with'. However, had it not been for those qualities and attributes, it is most unlikely that, at the age of sixty, she would have grasped the chance to visit some poor communities in rural Kenya and then gone on to found a charity, with which she worked for seventeen years and which is still serving the Kenyan people today.

Elizabeth had a deep conversion experience in her early thirties, whilst listening to Archbishop Trevor Huddleston on the TV, and subsequently became involved in the early days of the charismatic movement. She endured a difficult marital break-up, being left to bring up her family alone, and then moved with the children to Oxford in 1979. A valuable friendship, forged with Michael Green, an evangelical theologian who had previously been Principal of St John's College Nottingham and was at the time rector of St Aldates Church in Oxford, proved to be the catalyst for Elizabeth's African adventure.

Her first visit to that continent came about because she had met a Kenyan Pentecostal pastor in 1984, to whom she had given accommodation in Oxford while he was attending a course of study. She learned from him some of the needs in his home area, in the west of the country, and of his desire to build a Bible college at Oyugis. The following year, Michael Green was due to go out to that region and Elizabeth asked him to investigate the situation near Oyugis. For reasons beyond his control, Michael had to cancel the trip and Elizabeth felt that she ought to go instead. Thus, something memorable was brought to birth.

We should digress here because the words used to describe Elizabeth, listed above, do not tell the whole story – she may have been intrepid but she was not impetuous; she may have been determined but she was also prayerful; she was a strong personality but she also looked to others for help and for confirmation of the rightness of a decision. Notes that she made, about a trip to Poland in 1982, illustrate the balance between these different sets of qualities [no facts have been changed but a little bit of literary licence has been taken in piecing the text together to create a coherent narrative]: *In November 1981, I was meditating on The Good Samaritan and praying for Poland. At that time, it [the country] was in great difficulties with communist Russia. There* were grave food and supply shortages. 'Solidarity' had been launched and the Gdansk dockyard had gone on strike. We [knew something of the situation first hand because we] had friends there, whom we had visited.

God told me to take a lorry to Poland with relief goods. I answered God, 'What, me? I am just an ordinary housewife.' However, the following evening I was due to attend a meeting with leaders from three different churches and so, whilst there, I asked three of the leaders, whom I knew well, what they thought. They all said, 'Yes, you should do it.'

[Elizabeth doesn't say *how* God told her but she appears to have had some sort of dialogue with Him whilst praying. Her modest reaction to the instruction and her immediate decision to submit to others and to seek confirmation were commendable and are both worthy of recall, should any of us find ourselves in a similar position.]

From there onward, God led us step by step. The first thing I did was to ring the editor of the local newspaper, who had recently become a Christian, and he arranged to send a reporter and a photographer. On the day in question, without my knowing it, a friend was told by God to 'go down to the house of the potter' [Elizabeth was a potter] and he arrived at the same time as the newspaper people and was able to pray in the background.

We got front-page news and a cover photo and people started ringing up and coming to offer their services. They were from every church and denomination. I was put in touch with many Polish people in Oxford and someone with secretarial experience offered to create an office and to man the phones.

Every morning we prayed and told God about our needs. St Matthew's Church offered to receive and to sort all the goods, as they came in, and we arranged for space in a barn outside Oxford in which to store them. We also arranged a street collection for the work but, on the day, there was thick snow and no traffic could move. Nevertheless, we went ahead and collected over £1500.

She then talks about being offered a transport container and packing boxes and amassing clothing, medical equipment, toys and food. She relates the acquiring of two vehicles (a caravanette and a lorry), packing and sending off the lorry for sea transport to Gdynia (close to Gdansk), the long wait in London for visas for those who would be travelling, the road journey that took several days, their arrival in a country experiencing serious unrest, curfews and protest marches and the process of getting the container released at Gdynia.

The plans were complex – some unloading, storage and distribution near Gdynia and some materials to be taken another 400 km to Warsaw. In the midst of it all they made two mistakes: With all this, we had not had the chance to go to the police to register, which later got us into trouble. We sent the lorry off to Warsaw and we followed (in the caravanette). On the way out of town we stopped to see the monument, designed by Yatzek, in the square before the *shipyard gates, and I was taking a photo when plain clothed policemen came and arrested us. We had to spend two days waiting to be interviewed by the magistrate, who finally let us go after we had paid a fine.*

It took time to locate the materials in Warsaw and to make arrangement for their distribution. They were then delayed by mechanical trouble on their exit from the country and had to get visas extended, finally getting home many days later. Despite this being something God both initiated and assisted with, every step of the way, Elizabeth learned many lessons. The immigration service in Gdansk had warned her that she would not be allowed to return to Poland and so the next container of supplies from England was taken by Poles and she never tried to go back. It certainly behoves us to be 'wise as serpents and innocent as doves'.

Four years later, on that first visit to Kenya, she adopted a more considered approach. An investigation of the needs 'on the ground' led her and other members of the St Aldates congregation to conclude that they should encourage community development for rural poor farmers, rather than the building of a Bible school.

By the end of 1986, Elizabeth had already visited Kenya three times and, as well as establishing relationship with many in the region, a training project had been set up; Amani UK had been born; and the work had attracted its first long-term volunteer. Books on various subjects, including agriculture, had also been obtained, for distance learning and support and for training local leaders and farmers in three different districts.

In a sermon that she preached in 1997, Elizabeth comments on that beginning: *When I first went to Kenya at the age of sixty, and saw the poverty of the rural poor, I felt that I should go out there. I shared my vision, of the needs of the whole man, with the body of Christ and asked the Christians and Churches that I knew to support me in prayer... I thought I would go for two to three years, and lived in a tent with my first volunteer whilst we got to know the people. After a time, when I could not see the future and was struggling, a colleague wrote from the UK, 'I think God is saying to you, "complete the work that you have started".' It kept me going through difficult times and so, eleven years later, I am still there.*

No work to which we are called by God will be without its difficulties and it can be vital to find people who will 'stand with us' in it. Their encouragement is often crucial to our survival. It is also entirely normal, at the outset, when experience is limited, to commit to a shorter, more manageable timeframe. As she states, Elizabeth's accommodation was a tent and we know that she was forced to return to the UK towards the end of 1986, suffering from hepatitis, and that the volunteer had to return to the UK in early 1987 after failing to get a work permit. However, the indomitable Elizabeth was back in Kenya a few months later, accompanied by a group of student volunteers and another tent, visiting schools, farmers and sick children and holding dressmaking classes.

A local landowner gave her a large piece of apparently useless land, at the top of a steep hill, but to Elizabeth it was a godsend. Later that same year, the charity's first building was started, providing accommodation for two staff, an office, a kitchen and a garage. The following year, a weekly ante-natal and baby clinic, under the auspices of the local diocese, began on the veranda of the completed building, with teaching meetings being held under a nearby tree. Then a circular chapel, with roof and open walls, was constructed, providing a dedicated space for worship and prayer.

It would be possible to go on to detail the progress, from those humble beginnings, over the following years, and to describe the various crises that threatened to engulf the project, along with the solutions that were found. But, what is most important here is to chart the way in which Elizabeth herself was led by God to spend the last quarter of her life intimately involved in the lives of the people of poor communities in rural Kenya.

Jane and John Woolmer, Elizabeth's daughter and son-in-law, wrote the following, in their book *The Grand Surprise*, about the legacy Elizabeth left and the inspiration that she was, both to those she worked with and to her wider family:

For some seventeen years, she lived much of the year in Kenya – first in tents and then in permanent buildings. The call involved her in a great deal of sacrifice (in health, with regular bouts of malaria; in finance; in struggles with local jealousies and against financial corruption) but there were many gains. The lives of poor farming families have been transformed by learning how to use their land better and, in some cases, by the precious gift of a cow! Many people have learned useful [new] skills; many have been employed; evangelism has been undertaken, particularly through the JAM Factory (Jesus And Me), which has inspired many young people and now has an independent life of its own. Medical health teaching has been delivered, especially concerning HIV, and many families now have improved and enriched diets.

Elizabeth's dedication has [also] inspired her grandchildren. All of our [John & Jane Woolmer's] family have spent serious time in Africa as a result of her lead, which has also influenced their faith. Rachel [John & Jane's eldest daughter] started the JAM Factory on one of her summer visits. Susie [another daughter] spent a lot of time in Uganda and launched a women's charity in Kabale. Tim [their son] helped to lead an effective mission in an area near Elizabeth's project and Katy [the youngest daughter] spent part of a gap year teaching in Tanzania. My [John Woolmer's] own call to be involved in short-term missions to Africa was made much clearer by seeing Elizabeth's inspiration and sacrifice. [Years later, Katy and her husband are full-time missionaries in Tanzania, working for CMS and leading a charity called Neema Crafts.] (Woolmer, 2004)

Elizabeth knew her limitations and, over the years, links were forged with a variety of other Kenya-based and UK organizations, to supplement and enrich the development programme and to supply complementary gifts and abilities to the work. She was also supported financially by a German Lutheran charity called 'Bread for the World'.

In 2000, Elizabeth's mother died at the age of ninety-eight and, whilst back in the UK, Elizabeth was introduced to Derek Hopwood, the Pastor of Holy Trinity, Hazlemere. She learned that an intended trip to Zimbabwe, by a group of school leavers and staff associated with the Church, had had to be cancelled and they were looking for an alternative destination. At Elizabeth's invitation, the group duly switched its attention to Kenya and went out to work with JAM. The link to Holy Trinity Hazlemere proved pivotal to the future of the work in Kenya with further teams of adults and young people going out from there over the next two–three years and one such adult, Jim Leftwich, emerging as the person best suited and equipped to take over from Elizabeth.

By 2002/3 Elizabeth was seventy-seven and ready for someone else to assume her responsibilities. Jim stepped up and was just in time to discover that a serious fraud had been perpetrated by a Kenyan worker on the ground. Elizabeth played a key role in the joint operation to resolve this issue – her wisdom and seasoned advice were crucial in the plan for protecting the work and in making the difficult decision to restructure Amani, splitting the project into two separate and independent units, both of which are flourishing – one led by UK trustees with local African leaders and the other administered entirely by locals.

She was an ordinary woman whom God used for an extraordinary purpose and her story shows that a new beginning can occur at any point in life – reaching retiring age is no obstacle to God. People at that stage may reflect on their lives and realize that there are things they had always felt drawn to but never followed up. Despite her intrepid nature, it still took courage on Elizabeth's part to get up and go to Africa. Many of us are less inclined towards adventure and may need more resolve and greater certainty before we step out but let us be encouraged by Elizabeth's example.

Sources:

- Testimony and recollections of John & Jane Woolmer and Jim Leftwich;
- Amani UK Website (Amani UK - Charity No. 1073357);
- *The Grand Surprise* (Woolmer, 2004).

189

Chapter 12

What Happens After You Are Called – Re-telling an Old Story

When you are aware of God having spoken to you about a long-term calling or a short-term commission, change is in the wind and a new chapter in the story of your life is about to begin. Needless to say, there are myriad alternative scenarios that we could dream up to try to describe what might happen next but most can be distilled into a set of general principles. If you are aware of those, you are likely to avoid major error. Instead of launching into a list, however, let's look at a real-life example, in which many of the principles are illustrated.

Nehemiah gets a call and feels its 'weight'

The year is 444 BC and it is now fourteen years since Ezra, the priest and scribe, left the capital of the Persian empire with 1800 Levites, in order to restore both the rule of law and the structure of worship for the people of Israel in Jerusalem.

It is also just over ninety years since Zerubbabel, of the royal line and directly descended from King David, along with Joshua the high priest and 50,000 Jews, had left the capital of what was then the Babylonian empire, with the Emperor Cyrus' blessing, in order to re-colonise Israel and rebuild the temple in Jerusalem.

By the time we get to 444 BC, it is more than 160 years since the Jews were first taken into exile in Babylon by the Chaldeans. In the meantime, Babylon has been conquered by the Medes and Persians and, over the years, by God's grace and through the prophecy of men such as Jeremiah and the wise governance of men such as Daniel, the Jews have prospered. Indeed, a great many Jews chose never to return 'home'.

Nehemiah, a Jew who had been born in captivity (obviously!), is going about his daily duties in Susa, the Persian capital, as cup-bearer to King Artaxerxes. It is interesting to speculate on how he came to that position – Artaxerxes was the stepson of Queen Esther who, aided and abetted by her older cousin Mordechai, had thwarted Haman's plan to exterminate the Jews.

191

Artaxerxes had grown up to be sympathetic toward the Jewish people and their culture and many think it was the direct influence of Esther that led to Nehemiah's appointment, as someone who was known to be both trustworthy and loyal.

There were both good and bad aspects to the job of cup-bearer. It was a senior and very responsible position, which was good. It afforded a relaxed relationship with the king because the cup-bearer was a close confidant, which was very good. However, you literally never knew whether the next taste of the king's wine would be your last – if someone had the notion of getting rid of Artaxerxes by poisoning his drink, Nehemiah's job was to save the king by sacrificing himself, which was not so good.

All had not been going well back in Jerusalem – bulletins from the province spoke of hostility from the Samaritans, disagreement among the Jews, long periods of inactivity on the building projects, a breakdown in the rule of law and a lack of religious zeal – and when some Jews arrive in Susa, from Judah, Nehemiah makes a point of asking them for news. Nehemiah 1:1,3 tells us, 'in the month of Chislev... Hanani... and certain men from Judah... said to me, "The remnant there in the province who had survived the exile is in great trouble and shame. The wall of Jerusalem is broken down, and its gates are destroyed by fire."'

Their words have a devastating effect on Nehemiah – if he hadn't realized, up to this point, the degree to which his own heart's desires were tied up with the state of his homeland, he definitely knew it now. Nehemiah may be trustworthy and loyal but he now finds himself conflicted.

First response – pray

Nehemiah 1:4 says, '*As soon as* I heard these words I sat down and wept and mourned for days, and I continued fasting and praying before the God of heaven.'

This was a big deal because it caused Nehemiah, as stated in the next few verses, wholly to identify with the people of Israel, to put himself in their position, to confess their sins as though they were his own, to invoke the promises made by God to Moses and to call on the God of heaven to grant favour with the only person he knew to be humanly capable of affecting the situation.

His prayer, set out in verses 5-11, is remarkable not just because of its heart-felt honesty and fervour but also because it shows him, though several generations removed from those who were originally exiled from Judah, to be a student of the Hebrew scriptures and familiar with the ways of God. It was not an outbreak of emotionalism, it was a deep longing for God's purposes to be worked out. Nehemiah found himself in step with the God who had spoken to Moses both about the consequences of unfaithfulness and the redemption that would result from Israel returning to the Lord.

When was the last time something like that happened to you – when you became so concerned for a situation that you felt compelled to embark on a period of fasting and prayer for its resolution? Calls can come completely 'out of the blue' but it is more likely that the recipient has already been 'sensitized' in some way to a need or a situation. When God speaks to us we will usually have some familiarity with what He is talking about or be aware of the importance of the opportunity or the project or the role. The word from God has the effect of highlighting that importance and it awakens a heightened sense of interest – what we were previously aware of somehow assumes a vividness and immediacy that it didn't have before. There is an imperative to recognize its importance.

Elsewhere in this book, I have used the word 'resonance' to describe this phenomenon – there's a coming together of, on the one hand, facts and observations and possibly words spoken to us and, on the other hand, an intervention on the part of God's Spirit, which creates a reaction in us that is out of proportion to the facts themselves but is actually more proportional to how God himself is feeling about the issue. We have a nature that is 'de-sensitized' to the heart of God and which generally doesn't allow us to see things as He does – from time to time, He gives us a glimpse.

The first thing we must do when this happens; when we sense that God is speaking to us about a need or an opportunity or a project or a role – our very first response, having heard what might be a call – is to take it seriously and pray. Prayer is utterly vital because, if God is speaking to us, we need to speak back to Him and to 'discuss' the issue. We can expect that He, having either initiated a conversation or responded to some request from us, will have important information to pass on concerning both the need and our conduct.

Second response – ask God for a strategy & then obey it

Was Nehemiah aware of a 'call' on his life as he prayed these prayers? Did he know what God was telling him to do? If it wasn't altogether clear by this time, it was most definitely taking shape but, despite having a good job and being in a relatively comfortable position, Nehemiah was still in service to a ruthless regime and thus not free to make his own decisions. He did not fire off a quick prayer and then hope for the best, he 'wept and mourned for days, and [I] continued fasting and praying before the God of heaven.' In other words, he gave the call time to sink in and time for God to continue the conversation. He needed to know what he should do and, if a solution was to be found, other influential people, who did not worship the God of heaven, would also need to see the need and commit to action.

God seems to have told Nehemiah to hold back from making this thing known and we can learn a lot from his restraint. He was wrestling with very strong inclinations and becoming more and more determined that something decisive must be done for the Jewish cause but, other than seeking to understand the facts about life back in Judah, we have no indication that his inner turmoil showed itself to anyone other than his immediate family and friends.

He certainly took care not to betray his inner feelings when in the presence of the king but, about three months later, there came a day when he could not bury them out of sight any longer. Nehemiah 2:1-5 says, 'In the month of Nisan... I took up wine and gave it to the king. Now I had not been sad in his presence. And the king said to me, "Why is your face sad, seeing you are not sick? This is nothing but sadness of the heart." Then I was very much afraid. I said to the king, "Let the king live forever! Why should not my face be sad, when the city, the place of my father's graves, lies in ruins, and its gates have been destroyed by fire?" Then the king said to me, "What are you requesting?" So, I prayed to the God of heaven. And I said to the king, "If it pleases the king, and if your servant has found favour in your sight, that you send me to Judah, to the city of my father's graves, that I may rebuild it."'

There it is – the actual moment when a word from the Lord which, for a period of weeks, had been altering a man's perspective on life, bringing him conviction about what he must now do and giving him anguish of heart, is spoken out. And it's as if it hangs in the air.

We have to pause because there is a yawning gap between the end of v5 and the beginning of v6 – between making the request and getting the answer; between articulating the audacious plan and getting it approved (or otherwise). When dealing with a call or a commission, there is always a moment a bit like this – maybe not quite so dramatic but wherever God's Spirit has taken initiative to deliver a message and it has resonated with the spirit of a man or woman and a new purpose has been planted deep in his or her heart, there is a point when it has to be communicated and it is 'out there'. It's a point of no return.

Nehemiah has not only told the king what *he feels about* the state of life in Judah, he has declared what *he believes God wants him to do about* the situation. What was formerly a *concern* has now officially become a *call*. Please note what he says in verses 4-5, immediately after the king asks him what he's requesting, 'So I prayed to the God of heaven. And I said to the King...' It's a good principle – pray first, speak later.

If God has spoken, He knows what you need

We are not told how long it took Artaxerxes and his wife to respond to Nehemiah's request but a conversation follows during which details of the trip are agreed and then letters are written, building materials and other supplies are gathered, a travelling party is prepared and an accompanying escort is

194

provided. As always, God demonstrates His command both over those who believe and those who don't believe and He ensures that sufficient resource is allocated for the job that must be done.

Some things that God asks us to do are short term and the doing of them is not a resource-hungry process – indeed, we might be well able to go forward and reach the objective using existing resources. But some things are longer term and might be life changing and most definitely require resources that we do not currently possess. It is perfectly possible that to embark on the call will threaten our livelihood or require a change of status or entail a change of direction.

The operative words are 'change' and 'threat' and we are not good at handling either of those. I cannot offer you comfort at this point, except to say that this whole process is about you and God and He knows you intimately and will not let you down. Furthermore, He is cleverer than you or me and, although we might think we can see the next couple of moves in the game, He can see all the way to the solution. All 'calls' that He issues are challenges and the biggest aspect of the challenge is whether you will trust Him, particularly through difficulty and opposition.

Good works can attract bad people

The king's letters authorise Nehemiah's safe passage to Judah, appoint him as de facto governor of the province [5:14] and authorise him to take control of the building process. But, as soon as he arrives, another key principle of 'what happens after you sense a calling' is demonstrated: wherever God's purposes are out in the open the opposition will begin to show itself.

We are told that, no sooner has Nehemiah handed over to the existing governors of the province the letters written by the king, 'Sanballat the Horonite and Tobiah the Ammonite heard this, [and] it displeased them greatly that someone had come to seek the welfare of the people of Israel' Nehemiah 2:9,10. Why these two? The Horonites and the Ammonites were two of the Canaanite people groups that God had driven from the Promised Land when He had allocated it to the Israelites. Given the absence of Israelites, due to the exile, Sanballat and Tobiah (and Geshem) had seized the opportunity to acquire influence. They had been appointed as regional officials, serving under the king of Persia, and they did not want anybody to threaten their power base.

That they were only interested in their own personal power and influence, rather than using their responsibility to develop and improve life in Jerusalem, is shown by there having been no house building or wall repairs or other infrastructure improvements in the city for many years, until Nehemiah came on the scene. The exiles who had returned previously were living in towns and villages outside a civic centre that still lay in ruins. Evidence for that conclusion is found in Nehemiah 7:4 – after the wall had been finished and Nehemiah was posting guards on the new gates we read, 'The city was wide and large, but the people within it were few, and no houses had been rebuilt.'

Start well – obey the strategy and gather the facts

Having arrived back 'home', Nehemiah did not move in with 'all guns blazing' – he was extremely circumspect. You have to think that, at the outset, God had instructed him how to proceed and to take great care over communication. He says, 'I went to Jerusalem and was there three days. Then I arose in the night, I and a few men with me. And I told no one what my God had put in my heart to do for Jerusalem.' Nehemiah 2:11,12. He carries out a detailed inspection of the city walls, lasting several hours, with nobody to observe or interrupt, and then returns. 'And the officials did not know where I had gone or what I was doing, and I had not yet told the Jews, the priests, the nobles, the officials, and the rest who were to do the work.' Nehemiah 2:16.

This was a wise strategy, especially since it was clear to Nehemiah that both teamwork and complex project management would be required if anything meaningful was to be done about the walls. Before launching into action and possibly inviting questions that he would not be able to answer, it behoves him to gather the facts; to understand the full extent of the task, to get some idea of manpower requirements, to plot likely timescales and to calculate probable costs.

As we have stated previously, it is quite rare for God to issue a calling to someone without it being necessary for that someone to team up with others. They will either need to enlist the help of other people or to fall in with those whose vision requires a someone with their particular aptitude and passion. In Nehemiah's case, there is nobody else with vision and no other initiatives have been taken. He knows that God has called him to exercise leadership and project management and he knows that, even with the willing help of the Jews, the priests, the nobles, the officials and the rest, it will require the strong arm of the Lord – as he says in 6:16, 'When all of our enemies heard of it [that the wall had been finished], all the nations around us were afraid and fell greatly in their own esteem, for they perceived that this work *had been accomplished with the help of our God.*'

As Nehemiah undertakes the work of rebuilding the walls and of introducing much needed social reform among the Jews, whilst at the same time fending off the unwelcome attentions of Sanballat, Tobiah, Geshem and their associates, we see various other principles demonstrated.

Fear God, not the enemy

When I compare Nehemiah to myself and to most of the people I have ever known, his single-mindedness, motivation, refusal to look for gain or reward and refusal to be intimidated by those who were opposed to the work are really impressive! He attributes it to a 'fear of the Lord'.

Nehemiah 5:14,15 says, 'Moreover, from the time that I was appointed to be their governor in the land of Judah, from the twentieth year until the thirty-second year of King Artaxerxes, twelve years, neither I nor my brothers ate the governor's provisions. But the former governors who were before me laid burdens on the people, and took from them bread and wine, besides forty shekels of silver. Yes, even their servants bore rule over the people, but I did not do so, because of *the fear of God*.'

So important was this quality to Nehemiah that, when he was looking for somebody to be overseer of Jerusalem, at the conclusion of the building work, he says the following: 'Then it was, when the wall was built and I had hung the doors, when the gatekeepers, the singers, and the Levites had been appointed, that I gave the charge of Jerusalem to my brother Hanani, and Hananiah the leader of the citadel, for he was a faithful man and *feared God more than many*' (Nehemiah 7:2). Despite their other skills, it was a fear of the Lord that, in Nehemiah's opinion, made people into good and reliable leadership material.

There is a telling statement in Proverbs 1:7: 'The fear of the Lord is the beginning of knowledge; fools despise wisdom and instruction.' If, as we have stated previously, God is in the habit of commissioning and calling people who will be required to gain knowledge and to learn new skills in order to fulfil His intentions, this quality of 'the fear of the Lord' assumes critical importance. The inference is that, *not* to have it makes us foolish and unable to gain wisdom and heed instruction. Both the person of Jesus and the conduct of the early Church uphold this same principle:

- Isaiah prophesied of Jesus in chapter 11:1-4, 'There shall come forth a shoot from the stump of Jesse, and a branch from his roots shall bear fruit. And the Spirit of the Lord shall rest upon him, the Spirit of wisdom and understanding, the Spirit of counsel and might, the Spirit of knowledge and *the fear of the Lord*. And his delight shall be in the fear of the Lord. He shall not judge by what his eyes see, or decide disputes by what his ears hear, but with righteousness he shall judge the poor, and decide with equity for the meek of the earth.'
- Then, in Acts 9:31 we read, 'So the church throughout all Judea and Galilee and Samaria had peace and was being built up. And *walking in the fear of the Lord* and the comfort of the Holy Spirit, it multiplied.' So, when the Holy Spirit was poured out and the Church was born, the condition under which it flourished was a healthy fear of the Lord.

Taking all these references together, it looks as though we have discovered the magic ingredient that, if we have it, will ensure success. The fear of the

Lord is not just an inhibitor, in the sense that it acts as a check or a balance or a guide, it is a catalyst for growth, a key to understanding, an antidote to intimidation and a powerful motivator for fulfilling God's purposes.

Let's be honest – when we are engaged in the Lord's work, there will be regular temptations to promote our own wellbeing, to enhance our personal standing and reputation and to increase our wealth. There will also be attempts either to divert us from the path or to stop us in our tracks through fear or discouragement or altered objectives. Only a healthy fear of the Lord has the power to fend off what would otherwise be an inevitable fall from grace. The pages of the Bible, and of history since that time, are littered with the corpses of those who failed to maintain theirs in good health.

In Nehemiah's case, he had been appointed governor by King Artaxerxes and so his enemies could not challenge that position. So, their only options were either to resort to violence or to question his integrity by suggesting he intended to overstep the authority conferred on him. However, Nehemiah's fear of the Lord ensured that he was not intimidated or diverted from his primary task when both these methods were attempted.

Nehemiah 6:1-14 describes the attempts made to remove control of the work from Nehemiah's hands. First, a series of seemingly innocent invitations came from Sanballat, Tobiah and Geshem, to meet and talk 'in the plain of Ono' but Nehemiah knows that 'they intended to do me harm'. If this had been a pantomime we'd have seen the obvious clue in the place name, telling him what his response ought to be! When that attempt failed, the bad guys followed up with an unsubtle letter of accusation, suggesting that Nehemiah's intention, in rebuilding Jerusalem, was to seek kingship.

His response, in writing, to their letter is most refreshing - 'No such things as you say have been done, for you are inventing them out of your own mind' (verse 8). Sometimes we need to be strong and unequivocal in our response in order to shut down the nonsense that is aimed at thwarting the work of God. One of Nehemiah's great strengths is his continual conversation with God that provides him with ongoing instruction and helps to discern peoples' true intent. As he says, in verse 9, 'For they all wanted to frighten us, thinking, "Their hands will drop from the work, and it will not be done." But now, O God, strengthen my hands.'

Take sides and stand up for justice & righteousness

Chapter 5 of Nehemiah deals with social and economic reform among the returned exiles and concludes with testimony to the example set by Nehemiah himself. Although his primary task was to rebuild the city's defences and to attend to essential infrastructure, his secondary task was to attend to the welfare of those for whom he had been given responsibility. Not to have addressed the issues of inequality and oppression that were prevalent among the Jews would have undermined the value of restoring the walls and the gates.

The Jewish nobles and officials, who were wealthy compared to most ordinary people, had been exploiting their poorer brothers. Those with limited resource struggled to feed their families and to pay their taxes and had borrowed money. For many, their only recourse had been either to mortgage their land or to sell their children into slavery, or both. In lots of cases, fields and children had been sold to non-Jewish people and, as part of a commitment to reform, Nehemiah had been redeeming them from the surrounding nations. The Jewish nobles and officials, on the other hand, were gobbling up pieces of land, exacting usury on loans and making a profit by trading property and slaves with people of the nations around. As Nehemiah 5:1 says, 'there arose a great outcry of the people and of their wives against their Jewish brothers.'

Nehemiah's response is brilliant – 'I was very angry when I heard the outcry... I took counsel with myself, and I brought charges against the nobles and the officials. I said to them, "You are exacting interest, each from his brother." And I held a great assembly against them and said to them, "We, as far as we are able, have bought back our Jewish brothers who have been sold to the nations, but you even sell your brothers that they may be sold [back] to us!" They were silent and could not find a word to say. So I said, "The thing you are doing is not good. Ought you not to walk in the fear of our God to prevent the taunts of the nations, our enemies? Moreover, I and my brothers and my servants are lending them money and grain. Let us abandon this exacting of interest. Return to them this very day their fields, their vineyards, their olive orchards, and their houses, and the percentage of money, grain, wine and oil that you have been exacting from them." Then they said, "We will restore these and require nothing from them. We will do as you say".'

Note that Nehemiah's main objective is that the Jewish officials should 'walk in the fear of our God'. He knows that, otherwise, having been shamed into changing their behaviour, they will soon revert to lining their own pockets once again.

If it's God's work, He will come alongside to help

God doesn't give us 'noddy' tasks to do – His commissions and calls will often stretch us, not only requiring that we find others to assist but also, from time to time, presenting a workload that either seems too heavy or too difficult. This was the case for Nehemiah – he had produced a detailed plan and secured a large team of workers but the work was hard and tiring and long and there was constant threat from cunning enemies that spread fear and sapped people's strength.

Nevertheless, we are told in Nehemiah 6:15,16, 'So the wall was finished on the twenty-fifth day of the month Elul, in fifty-two days. And when all our enemies heard of it, all the nations around us were afraid and fell greatly in their own esteem, for they perceived that this work had been accomplished with the help of our God.'

What a wonderful statement – '[they] fell greatly in their own esteem'! Thus, it is and will ever be for all who oppose the purposes of God. So, as we've said above, do not be afraid when people oppose your 'good work' because your God will fight for you.

Finish well – it's as important as starting well

Nehemiah 5:14 suggests that Nehemiah spent twelve years as governor of Judah before returning to Susa. In chapter 13:6,7, after an unspecified amount of time, we are told that he asked leave of King Artaxerxes to go back to Jerusalem. Given what he found there we have to assume he had received news of double dealings by senior officials and a failure by many others to comply with God's rules.

God's good works, that He gives us to do, will always require us, and those with whom we are working, to align more closely with His ways. And we know, from our own experience, that reform of lifestyle and operating by different rules, followed by long-term compliance, is extremely difficult to achieve. I have often lamented that, even among those who own Jesus as Lord, too few people exhibit the effects of Jesus' Lordship and even fewer demonstrate lasting change.

Nehemiah was not prepared to see all the good work go to waste and therefore, having travelled back to Jerusalem, he investigated and discovered four major problems. He went on to determine who were the guilty parties and, having established the facts, he began to 'throw his weight about'. He was fully justified in doing so because, after the wall had been finished:

- Ezra had read the law to the assembled multitude of Israel [chapter 8];
- The people had confessed their sin and committed themselves to God in prayer [chapter 9];
- A solemn covenant had been drawn up, the obligations of which were very clear [chapter 10]:

  o to separate themselves from the people of the nations around;
  o not to trade on the Sabbath;
  o to give regularly to the service of the house of God and for those performing the service;
  o and to bring in their tithes and the first fruits of their produce and their herds.

- A census had then been taken and the wall had been dedicated [chapters 11 & 12].

But, what were the four things that Nehemiah found on his return to Jerusalem [chapter 13]?

- A senior priest, who was related by marriage to Tobiah, had prepared a place for Tobiah within the courts of the house of God – admitting a declared enemy of both God and His people into the very place that had been sanctified for worship. It is noticeable that Nehemiah did not hold back – offending people or hurting their feelings did not concern him because he feared the Lord. He threw all of Tobiah's furniture and belongings out of the chamber and then gave orders to have it cleansed of his presence;
- The Levites, and others appointed to minister in the temple, were not being provided for. Remember that these people were supposed to be 'paid' for their service by receiving portions from sacrifices and offerings. The offerings were not being made, the Levites had gone back to their fields and the service was not being performed. So, Nehemiah re-established the correct practices;
- The Sabbath rules were being transgressed by merchants of various nationalities, selling all kinds of produce, who were being admitted to the city and carrying on normal business on that day. Once again, Nehemiah's solution took no prisoners – he closed the gates of Jerusalem at dusk on a Friday and forbade them to be opened until the Sabbath was over. He also threatened those who chose to camp outside the gate with punishment and confiscation of their goods;
- Worst of all, many of the Jews had married 'foreign women' and the language and culture of the forbidden nations had become ingrained in their families. It even turned out that the grandson of the high priest had married the daughter of Sanballat, one of the arch enemies of all God's purposes for Jerusalem. Nehemiah treated the perpetrators harshly, squaring up to them physically, and in a classic example of biblical understatement, 'cleansed them from everything foreign'! – Nehemiah 13:30.

What a story! It was by no means an easy call, either to receive or to carry through, but there are not many other biblical characters with as much resolve and determination as Nehemiah. He is quoted as saying, at the end of the narrative, 'Remember me, O my God, for good.' Nehemiah 13v31. Rightly so, because he finished well.

It is my hope that we too, being able to connect with, receive, embark on and complete calls from God, will also finish them well and find ourselves progressively coming to resemble the likeness of Christ.

Chapter 13

What Happens After You Are Called – Telling a New Story

Yours is a new and different story

We have just been relating what happened to Nehemiah. We could not have done that if Ezra hadn't written it all down for posterity. The books of Ezra and Nehemiah were not originally separate from each other, they were one. Each has exactly the same structure as the other and, although Ezra travelled back to Jerusalem about fourteen years before Nehemiah, they worked together once Nehemiah arrived there and Ezra, being a scribe and meticulous by nature, is credited with putting it all down in writing.

Each life is a unique story, unlike that of any other person, and its twists and turns, setbacks and failures, positive interventions and successes read like no other story. That's why all those whose short biography is included in this book either had or still have different narratives to relate. They responded and reacted differently from each other, they possessed or possess different sets of skills and abilities and each had or has a different set of objectives from the Lord.

No two people you read of in the Bible have the same story because God revealed Himself to them and led them differently and did His sovereign work in them His own unique way. Similarly, no two people that you speak to today, who can testify to having a sense of calling or to having undertaken tasks in direct response to God's leading, will tell you the same story.

We have suggested throughout this book that the receipt of a call or a commission from God could come in a variety of ways – it's not necessarily going to be like Mission Impossible with a divine voice saying, 'Your mission, Ethan, should you decide to accept it, is…', but it might be a Bible verse that leaps off the page or a comment heard in conversation or a point made in a sermon or a sense that comes in a dream or a growing realization of something that grips you with purpose or a task that in the doing seems to resonate with who you are.

It doesn't really matter *how* it is received. What really matters is that you are aware of having heard or sensed something important. In other words, there was a time when you didn't know it, but now you do know it. Furthermore, now that you know it, God's word needs to be allowed to do its work in you and you need to prepare your response.

Prepare for a new adventure

Since you have heard something from Him and, as a result, will be 'about your Father's business', stop and take stock of the situation. When He speaks, His words always have life-affirming, character-building and relationship-developing qualities and so, as well as kingdom development, there is already the promise of personal development.

However big your objection to being changed and developed and however many are the apparent obstacles, God's words always have purpose and they possess the innate power to *create* and so, in terms of both kingdom and personal development, there is already the promise of new things coming into being, things that are not there at present.

God is experienced at making things out of nothing – He used words to create the world in the first place ('Divine Fiat') and we must not lose sight of the fact that His word will come to us accompanied by the power to bring into being the thing He has said. So, do not take the voice of the Lord lightly.

This is the beginning of a new adventure and, as with any adventure, there is preparation to be made, advice to be sought, equipment to gather and good practice to imitate. I am going to suggest, over the coming pages, that success may depend on carefully attending to some or all of the following:

- Decide what to communicate and who to communicate with – be wise about who you tell and what you tell them;
- Deal with self-doubt but be realistic about your personal capabilities – remember that God usually gives people things to do that require them to learn new skills;
- Take confidence from the fact that God has spoken to you and then seek and be expectant for Him to provide both confirmation of the call and ongoing instruction about the *what*, the *how* and the *when* – it's His work;
- Engage with an active support network – it may be just one or two other individuals or it may be a group – because the successful realization of a call or commission usually requires the encouraging presence and possibly also the practical help of others. There are several aspects to this:

  o Learn what it means to 'stand with' someone, as was described in Chapter 8;

- o Know what role(s) you need to play - you may be the one to whom a call has come or you may know someone for whom that is the case. As such, you might be the one seeking support or the one being asked to give support to another;
- o If you are the one to whom the call has come, construct a truthful and coherent 'story' to describe what is happening – anchored in reality, devoid of delusion, honest about objectives and outcomes – and then tell it. Doing that will help you to make sense of what is happening;
- o If you are supporting another person, tease out and listen generously to their story and then 'look out for them';

- Determine whether you yourself need some additional skills and/or whether another's complementary skills, are required. You will have to trust Him for what you yourself need, because the call is almost always to something that we are not yet and a lack of skill has never been a disqualification. Exodus 28-32 makes clear that all those *whose hearts stirred them to be part of the work* and to whom God gave a 'spirit of skill' were able to learn the necessary skill;
- Adopt the 'business plan' approach – always be aware of the now, the not yet and the space in between;
- Prepare to be changed – like everyone else, you will be change-averse to some degree but the call will inevitably affect some or all of lifestyle, attitude, knowledge, skill set, livelihood and world view and, if the outcome is to be successful, you will have to be altered for the better;
- Get ready to cope with delays and reversals and a timescale that is dictated by God because, among other things, the journey is sometimes as important as the end result and He knows what has to be learned along the way;
- Get ready to face opposition – if it's His work it will, by definition, be opposed.

Your story will be different but, if you are going to make sense of the process and maintain an honest and objective grip on reality, it will be helpful (and sometimes vital) for there to be witnesses. It is your choice as to who is invited to share the adventure, as it unfolds, but narrative integrity and personal accountability facilitate and enable effective progress.

A time to be silent and a time to speak

Nehemiah showed himself a master at knowing when to keep things to himself and when to share the facts. When God speaks – or you think He has spoken to you – it is between you and Him. How should you conduct yourself and what should you say? The best answer is to ask Him and then do what He tells you.

The Bible is chock-full of instances where God gave angels or men or women or children something to say and instructed them who to say it to – it could be the delivery of a message; an explanation of what has already happened; an explanation of what is about to happen; the passing on of instructions; the telling of a story or parable to illustrate a truth; the proclamation of some good news etc. – but there are also instances where the opposite is true... in other words, where we are supposed to keep quiet.

Jesus, for example, on several occasions, specifically told people *not* to say anything about what had just happened. He had good reason for issuing such an instruction – He knew that, if news got out about what he'd just done, His movement would be severely restricted:

- Mark 1:40-45 – 'A leper came to him, imploring him, and kneeling said to him, "If you will, you can make me clean." Moved with pity, he stretched out his hand and touched him and said to him, "I will; be clean." And immediately the leprosy left him, and he was made clean. And Jesus sternly charged him and sent him away at once, and said to him, "See that you say nothing to anyone, but go, show yourself to the priest and offer for our cleansing what Moses commanded, for a proof to them." But he went out and began to talk freely about it, and to spread the news, so that Jesus could no longer openly enter a town, but was out in desolate places, and people were coming to him from every quarter.'
- Mark 7:31-37 – Some people brought a deaf man to Jesus: 'Immediately his ears were opened, and the impediment of his tongue was loosed, and he spoke plainly. Then He commanded them that they should tell no one; but the more He commanded them, the more widely they proclaimed it. And they were astonished beyond measure, saying, "He has done all things well. He makes both the deaf to hear and the mute to speak."'
- Mark 8:25,26 – A blind man at Bethsaida: 'Then He put His hands on his eyes again and made him look up. And he was restored and saw everyone clearly. Then He sent him away to his house, saying, "Neither go into the town, nor tell anyone in the town."'
- Mark 9:9,10 – The transfiguration: 'Now as they came down from the mountain, He commanded them that they should tell no one the things they had seen, till the Son of Man had risen from the dead. So they kept this word to themselves, questioning what the rising from the dead meant.' NKJV

The final example illustrates that, although Peter, James and John were forbidden, in the short term, to speak about what they had seen, there would be a time when it was permitted to do so. God's instructions regarding communication are usually strategic in nature.

Dealing with internal and external opposition

Realizing a calling, once you have received it, is a major subject. Even if the *what* is fairly clear, the *when* and the *how* can be problematic.

The short biographies, inserted throughout this book, describe real people who are all very different from each other in terms of background, personality, skill set, cultural context and objective. The pathway that each has followed has been different and the obstacles varied. Some let their call lie dormant for a long time before picking it up again and running with it – indeed, for some, the major challenge has been how to get started. For others, enterprise and determination has not been lacking but they have encountered significant opposition.

If God has a purpose – and you need constantly to remind yourself that it's His work and He initiates it in us – you can be sure there will be opposition and it can come from inside or from outside or both. What might surprise you is that opposition from inside is often more dangerous than from an external enemy. As we said in Chapter 2, after receiving a sense of calling it is likely that, within a very short time, several other thoughts will try to counter it – 'That can't be right' or 'I'm not trained to do that' or 'I'm not good enough' or 'I could never make a living doing that' or 'That role/position is too up-front or important or senior for someone like me'. Even if the call is to something short term and relatively simple there will still be a tendency to find obstacles – 'I've never done that before' or 'I'm not eloquent enough' or 'I'm no good at handling conflict' or 'They'll never believe me' or 'Nobody else seems to be thinking this way'.

There is nothing unusual about this type of response and the list of biblical characters who expressed something very similar is legendary:

- Moses to God – 'Who am I that I should go to Pharaoh and bring the children of Israel out of Egypt?' 'But behold, they [the people of Israel] will not believe me or listen to my voice, for they will say, "The Lord did not appear to you".' 'Oh, my Lord, I am not eloquent, either in the past or since you have spoken to your servant, but I am slow of speech and of tongue.' 'Oh, my Lord, please send someone else.' Exodus 3&4
- Saul to Samuel – 'Am I not a Benjaminite, from the least of the tribes of Israel? And is not my clan the humblest of all the clans of the tribe of Benjamin? Why then have you spoken to me in this way?' 1 Samuel 9
- Isaiah in response to his vision – 'Woe is me! For I am lost; for I am a man of unclean lips; for my eyes have seen the King, the Lord of hosts!' Isaiah 6

- Jeremiah to God – 'Ah, Lord God! Behold, I do not know how to speak, for I am only a youth.' Jeremiah 1
- Zechariah to the angel – 'How shall I know this? For I am an old man, and my wife is advanced in years.' Luke 1

However, it is vital that self-doubt is dealt with quickly or else the word of God may be delayed or compromised or lost. In two of the cases above, God was angry with the unbelieving response and it led to unnecessary trouble – in Moses' case he ended up with Aaron sharing in the leadership, with disastrous consequences at Sinai, and in Zechariah's case he was struck dumb for nine months. You can turn out to be your own worst enemy by giving air time to those negative voices.

We do have an enemy who hates to see God's purposes fulfilled and he can make life difficult for us but, as Nehemiah's story illustrates, he is no match for God's power, zeal, creativity and enterprise. Most of the instinctive objections that come to mind, when you contemplate what God is calling you to, relate to your own ability to fulfil it. Which is okay because it shouldn't be your own enterprise and determination that wins the day.

As to the objections that come from outside, as long as you don't disobey God's strategy, they will only be what He has determined to allow. As such, the opposition is likely to come from the particular enemies that He has already determined to deal with by means of your call. If God has a purpose and initiates a scheme for you to assist Him, don't doubt that, subject to your willingness, He will also assume responsibility for its completion. We are dependent on the God who initiated it to bring it about.

You will need an evolving strategy to deal with those who oppose you from the outside – both for the subtle and the blatant opposition. As was the case in Nehemiah's day, God will instruct you what you are to say and do in response to each event.

Whilst that might sound like an opt out from providing you with instructions, it isn't. The Bible is clear that God wants us to be 'on our toes' at all times and prepared to ask Him about everything. Even when the current set of circumstances or events is exactly similar to what happened on a previous occasion, God is likely to give different instructions the second time around.

In 2 Samuel 5:17-25 we find the story of two battles, between Israel and the Philistines, which occurred within days, or at most weeks of each other, both in the Valley of Rephaim. David did not receive help from a heavenly visitor, like Joshua did outside Jericho, but on both occasions, we are told that he 'enquired of the Lord'. Although the circumstances of both battles were almost identical and the result of following God's instruction the first time was a decisive victory, David did not fall into the trap of using the same methodology for the second encounter. God's instruction for the second battle was radically different to the first and, as had been the case for Joshua, it was a strategy both unique and un-guessable.

Prepare to be tested

Because, as Paul says in Romans 10:17, 'faith comes by hearing and hearing by the word of Christ', we are required to exercise faith from the moment we receive a call. The visible substance of what God calls us to is not seen until that call is worked out successfully and so our faith will inevitably undergo testing in the meantime.

I hesitated to put this section in because, after dealing with various kinds of opposition, it may seem as though we are emphasising how difficult it is to realize a calling! However, having outside agencies or inner doubts and fears threaten the call is a bit different to having our faith tested because, in this case, the person doing the testing is not you or an enemy, it is God and He is doing so in a calculated and specific manner.

He tests us to see whether we really trust Him and are prepared to depend on Him because, when He deliberately entrusts His work to us and (to some degree, along with it) both His reputation and the outcomes He cares deeply about, it becomes a high stakes operation. His ways are very different to ours and here is the paradox: those who are intent on personal gain and/or building their own reputation may encounter less hassle from God than those whose express purpose is to please Him and to be useful!

Job, David and Jeremiah, to name but three, all complained about the wicked appearing to prosper:

Job – says in Job 21:7, 'Why do the wicked live, reach old age, and grow mighty in power?' And then again in verse 17, 'How often is it that the lamp of the wicked is put out? That their calamity comes upon them? That God distributes pains in His anger?'

David – says in Psalm 73:3-5, 'For I was envious of the arrogant when I saw the prosperity of the wicked. For they have no pangs until death; their bodies are fat and sleek. They are not in trouble as others are; they are not stricken like the rest of mankind.'

Jeremiah – says in Jeremiah 12:1, 'Righteous are you, O Lord, when I complain to you; yet I would plead my case before you. Why does the way of the wicked prosper? Why do all the treacherous thrive?'

In contrast, the lives of those who want to be, or already are, useful are governed by the principle outlined by Jesus in John 15:1,2 where He says, 'I am the true vine, and my Father is the vinedresser. Every branch in me that does not bear fruit he takes away [Gk. 'airo'], and every branch that does bear fruit he prunes [Gk. 'kathairo'], that it may bear more fruit.' Whilst the first verb indicates removing something completely, because it is no longer useful, the second means removing something (usually dirt) in order to leave what is left behind in a cleaner and more useful condition. The thrust of Jesus' words is seen in the adjective that comes from the verb 'kathairo' – 'katharos' meaning 'blameless', 'pure' or 'free from sin and guilt'. So, the productive branch undergoes a cleaning process, making it able to be more productive.

It is not possible to dress this up to look pretty; pruning is not a pleasant process because it always involves the cutting away of material. What is more, the principle of testing is right there in both Old and New Testaments and we see two important aspects of it in the following pairs of references:

Abraham – Genesis 22:1,2 says, 'After these things God tested Abraham and said to him... "Take your son, your only son Isaac, whom you love and go... offer him as a burnt offering on one of the mountains of which I will tell you".' We know that Abraham was prepared to obey but the angel of the Lord stayed his hand at the vital moment. And Hebrews 11:17,18 says, 'By faith Abraham, when he was tested, offered up Isaac, and he who had received the promises... figuratively speaking, received him back (from the dead).'

Joseph – Genesis 37, 39 & 40 chronicles the injustices that Joseph suffered on his way to being asked to interpret Pharaoh's dreams. The being sold by his brothers; the false accusation of Potiphar's wife; and the long period in prison, when he was essentially a forgotten man, are well known. But Psalm 105:16-19 says, 'When he [God] summoned a famine on the land and broke all supply of bread, he had sent a man ahead of them, Joseph who was sold as a slave. His feet were hurt with fetters; his neck was put in a collar of iron; until what he had said came to pass, *the word of the Lord tested him.*'

So, we see that, when the word of the Lord comes to us and calls us, there may be waiting involved before God makes actual the things He has spoken about and we can expect that word also to test us. Furthermore, rather than complain, we are bidden to remain rock solid and to rejoice. James 1:2-4, 12 says, 'Count it all joy, my brothers, when you meet trials of various kinds, for you know that the testing of your faith produces steadfastness. And let steadfastness have its full effect, that you may be perfect and complete, lacking in nothing... Blessed is the man who remains steadfast under trial, for when he has stood the test he will receive the crown of life, which God has promised to those who love Him.'

Being tested is not pleasant but it is proof that we are children of our Father and He has recognized the potential in us to be, not just okay but, really useful. He is not vindictive toward us, determined to make life more difficult by deliberately putting obstacles in our path. No, something quite different is going on and we see it clearly in God's call to Jeremiah: after having told Jeremiah he was to be a prophet and having reassured him by saying, 'Behold, I have put my words in your mouth', God establishes a principle by stating, 'I am watching over my word to perform it'. Jeremiah 1:9,12.

God does not speak a word or issue a call and then stand back. He actually takes delight in the one who is called and He is then closely attentive – including to any testing – until the word is fulfilled. His relationship with us is personal and He wants to watch closely to see how we handle the tests because they are as much about our sanctification as are the calls themselves. We should also take reassurance from the fact that, if God's calls and commissions are tailored to the individual then so are His tests, they are definitely not random.

Always look expectantly for confirmation

Given that the initial word from God, or call, that you heard might have come 'out of nowhere' – one of those times when you didn't know something but then, an instant later, you did know something – and you cannot recall having asked Him for anything or having been in a state of expectancy, you might want some kind of surety. There is no instance in the Bible, that I can think of, where God refused a request for confirmation from someone to whom He had just spoken. He expects us to ask questions and He knows we will need clarification before acting.

What is important is not that we ask but that we ask *in faith* – for example, there appears to be a significant difference, in Luke 1, between the 'How shall this be…?' question that Mary asked Gabriel and the 'How shall I know this…?' question that Zechariah asked the angel of the Lord. In Mary's case, it was a genuine desire for clarification that resulted in her being given more detail of what, how and when. In Zechariah's case, it was unbelief and resulted in him receiving a rebuke and being unable to speak for nine months.

In Exodus 3 & 4 is the call of Moses. There was a long conversation between him and God, during which legitimate questions were asked and a series of amazing confirmations were granted but it tipped over from a genuine desire for confirmation into unbelief and we find God becoming increasingly frustrated with Moses' excuses and general unwillingness to accept the mission, culminating in God reluctantly allowing Aaron in on the gig.

In Judges 6 there is the call of Gideon, while he is threshing corn in a winepress out of fear of the Midianites. Then we have the famous account of Gideon twice putting out a fleece to gain confirmation of what God had said and there is no indication of God being reluctant to act on those two requests.

The desire for confirmation is simply a desire for God to speak again about the thing He had first talked to us about. We just want to be sure it was Him and that we heard aright. He is really creative when it comes to communication and He has many, many ways of attracting our attention – still, small voices; dreams & visions; timely advice from a messenger be it an angel or a wise friend; an audible voice; a strange occurrence that demands attention; an observation that has to be investigated; or simply through the reading of His word. If He is calling you to something, you can guarantee that He is also determined to provide clarity and will go to great lengths to get His message across.

Sanctification and change are inevitable if you want to succeed

The outworking of God's call to salvation and the consequent commitment we make to Him leads to two things: firstly, a quality of life in Christ, characterized by certain persistent attributes, and secondly, good works, prepared beforehand for us to enjoy.

This inevitably means that we are transformed, a bit at a time, by regular applications of grace; by frequent repentance; by lifelong learning; by not being good enough but constantly getting better; by prayer and supplication and by hard work and dedication (among other things), into someone who is more like Christ.

So, it is true to say that being useful to God, and achieving lasting results from the things He gives us to do, inevitably requires our 'sanctification'. It is also true to say that giving us things to do and changing us in the doing of them is one of God's chosen methods of sanctification. In other words, God deliberately uses the process of 'calling' to make us more like Himself.

Nobody has ever said that the process of sanctification is easy – by definition, it involves us being made into what we are not and have never yet been. But the inevitable result is that we progressively become more 'us' (if you'll forgive the philosophizing). However, substantial changes do not usually happen by instinct or by better application of our existing ways and the process is most likely to involve us facing up to those longstanding personality and behavioural traits that have been obstacles for a long time.

It is possible that you have been fighting for years against things in yourself, which you know are inhibitors, and they are still tripping you up. It is also possible that, in your moments of maximum honesty, you know you could have been fighting harder. Either way, you should actually feel very encouraged if God calls you to do something and it brings you face to face with those inhibitors because it means He must have a plan to deal with them and this new task or commission will provide the necessary motivation for you to let Him do so.

This may seem obvious but the change process is usually cyclic, i.e. it involves some kind of repeat sequence, such as:

- Seeking God & listening for His response – followed by…
- God's Spirit calling out to us – followed by…
- Hearing and checking what we have heard – followed by…
- Resonance with our spirit – followed by…
- Agreement, repentance and commitment to change – followed by…
- Moving on & making progress – followed by…
- Listening again…

What I am saying is that we usually make progress a bit at a time – we iterate towards the answer – and it is helpful to be aware of where we are in the sequence at any particular time. Because we are so change-averse, God usually reveals things to us in stages. We can't handle everything at once and so don't be alarmed if you think you've made some progress, but not enough. He will speak to you again and take you another step.

Some of the change will be spiritual and behavioural and attitudinal but some will be related to the acquiring of new skills and abilities. Much of this change happens 'on the job' i.e. God doesn't require us to be perfect before we embark on something, although we do need to be sensitive to what He is giving us permission to do and (conversely) what we do not have permission to do.

If there is one thought to hold onto at all times it is that we must *always* be listening to what God has to say – His instruction and guidance is the basis of our faith and will *constantly* be required if we are to navigate the task to a successful end.

Find confidantes and tell them your story

In the midst of sanctification and change there will be times when we feel inadequate or out of our depth; times when we have to swim against the tide and suffer the disapproval of those around us; times when stuff doesn't work out; times when others let us down or we let ourselves down. We will not get through it without a support network – people to 'stand with' us and to intercede for us.

Even if there were no adverse conditions, a support network is extremely valuable. We all have a constant need for courage, confirmation and correction. Nobody should be operating in total isolation, it's too dangerous. We are too prone to error or to discouragement, if left to our own devices. Proverbs 18:1 says, 'A man who isolates himself seeks his own desire; He rages against all wise judgment.' It is encouraging us to be willing and brave enough to allow others to offer input and correction.

It is a sad fact that, however much we try not to be, we are full of our own importance and therefore may not heed certain aspects of what God is saying – particularly the bits that promote Him and demote us. One of the reasons why Jesus was so complimentary towards John the Baptist is because of John's refusal to pursue personal glory – when asked to comment on Jesus' seeming rivalry, he said, 'A person cannot receive even one thing unless it is given him from heaven... I am not the Christ, but I have been sent before Him... therefore this joy of mine is now complete. He must increase, but I must decrease.' John 3:27-30.

Each of us needs a few wise people with whom to consult. By 'wise', I mean people who love God and are experienced at hearing Him for themselves; people without any vested interest in what we do, i.e. not predisposed to taking a biased view of what we think God might be telling us; people who speak the truth and are unafraid to tell us like it is; people who, from time to time, will genuinely seek God on our behalf and have our best interests at heart; people who will 'look out for us' and give timely warning of danger.

It will not necessarily always need to be the same set of wise people – needs and requirements shift and God can help us adapt or find new people or locate a specialist, etc.

If we are committed to seeking God's will and have a little of John the Baptist's attitude and there are a handful of people to whom we can go and whom we trust, the conditions are favourable for courage, confirmation and correction.

The decision to do something or to go somewhere or to take on a particular role will always be ours to make but we ought not to be afraid of being challenged. We need good reasons for our actions and we need to be sure of our guidance. If you sense that God is leading you in an unusual direction, He will always be prepared to provide confirmation. If those around you are disquieted by what you are saying, it doesn't necessarily mean you are wrong, but you might be! It's always a good thing to test it.

So, let's say you have found a few confidantes – why am I then urging you to tell them your story? It has to do with 'sense-making'. My friend Nick Isbister explains it much better than I can. I am taking several snippets from the chapter on 'Narrative Identity', in his book, *The Story So Far* and amplifying the language slightly, so that it is more immediately accessible in this context (Isbister, et al., 2018):

'Everyone constructs what things mean to them through the variety of stories they tell themselves. Our narratives can be partial. They can be tentative. They can be inconsistent. They can be grandiose. They can be accurate and they can be delusional. They can encompass a number of perspectives and cast us as the agents of the narrative, or as the victims. Our stories can be highly individualistic, even solipsistic [egocentric], *or they can situate us as part of a tribe, or a group, or a class or a nation, or an era...*

'We each choose how we see ourselves and how we see our place in the world... When we talk about our lives... we are not merely chronicling [in other words, listing a series of events], *we are also telling the story of our lives. When*

we narrate something, we naturally include a sequence of events and the connection between them... narrative always has two things – "episodes" [i.e. one thing after another] and some sort of "configurational dimension". The configurational bit is what gives each of the episodes their significance. The story includes a description of the outward events and it usually expresses, or at least hints at, some of what is going on inside the story teller. The fact that the events being spoken about are not just random or scattered is what allows those who are listening to "make sense" of the story.

'When we ask someone to tell us their story, it is important that a connection is made between the teller and the listener. The listener usually knows if the story is authentic and, in practical terms, it is important that what is said both makes sense to the teller and rings true to the listener.'

I would sum up the argument as follows... Constructing a coherent story, that is anchored in reality and devoid of delusion, that doesn't omit key episodes and is honest about objectives and outcomes, is an extremely valuable exercise. The process of constructing the narrative causes the teller to face up to where the holes and inconsistencies are. It sorts out the counterfeit from the authentic and it either makes sense or it doesn't. The object of the storytelling exercise is sense-making for the teller and for the hearer(s).

As the adventure unfolds, the story continues to be written and retelling it from time to time helps to keep a firm grasp on the truth and makes the teller better able to focus on the key objectives. The confidantes need to be trusted and encouraged to report back what they are hearing – if they are genuinely able to hear God for themselves and they have your best interests at heart, they are very likely to provide timely interventions and the necessary encourage-ment.

Teamwork or at least some complementary skills

There are times when the thing that the Lord requires can and should be done by one person – you alone. But on many occasions the task will require more than just you - it may be that, in due course, once confirmation has been received and the nature of the task is understood, you will be prompted to look for complementary skills in other people and the task will be undertaken by a team.

In Chapter 6 we talked a great deal about complementarity and teamwork and alluded to the fact that Paul's several discourses on the use of spiritual gifts in the Church, where he uses the analogy of the Body, do not suggest that God has sanctioned only a very limited number of gifts.

The Church worldwide comprises all of His called-out people and, in its glory and diversity, is intended to be God's instrument for establishing His kingdom. We who are 'called out' and part of that gathering, each eagerly waiting to emerge as 'sons' [Romans 8:23], are to be a demonstration of His wisdom and glory both to the creation [Romans 8:19] and to the principalities and powers [Ephesians 3:10].

How is that going to happen unless we each start to express ourselves in the ways that He directs? And how is the Church to be seen for what God intended unless we learn to work together, in concert, each 'member' using his/her unique combination of God-given, Spirit-inspired skills and talents ('gifting')?

Instead of trying to piggy-back on someone else's calling or look for another person (be it a friend or a church leader or a spouse or a mentor) to tell us what to do, why don't we turn aside and ask the One who knows and then follow His directions about either calling others to help us or joining in with a project that needs us?

If we follow that route, there really will be stories to tell.

Bio #6 – Kate

Kate's family background was extremely privileged. She was brought up in a large stately home with her parents and two younger brothers. For the first few years of her life, her parents, although present, did not have much hands-on involvement, leaving the day-to-day care in the hands of nannies. From the age of seven or eight she remembers her father spending quite a lot of time with her and the boys and she became quite close to him but she had no emotional attachment to her mother.

Despite the lack of intimacy – as she says, 'my family didn't do emotions, especially not the negative ones' – Kate's upbringing was very free. The children were always outside, running wild in large grounds and very happy, but when required to relate to others, outside the family, she was extremely shy. This was in no small part due to her learning difficulties and an inability to communicate them to those around her. She describes her experience of education, from as far back as she can remember, as 'always having to swim upstream'. Every subject, with the exception of mathematics, was a problem and the only thing that alleviated the stress was her ability at sport and being able to run very fast.

Around age twelve she took courage to approach her parents and tell them that she thought she might be dyslexic. Their response was, 'Nonsense, darling, you're just not academic'!

She passed some GCSEs but A-levels were thought to be a step too far and so she was sent to a finishing school in the South of England, where something at last went right. Although Kate's self-esteem was extremely low she learned to cook and, by some miracle, that proved to be a clear pointer to the future that God was preparing, she earned a cordon bleu qualification and a certificate in wine. It must have been a miracle because she couldn't read the recipes properly!

Soon after that, aged nineteen, she was given the opportunity to be the chef at a ski chalet in France, looking after and cooking for twelve people for the winter season. It didn't take the company that hired her very long to realize that Kate's learning difficulties were affecting her performance – she wasn't following recipes correctly, finding afterwards that she had skipped a line or two, here and there, sometimes with disastrous consequences, and she was given one week to improve or else she would be sent home. The following morning, at about 6 a.m., as she went out to buy bread for breakfast, she heard

God speak to her and says it was so clear it was like an audible voice. He simply said, 'It will be OK'.

She decided to change her methodology and spent hours studying, in advance, recipes for the food she was intending to cook, writing down every step and adding exact timings at each point. With the result that every day she knew precisely what she had to do, her performance dramatically improved and she managed to complete the season.

She had done a secretarial course in London, after leaving the finishing school, and for a period of about five years she had a succession of different jobs, both in administration and as a cook. Getting a job was not nearly so difficult as keeping a job – she spent most of the time in employment waiting to be sacked and being sacked was very often the outcome. This period culminated, at the age of twenty-three, in two very different experiences.

Firstly, there was one that Kate describes as 'horrific', working as a temporary chef at a financial PR company. Her job was to make lunch each day for the directors. She had developed a sort of sixth sense that told her when someone was planning to sack her and she had such a feeling from about the second day on this particular job. She found it impossible to communicate with anybody in the company and so the strategy she adopted was to try to capture as many of the good recipes as possible before the axe fell. She spent hours drawing pictures and writing out methods for anything that might have future value. Once again, her enterprise won her a reprieve and she actually lasted six months before being pushed out, by which time she could leave with an impressive portfolio of recipes.

Secondly, having always been a churchgoer and knowing she had a desire for God, but without ever really knowing Him, she elected to attend an Alpha Course being run by a local church. It was one evening per week for twelve weeks, involving a meal, some teaching about the Christian faith and then discussion in small groups. For Kate it was a revelation and after some weeks, when the participants all spent a day together with the organizers, reflecting on what they had learned, she decided to give her life to Jesus. In contrast to what was happening at work, this was an overwhelmingly positive experience and marked a pivotal point in her life. She embarked on an entirely new relationship with God but it turned out that His priorities for her didn't involve an instant solution to her everyday learning problems. The severe dyslexia, as yet undiagnosed, continued to be a major stumbling block and her self-esteem constantly suffered.

After a few years in which she tried various occupations, including teaching, Kate decided to take the food route full-time. Her privileged background came to her assistance in making important social connections such as with the family of an American-born billionaire, who owned, among many houses around the world, an enormous country estate in the UK. They wanted a chef for the winter and Kate was duly appointed. She took with her a portfolio of recipes that she was familiar with and was able to work mostly from memory, sometimes further developing a recipe she already knew and occasionally fitting in a new one that caught her imagination. She did well and was commended for her skills. Then, in the summer months, she landed a job cooking for a family whose name appears on a major chain of UK retail outlets. Again, she was able to display an impressive repertoire of skills, relying primarily on what she had already learned and adding to that knowledge in a controlled way that didn't require a lot of reading.

When she was thirty, Kate moved on to be head chef of an Arts Café, where her cooking received the accolade of 'Best Café Food in Edinburgh' – it was one of those rare but welcome times in her professional life when the hard work seemed worth it. Nevertheless, such successes always come at a price and for Kate it was constantly having to work all week and all weekend. She was becoming dissatisfied with the lifestyle but was nevertheless willing to submit to what she felt God wanted.

She was also, at this time, going out with someone who typically spoke in very long sentences, sprinkled with uncomfortably long words. Kate regularly found herself hearing the first part and the end part but missing everything in the middle, which made joined-up conversation difficult. One day he told her the relationship was over and, when asked why, said it was because he thought she was dyslexic. Instead of having a devastating effect, this actually gave her hope because someone else had come to the same conclusion as her. A subsequent test by a clinical psychologist confirmed the diagnosis and it proved to be a springboard towards realizing her calling.

In her personal walk with God, Kate had been thinking and praying about healing. Like Jesus' disciples, she really wanted to be sent out to pray for the sick and see people made well. One Sunday, soon after having been left by her boyfriend, the vicar said, at the close of the service, 'someone here has been praying for a gift of healing and, if that is you, you should come forward and we'll pray for you'. Kate started to go towards the front of the church and, at that moment, for the second time in her life, she heard God speak to her in a voice that seemed audible. He said, 'I want you to be a nutritional therapist.' Within seconds, she knew it was not now necessary for anyone to pray with her and so she stopped walking towards the front of the church and returned to her seat!

Kate knew what a nutritional therapist was because, for health reasons, she had once been to see one. However, she knew that she could not fulfil such a calling without a series of qualifications, none of which she possessed. So, she was faced once again with an obstacle that her learning difficulties would struggle to overcome but, crucially, she knew that God had spoken and had answered her prayers about healing because here was a vocation that sought to address health issues that are brought about or are adversely affected by diet.

As is usual when God issues a call, it was not long before doubts arose in her mind, both about her own capabilities and how He could possibly make it happen and so, the following day, she resolved to 'put out a fleece'. She only knew of one nutritional therapist – the person she had visited some time previously, a woman both well-known and influential in the profession and who had written several books. She said to God, 'I am going to telephone her and, if you have really spoken to me and you are going to make this happen, I want her to pick up the phone herself.'

At the time, Kate didn't quite realize how naïve this statement was – the woman in question had receptionists and administrators to answer calls and to queue people up to be granted an appointment. Nevertheless, Kate dialled the number of the clinic and the call went straight past the reception phone and rang on the therapist's private line in her kitchen at home! The recipient of the call was duly shocked and said to Kate, 'How did you do that? This is extraordinary, I have a receptionist!' But, having recovered her composure, she answered Kate's questions about the steps she needed to take towards taking up the profession and the A-levels and other qualifications that would be necessary.

Half an hour after putting the phone down Kate realized there was another important question that, in the stress of the moment, she had not asked. So, she prayed again and said to God, 'if you made it happen once, please could you make it happen again?' Then she dialled the number of the clinic for a second time. Once more, to the therapist's obvious consternation, the call came straight through on the private line in her kitchen and Kate got the answer she was looking for.

There then followed an epic period of re-education, lasting just over three years and supported by a chef's job at the Bristol Cancer Help Centre. The educational part started with Kate giving up her job in Edinburgh to tackle a Science Access Course, which she did full-time from May to Sept, achieving the equivalent of two A-levels and winning A grades. Then, she began a degree course at the end of September, which required her to attend lectures for one weekend per month in London and to write essays continuously.

Securing a job at the Cancer Help Centre in Bristol was another miracle of timing. It was the only place that Kate knew of where nutritional principles were as important as a high standard of cooking and, over the years, she had enquired about a job there on many occasions. Each time she called or wrote, they had a full complement but, on this occasion, as she prepared to begin her degree, a vacancy appeared. She applied for it, was accepted and within three months was made head chef.

She was living in Bristol, attending a community church in the city and going up to London once a month. The community church had home groups and Kate's group decided to embark on a programme of reading the Bible in three months, which meant completing ten chapters every day. This would have been a tall order for someone who was good at reading but, for someone with dyslexia it was a daily mountain to climb. Kate had an audio Bible and so she decided to listen to it being read and to follow the text with her finger. She completed the whole Bible in the three months and then immediately started again and, this time, she found that she didn't need the audio. From that time on, she experienced a significant improvement in reading ability.

The essays, however, were another matter and writing them didn't get any easier. She struggled on, consistently getting below average grades until it came time to write the final dissertation. This was such a challenge that Kate gave up her job at the Help Centre in order to work on it full-time. She researched meticulously, worked long hours and even went to the library to read and to study the content and style of output from other successful students from previous years. Eventually she completed a first draft and showed it to a friend who had experience of proofreading and correcting academic papers and dissertations.

The response that she received was quite a shock – her friend told her that what she had written was Masters standard but was being let down by too limited a vocabulary. They worked on it together for a day and Kate then submitted it. When the results were announced, she learned that what she had written was of an exceptionally high standard and she had won an award for the best dissertation of the year. It was called 'The Shekinah Award', which is a Hebrew word meaning God's Glory or God's Presence!

Kate rang her parents, to tell them what had happened and that there was to be a prizegiving ceremony. They told her she needed to call the college back straight away and make absolutely sure it was true, so that she wouldn't be disappointed on the day.

There was no mistake, the prize was duly awarded to her and she emerged with the qualifications that she needed in order to set up shop as a nutritional therapist. God's ways are indeed hard to fathom because there then followed nearly five years of difficulty, where she was scratching around for a living, but He kept speaking to her and encouraging her to keep going. She got married and then, about a year later, the business began to take off and she became very busy doing what she had always wanted to do – helping people towards health and wholeness.

Kate still continues to develop her role as a therapist and the testimonials show that, alongside giving professional nutritional advice, she often discerns the underlying reasons for someone's condition, has frequent opportunities to pray for people, and has seen God intervene in their lives.

Chapter 14

In Conclusion

God is looking for craftsmen

Celebrating uniqueness

Exercising craftsmanship is not the same as mass production – something made by a craftsman has unique qualities and what he/she fashions might be the only example of its kind that has ever existed.

God's call to an individual has unique characteristics because each individual has been created to be different to all other people and His relationship with that individual must necessarily have unique aspects to it. During a person's lifetime, God's calls will be tailored to match the unique combination of skills, aptitudes and passions of that individual. Then, at the close of their life, the name He bestows on each person, that only He and they will know, will not be the same as for any other.

The outworking of an individual's call will similarly be unique – we are pieces of an intricately patterned jigsaw, not 'tiles' of uniform shape that are laid in sequence.

Celebrating the craftsmanship, not the object

In our day and culture, we have all but lost our appreciation of the person who crafts an object and of the creative process – we tend to focus on the utility of the object, rather than the discipline and skill that went into making it. We give honour to the object and not to the builder – to what is done rather than to those whose obedience and skill led to it being done.

In God's economy, the outcome is important but it is as much about the person who is called and the process of working out that calling as it is about the result. It matters whether we hear and obey; how we undertake the work; how successfully we relate to and collaborate with those having complementary skills; whether we resist the opposition and if we stand firm through the tests. He is all about relationship and communication and so He cares desperately about HOW the calling is worked out and by whom.

I started this book by saying: God is a craftsman who is never idle and not usually silent; He creates with passion and with care and attention to detail and He made us in His image; and that the craftsman in Him has created a longing in us to be craftsmen – to produce quality work and to achieve lasting results. In Hebrews 3:3,4 it says, 'For Jesus has been counted worthy of more glory than Moses – as much more glory as the builder of a house has more honour than the house itself. (For every house is built by someone, but the builder of all things is God.)'

What is the 'builder of all things' telling you to do and will you do it in partnership with Him, employing His skill and excellence? Do you want to be a craftsman?

The object is transient but the one who calls is eternal

In Jeremiah 52, right at the end of the book, is an account of the fall of Jerusalem – the walls were broken down and the temple and all the grand houses were burned and destroyed. The precious artefacts from the temple were either broken up or carried off to Babylon and some of the more remarkable items are described. These are the things that Huram-abi made, many of which demanded new techniques to be developed.

What does this say about both the primary focus and the lasting nature of God's calls? Huram-abi was possibly the most accomplished craftsman in the physical trades that we meet in the Bible and he did work that endured and that had lasting purpose. But, when the objects he made were not being used honourably in Jerusalem and when those for whose benefit they had been made were not reaping that benefit, because the nation did not repent, God carried out His judgment and the results of Huram-abi's astounding skill – the outworking of his calling – were lost.

What lasts and what does not last? The relationship with God is more important than the projects He gives us to do and our partnering with Him in the creative process is more important than the results of the work that is done.

This life is transient but the next is eternal

Part of this life's purpose is to prepare for living alongside the God who calls. And the consensus, among those who have written about heaven, is that, if and when we get there, we will continue to do useful work.

I am not suggesting that useful work is all that we'll be doing – clearly, heaven is a place of entering God's rest, of worshipping Him because we can finally appreciate Him for who He is, of 'play' and enjoyment and of being with all those who love Him. There will be limitless opportunities to get to know Him and to 'walk and talk' with Him.

However, we bear His image and He has included us in 'the family business' and so our life alongside Him must surely include the things that are part of His nature, like being creative and inventive. It therefore seems intuitively reasonable that work is intended to continue beyond the grave and several passages in the Bible also point us toward that conclusion:

- In Genesis 2 God gave Adam a mandate to work and then brought Eve to him, as his helpmeet, before the fall into sin – hence, before death entered in; before thorns and thistles sprang up; and before sweat and toil took over from enjoyment and productivity. God had not wanted to 'curse the ground', He had made provision for fulfilling work always to characterise our lives;
- In His encounter with Satan in the wilderness, Jesus said, 'Be gone... you shall worship the Lord your God and him only shall you serve.' Matthew 4:10. Jesus is here addressing someone who pre-existed the created order and He mandates both worship and service, which means loving God, obeying His instructions and enjoying being with Him should be the natural state;
- Jesus' use of work language in John 5:17, where He says, 'My Father has been working to this very hour, and so I, too, must be at work.' (Cassirer, 1989), adds further weight to the notion that ongoing productive work should be the norm for those pursuing a relationship with God.
- In 1Corinthians 6:2 Paul is addressing the problem of people in the Church going to law against one another and submitting issues to a 'pagan court'. He says, 'Do you not know that the saints will judge the world? And if the world is to be judged by you, are you incompetent to try trivial cases?' Whatever this verse means, in terms of what those in heaven will be given to do, it certainly sounds like work.

God may have created us to co-exist with Him and intended that we enjoy being together but, here and now, it is often hard graft because of sin. Nevertheless, in the midst of a fallen creation, He has designed good works for us to do, so that in the doing of them we can discover a different, more productive and more enjoyable working partnership.

Part of that discovery process is coming to understand our own uniqueness and having times when our natural aptitude coincides with our personal passion. Thus, despite the difficulty of our ongoing service to God, we catch glimpses of what 'work redeemed' is meant to look and feel like.

Those glimpses and, God willing, longer passages of service, as we respond to and work out our callings, are part of the preparation for life in a different place where the restrictions don't exist and our inadequacies and shortcomings have been lifted out of the way. So, as we await that glorious transition, how should we conduct ourselves?

'Going & coming'

Psalm 121:8 says, 'The Lord will keep *your going out and your coming in* from this time forth and forevermore.' 'Going out and coming in' is a common Hebrew phrase that, in this context, denotes the whole of life. It has the same meaning in various other places, such as Deuteronomy 28:6, where God is extolling the benefits of 'faithfully obeying the voice of the Lord' – He says, 'Blessed shall you be when you come in, and blessed shall you be when you go out.'

In English we tend to use 'coming and going' to describe the general, almost haphazard, bustle of activity in a place or of a group of people. In the Bible, it is most often rendered 'going and coming' and has a more focussed meaning – the life or the activities of an individual or group, from this time onwards.

I prefer 'going and coming' because it is descriptive of going out to perform a particular task or to achieve an end and then coming back again. Indeed, the Hebrew phrase occurs in several places where the context is quite specific to the activities of an individual in the outworking of their calling. Here are a couple of examples, both of which have featured elsewhere in the book but are key to understanding how we must respond to God's call:

Solomon – started well, depended on God but finished badly

(1 Kings 3) – when discussing the spirit of skill earlier, we highlighted the fact that Solomon asked for wisdom and God gave him 'khokhmah'. Solomon prayed because he recognized God's call on him to be the king in place of his father, David, and he knew he did not possess the necessary skills. He was a relatively young man and the task before him was onerous, carrying with it a weight of expectation, huge responsibility and the not insignificant promise of God to establish a dynasty.

He says in verse 7, 'And now, O Lord my God, you have made your servant king in place of David my father, although I am but a little child. *I do not know how to go out or to come in.* And your servant is in the midst of your people whom you have chosen, a great people, too many to be numbered or counted for multitude. Give your servant therefore an understanding mind to govern your people, that I may discern between good and evil, for who is able to govern this your great people.'

This is what you must do when you recognize a 'call' – don't question God's judgment but, recognizing your lack of skill, pray for God's provision to fulfil

His purpose. He will give you what is necessary for 'going and coming'.

The uncomfortable truth about Israel's wisest king, however, is that having been given almost unlimited bounty and having established the basis of a lasting dynasty, he embraced foolishness and threw it all away. 1 Kings 11 tells us, 'King Solomon loved many foreign women… from the nations concerning which the Lord had said to the people of Israel, "You shall not enter into marriage with them, neither shall they with you, for surely they will turn away your heart after their gods." …for when Solomon was old his wives turned away his heart after other gods, and his heart was not wholly true to the Lord his God, as was the heart of David his father.' As a result, the kingdom was split.

Caleb – started well, depended on God (against the odds) and finished very well

Joshua 14 is one of my favourite passages in the whole of the Bible – look again at what Caleb actually said to Joshua at the point when the initial subduing of the land had been accomplished. He recalled the time, forty-five years earlier, when he had been sent by Moses to spy out the land and how, along with Joshua, he had 'wholly followed the Lord' and been promised an inheritance in the land.

He had carried that unfulfilled call of God with him for all that time and says in verses 10-12, 'And now, behold, I am this day eighty-five years old. I am still as strong today as I was in the day that Moses sent me; my strength now is as my strength was then, for war *and for going and coming*. So now give me this hill country of which the Lord spoke on that day, for you heard on that day how the Anakim were there, with great fortified cities. It may be that the Lord will be with me, and I shall drive them out just as the Lord said.'

In Numbers 14, after the debacle of the spies returning and the majority persuading the nation not to go forward into the land that God had promised to give them, God himself gives testimony about Caleb saying, 'Caleb, because he has a different spirit and has followed me fully, I will bring into the land into which he went, and his descendants shall possess it.'

Caleb himself had obviously heard God clearly those forty-five years earlier and had accepted God's challenge to possess a particular part of the land that was inhabited by giants. He had committed himself to overcoming the giants and to taking possession and God had honoured that promise by keeping him alive and by renewing his strength.

He was an old man by the time we get to Joshua 14 but his resolve had not weakened – the fulfilling of God's purpose was more important than his own comfort and safety and he knew that, along with the call comes the grace to succeed.

This is what you must do when you recognize a call and then see it seemingly thwarted – don't question God's methods or the delays that are not your fault; don't lose heart when you see yourself getting 'past it' but pray for God's provision to fulfil His purpose. He will give you what is necessary for 'going and coming'.

God's purposes and our response

God's purposes depend in part on our willingness to listen for and to heed His calls. It bears repeating that, if we don't heed Him, the tasks He intended us to perform, in a unique fashion, will not be performed in that way and possibly not at all. He exercises creative genius when it comes to getting the job done but He wants you and I to be part of the process and there are elements of what we each contribute that cannot be provided by anyone else.

If you have read the foregoing chapters, either wholly or in part, I can only now point you to a study of the biblical characters to whom God issued calls. Look at them, see how it happened and look closely at the journey they took. See how faithful God was, over protracted periods of time, to folk like Abraham, Jacob, Joseph, Daniel, Elijah, Mary, Peter, Luke & Paul, even though He didn't shield them from difficulty and reversals.

Look also for people who are only mentioned once but who grasped a prompting from God and performed a strategically important task – people like Simeon, Anna, the woman with the ointment, Joseph of Arimathea, Ananias & Agabus and see how many more you can find who received a call and ran with it.

Then commit yourself to active listening, with a heart of faith, and expect Him to awaken something in you or to give you a yearning to be involved in something or to present a need to you in a new light or even to give you an unequivocal instruction.

I believe this idea of 'calling' is right there, just under the surface, in most of us and I believe that we each want to *find our element* and so, in order to do so in anything other than a haphazard and almost accidental manner, why don't we ask the One who made us to lead us to it?

Bibliography

Amani UK - Charity No. 1073357. *Amani UK.* [Online] https://www.amaniuk.org.uk.

Cassirer, Heinz W. 1989. *God's New Covenant - A New Testament Translation.* Grand Rapids, Michigan : W B Eerdmans Publishing Co., 1989.

Crawford, Matthew. 2010. *The Case for Working with your Hands: or Why office work is bad for us and fixing things feels good.* s.l. : Penguin, 2010.

Guinness, Os. 1998. *The Call.* Nashville : Word Publishing, 1998.

Henry, Matthew. 1960. *Matthew Henry's Commentary on the Whole Bible in One Vol.* London : Marshall, Morgan & Scott, 1960. 0 551 05010 1.

Howard, Leslie. 1942. *The First of the Few.* RKO Pictures; General Film Distributors, 1942.

Isbister, Nick and Elliman, Jude. 2018. *The Story So Far - Introduction to Transformational Narrative Coaching.* Oxford : Isbister Press, 2018.

—. 2016. Transformational Narrative Coaching - Advanced Course. s.l. : Listening Partnership Ltd, 2016.

Luther, Martin and Pelikan, Jaroslav (Editor). 1955-1986. *Luther's Works, Vol. 22: Sermons on the Gospel of St. John Chapters 1-4.* s.l. : Concordia, 1955-1986.

Marshall, Tom. 1989. *Right Relationships.* Chichester : Sovereign World, 1989.

Medina, John J. 2008. *Brain Rules.* Seattle : Pear Press, 2008.

Men and Things, Women and People: A Meta-Analysis of Sex Differences in Interests. **2009.** 6, s.l. : Psychological Bulletin, 2009, Vol. 135.

Mitchell, Gordon. 2006. *R.J. Mitchell - Schooldays to Spitfire.* Stroud : Tempus Publishing Limited, 2006.

Morfin, Tim. 2015. *Out of the Ordinary.* Bradford : TLGBooks, 2015.

Motyer, Alec. 2011. *Isaiah By the Day.* Tain, Ross-shire : Christian Focus Publications, 2011.

—. 2016. *Psalms by the Day: A New Devotional Translation.* Tain, Ross-shire : Christian Focus Publications, 2016.

Robinson, Ken. 2010. *The Element - How Finding your Passion Changes Everything.* London : Penguin Books, 2010.

Schaeffer, Francis A. 1972. *He is There and He is Not Silent.* Carol Stream, Illinois : Tyndale House, 1972.

Schuurman, Douglas J. 2004. *Vocation: Discerning our Callings in Life.* s.l. : Wm. B Eerdmans, 2004.

Spangler, Ann and Tverberg, Lois. 2017. *Sitting At The Feet of Rabbi Jesus - How the Jewishness of Jesus can Transform your Faith.* Grand Rapids, Michigan : Zondervan, 2017. 978 0 310 33069 1.

Vineyard, Churches. 2019. *Legacy // An interview with Carol Wimber, Penny Fulton and Bob Fulton.* Vineyard UK&I, 2019.

Warren, Rick. 2002. *The Purpose Driven Life.* Grand Rapids, Michigan : Zondervan, 2002.

Woolmer, John. 2004. *The Grand Surprise.* Wells : Word For Life Trust, 2004.

Work Redeemed is Service to God. **Gillies, Chris. 2015.** Oxford : St Aldates: Faith & Work, 2015.

Yahav, Daniel. 2019. *Peniel Fellowship Israel.* [Online] November 2019. https://www.penielfellowshipisrael.com/an-altar-and-a-sacrifice-acceptable.

.

Lightning Source UK Ltd.
Milton Keynes UK
UKHW020847280222
399332UK00007B/146